D0561586

AGENTS OF INFLUENCE

Also by Henry Hemming

Agent M
The Ingenious Mr. Pyke
Together
In Search of the English Eccentric
Misadventure in the Middle East

AGENTS OF INFLUENCE

A British Campaign, a Canadian Spy, and the Secret Plot to Bring America into World War II

Henry Hemming

PUBLICAFFAIRS

New York

PublicAffairs
Hachette Book Group
1290 Avenue of the Americas, New York, NY 10104
www.publicaffairsbooks.com
@Public_Affairs

Printed in the United States of America

Originally published in Great Britain in 2019 by Quercus

First US Edition: October 2019

Published by PublicAffairs, an imprint of Perseus Books, LLC, a subsidiary of Hachette Book Group, Inc. The PublicAffairs name and logo is a trademark of the Hachette Book Group.

The Hachette Speakers Bureau provides a wide range of authors for speaking events. To find out more, go to www.hachettespeakersbureau.com or call (866) 376-6591.

The publisher is not responsible for websites (or their content) that are not owned by the publisher.

Print book interior design by CC Book Production.

Library of Congress Control Number: 2019946472

ISBNs: 978-1-5417-4214-7 (hardcover), 978-1-5417-4211-6 (ebook)

LSC-C

10 9 8 7 6 5 4 3 2 1

For Sam,
with all my love

'Foreign influence is truly the Grecian horse to a republic. We cannot be too careful to exclude its influence.'

Alexander Hamilton, 1793[1]

'Dreamed of, aimed at, and worked for, and now it has come to pass.'

Winston Churchill on the US entry into war, 1942[2]

Contents

Photo insert between pages 154 and 155

Preface

As a child, I remember hearing about the man who saved my father's life. It happened an ordinary summer's day, several years before the start of the Second World War. My grandparents had taken their accident-prone three-year-old, my Dad, to have lunch with a friend of theirs outside London. After the meal my grandmother was walking in the garden with the man they had come to see, Bill, when he asked where her son was. She had no idea. Without a word Bill raced over to the far side of the house, where there was a deep pond covered with a carpet of waterlilies.

From here the story I heard as a child might take a slightly different shape, depending on who was telling it. Bill arrives at the pond out of breath to find three-year-old Dad either walking into the water, drowning, or in the most colourful version he has disappeared beneath the waterlilies. Bill then wades, jumps or dives into the pond in his clothes, before staggering out with a spluttering child in his arms.

I remember this being my favourite part of the story, and the rush of relief I would feel at hearing that Dad had survived, and could go on to meet Mum, and my sister and I could be born. As the outline of this episode became more familiar with time, I began to feel as well a tacit bond to the hero of this tale, Bill, who went on to become

Dad's godfather. What he had done seemed to telescope the years between us, and it was strange to think that my life had hung for a moment on the actions of this elliptical figure, someone I knew very little about and would never meet.

Another story I heard about this man was that during the war he had asked my grandmother to work for him as a spy. But the best story about Bill – or William Stephenson, to give him his full name (not the name he was born with, for reasons we will get to) – was not one I remember being told. It was about how he was taken on by MI6, Britain's foreign intelligence agency, and sent to New York in 1940 on a controversial mission. He was to set up and run a secret British influence campaign that would change American public opinion and bring the United States into the war.

This is the story of the largest state-sponsored influence campaign ever run on American soil. Covert, sophisticated, eye-wateringly expensive, this undercover British operation has been described as 'one of the most diverse, extensive, and yet subtle propaganda drives ever directed by one sovereign state at another'.[1] The *Washington Post* called it 'arguably the most effective in history', 'a virtual textbook in the art of manipulation', and one that 'changed America forever'.[2] It has been linked to the birth of not only the CIA but the modern conservative movement in America. The figure running it, Sir William Stephenson, 'Bill' to his friends, the man who saved my father's life, later became known to the world as the 'man called Intrepid'. He was also hailed by Ian Fleming as one of the inspirations for James Bond.

But this Bond-like figure was not everything he claimed to be, nor was the operation he ran. Only now, with the release of newly declassified British records from the Foreign Office and the wartime special operations agency, the Special Operations Executive (SOE), and an array of corroborating material in American archives, is it possible to strip away years of historical bluff and bluster and tell the story of what Stephenson's undercover operation really achieved in the months leading up to the Japanese attack on Pearl Harbor.

By the time that happened, early on 7 December 1941, Stephenson was running what a CIA historian has called 'the largest clandestine foreign intelligence station ever established in the United States'.[3] At its peak this office employed just under one thousand agents, intermediaries, analysts, clerical staff, pressure-group leaders, journalists, pollsters, agent-runners, campaigners and document forgers, as well as two would-be assassins, an overweight astrologer called Louis and a female spy described by *Time* magazine as the 'Mata Hari from Minnesota'.[4] In the months before the United States entered the Second World War this unlikely team fed into the American news cycle a stream of 'fake news', as it was known then and now; they hacked into the private communications of US senators and representatives, produced forgeries, subsidized and directed protest groups, manipulated opinion polls, organized protests and wiretaps, and otherwise harassed those who stood in their way. At the time, many Americans suspected the British were up to something and imagined there might be collusion with the White House. Few could have guessed either the extent of what was going on or the impact it had.

When this British influence campaign came to life, shortly after the evacuation from Dunkirk in June 1940, one poll suggested that just 8 per cent of the American population wanted to go to war.[5] Eighteen months later, just weeks *before* Pearl Harbor, another poll showed that more than two-thirds of Americans had decided it was time to go to war against Nazi Germany.[6]

What happened then has a particular resonance now. For as long as we live in open and democratic societies there will be the concomitant risk of state-sponsored subversion on this scale, as the British showed in 1941 and as the Russians reminded the world during the 2016 US presidential election. Vast sums have been spent, and no doubt continue to be spent, on undercover operations designed to change the way people somewhere in the world think about a volatile political issue. These efforts to 'shape reality', to borrow from the motto of a modern-day company specializing in this work, are becoming a motif of our age.[7] Usually when we read about an influence campaign the story is told from the outside looking in. What we now know about the British wartime operation in America, 'a thorough, classical case of covert political warfare',[8] is different, and gives us a rare chance to step inside one of these covert operations.

'Fake news' has a long pedigree in American history. In the 1660s, in Kentucky, you could be fined up to 2,000lbs of tobacco if found guilty of spreading 'false news'.[9] By 1940, the term 'fake news' was being used in the press to describe invented or wilfully exaggerated news stories designed to serve a political agenda. The same is true today, even if the term has become more politicized than ever. Sometimes we worry that fake news has been planted by individuals, organizations or governments in an attempt to change the way we think. What follows is an account of when that happened on an unprecedented scale, and how it changed both America and the course of the Second World War.

At its heart is a human story centred on two men whose lives were changed forever by the decisions they made in the frantic months leading up to Pearl Harbor. One was Bill Stephenson of MI6. The other was America's best-known anti-war campaigner, the legendary pilot Charles Lindbergh. By the start of 1941, the British intelligence officer and the American icon were dug in on opposite sides of what had become a civil war of ideas. Throughout the United States the 'Greatest Generation' was caught up in the 'Great Debate'. What began as an argument between the 'interventionists' and the 'isolationists' about whether to go to war had become, by December 1941, as much about the European conflict as it was to do with race, immigration and, ultimately, what it meant to be American.

At stake for Stephenson and Lindbergh was the fate of their respective countries. In the heat of the historical moment they had to decide how much they were willing to risk, and just how far they would go. As much as this book is the history of an influence campaign and the way millions of Americans were encouraged insidiously to change their minds on a vital and divisive issue, it is also the story of how two flawed individuals reacted to the strange situation in which they found themselves, and how the choices they made went on to change the world around them.

PART ONE

APPRENTICE

11 JUNE 1940

Days Britain at war – 282
Allied shipping losses in the Atlantic (to date) – 1,135,263 tons
British Army strength – 1,650,000 men
German Army strength – 4,347,000 men[1]

18–23 MAY 1940

Gallup Survey: Do you think the United States should declare war on Germany and send our army and navy abroad to fight? Yes – 7%[2]

1

From a distance, there seemed to be nothing unusual about the ocean-going liner MV *Britannic* as it prepared to sail for New York. Over the ship's engines came the customary shouts of stevedores as the last of the cargo was loaded up from the Liverpool docks. A tang of petrol cut through the sea air, and beyond the colonnade of cranes you could see the Irish Sea, a glittering block of molten blue, reassuring in its familiarity. Everything was as it should be, except it was not.

On board the *Britannic* that day was a small army of workmen employed by the British government, more than a hundred children in sailor suits or starched white frocks, many of them holding teddy bears the size of lifejackets, at least sixty dark-suited diplomats, and two members of the British royal family, while down in the hold of the ship lay more than seven hundred crates of gold bullion, worth today just over £500 million. This mountain of gold and most of the men on the *Britannic* had one thing in common. All were being sent to the United States as part of a desperate, last-ditch effort to save Britain from defeat. The same was true of the British spy who had just stepped on board.

It was the morning of 11 June 1940. Britain was already at war with Germany, and by the end of that day would also be at war with Italy. As the translation of Mussolini's latest speech was typeset for the evening papers, Allied forces in northern France continued their retreat. Before them, young German men, some wide-eyed on methamphetamine, steered planes, tanks, horses, armoured vehicles and motorbikes deeper into enemy territory. Around them the world seemed to be falling in on itself. Poland, Denmark, Norway, Belgium, and Holland had been defeated. Now France was on the brink. After that, surely, Hitler would turn to Britain.

Earlier that day the country's new prime minister, Winston Churchill, just one month into the job, had written to the President of the United States, Franklin D. Roosevelt: 'We are preparing ourselves to resist his fury and defend our Island.'[1]

Island with a capital 'I'. In the urgency of the moment it was as if the British Isles had transcended geography to become a single sceptred isle, the citadel about to be stormed.

The next day, the prime minister would turn to a general and say, 'you and I will be dead in three months' time.'[2] Eight days before that, Churchill had given parliament a more robust vision of the future, promising that when the Germans came the British would fight on the beaches, and would never surrender. There is another part of this speech that is less known today but in some ways more telling. If the country was overrun, Churchill had also said, the British government 'would carry on the struggle, until, in God's good time, the New World, with all its power and might, steps forth to the rescue and the liberation of the Old'.[3] There was no longer any pretence. Britain's campaign to woo the United States was under way.

The *Britannic* pulled sleepily away from the Liverpool docks, while elsewhere around the country sandbags continued to be piled up in tidy formations, concrete was set on pillboxes, troops were drilled, often without weapons, and in Whitehall enervated civil servants finalized plans to move the machinery of government overseas when, or if, the Germans took London. Others oversaw the ongoing transfer of Britain's gold reserves to North America, including the king's ransom now hidden in the hold of the *Britannic*.

Up on deck, passengers watched the British coastline stretch out before them and shrink, until it was swallowed up by the sea and sky. Their minds would have been aswirl as they thought about the friends and family they were leaving behind, and the dangers of the crossing ahead. Since the start of the war the Allies had lost over a million tons of shipping to marauding German submarines in the Atlantic, and in recent weeks those losses had begun to rise.

The *Britannic* joined a convoy and began to sail west. After three days at sea, orderlies pinned the latest news bulletin to the ship's noticeboards. Crowds of passengers gathered round to find out what was happening in Europe. The news was bleak. That morning, the bulletin revealed, German forces had entered the suburbs of Paris.

France had fallen. Now Britain stood alone.

As German troops celebrated that night in the French capital, the *Britannic*, with its peculiar cargo of spies, diplomats, royalty, children and gold, was separated from its protective convoy for the first time since leaving Liverpool. Initially planes were dispatched from Canada to provide aerial cover, until, as reported in the *New York Times*, the 'fog became so thick that an airplane escort was unable to locate the vessel from the air'.[4] This elegant, ageing liner was on its own. The same was true of Britain. Salvation for both lay in the New World.

Those on board the *Britannic* had become familiar by then with the reassuring drone of planes overhead and the sight of the other ships in the convoy. The emptiness around them must have been eerie. A U-boat could strike at any time, and there was nothing they could do about it.

One of the passengers bracing himself for the shudder of a torpedo striking the hull was a forty-three-year-old called Bill Stephenson. Had you met him on board the *Britannic* you might have guessed he was a businessman. From the way he dressed and the cost of his cabin, you would have surmised he was fairly well-off. There is also a good chance you would have enjoyed talking to him. One man who had many reasons to bear a grudge against him later admitted, 'it was impossible not to like Bill Stephenson.'[5]

To look at, Stephenson was unimpressive. 'Very small in stature,' recalled one secretary, 'neatly put together' and 'a very still person.'[6] But unlike most short men 'he never struck his head up to look at you,' the author Roald Dahl remembered. 'He kept his chin right in and only his eyes, which were very pale, his eyes looked up at you and he never raised his voice, ever.'[7] Many remarked on this quiet intensity, this compression, and the sense that he seemed to be forever holding himself in. 'He always listened with total concentration to what I had to say,' recalled one employee, 'a sympathetic grin flickering at the corner of his mouth.'[8] In Stephenson it was as if a figure of restless energy had been wedged into the shell of a more watchful man.

It is unlikely that any of the people who met him on board the *Britannic* would have guessed either that he was a spy, or that he was on his way to meet the greatest challenge of his life, one that would catapult him into a world he knew worryingly little about. Stephenson had spent most of his adult life as a businessman. He was at his confident best in the world of investment: sizing up a new commercial venture, negotiating an improved stock option, securing collateral for a series of loans. In a matter of days he would start a new career as a professional intelligence officer.

Only a few days before boarding the *Britannic*, Bill Stephenson had formally joined Britain's foreign intelligence agency, MI6, and been appointed Head of Station for the United States, a country codenamed '48-LAND' in MI6 after its then forty-eight states. The stakes could not be higher. If he got it wrong, he might damage his country's chances of avoiding defeat. But if he got it right, consistently, he would play a part in its victory.

The *Britannic* swept out of the fog unscathed. Several days later, on 21 June 1940, the ship docked alongside Pier 54 in the heart of Manhattan's meatpacking district. It was a cool day, yet bright. The city's skyline was doused in a lemony light as the first passengers descended the gangplanks.

At almost exactly the same time, three thousand miles away in France, Adolf Hitler climbed into a railway carriage just outside Paris, where he laid down the terms of the armistice with France. This was the same carriage, and the same location, in which a German delegation had signed the 1918 armistice. Soon German radio stations declared a ten-day celebration of the Nazi victory, an announcement that finished with a promise of what was to come: 'we will sail against England' with an invading force 'like nothing the world has ever seen'.[9]

The crowd which had gathered to meet the *Britannic* was small and subdued. On the lower level of Pier 54, hidden from sight, hundreds of crates of gold were loaded onto armoured trucks and driven to the Federal Reserve Bank of New York. Overhead, passengers left the ship in a similar fashion: quietly and without revealing more than they needed to about why they were there or where they were going.

Bill Stephenson disembarked like the others, and at the end of the pier he was met by a driver. His luggage was loaded up, and he disappeared into the large-lettered commotion of New York, a city where people go to reinvent themselves. This is exactly what he had to do.

Among the many wartime additions to MI6, Bill Stephenson was unusual. His new colleagues tended to be well-off former naval officers who had enjoyed expensive childhoods, and might have been seen in the years before the war wearing 'spats and monocles long after they passed out of fashion'.[1]

Stephenson's upbringing was rather different. He had grown up in poverty in what was effectively the red-light district of a remote Canadian town, Winnipeg, in the Canadian prairies. He was four when his father died. At the age of fourteen he left school and found work in a lumber yard. His mother was an Icelandic immigrant, one of thousands who had left Iceland in the late nineteenth century in the wake of a volcanic eruption to start a new life in the heart of Canada. Stephenson grew up in a working-class Icelandic community rooted to the poorest part of town, Point Douglas, an area notorious for its frequent outbreaks of smallpox and typhoid. It was also the only district in which the city authorities tolerated prostitution. Growing up, the view from his house would have been similar, as a local historian has put it, 'to having a seat at an outdoor peep show'.[2] Stephenson's formative years were among men and women who rarely strayed beyond their neighbourhood, married within the community and dreamed of one day moving to a house within shouting distance of where they had been born. These were his people. This was his world. It was cloistered, dangerous and tough. He was surrounded by fellow 'goolies', local slang for Icelandic-Canadian, as well as bawdy houses, prostitutes and drunks. He grew up understanding the value of loyalty and the language of violence.

But almost as soon as he left Canada in his early twenties, it was as if none of this had ever happened. Years later, he reminisced pleasantly about a childhood spent 'on the prairies of western Canada', and how his 'family had pioneer blood that went back for generations'.[3] On his marriage certificate, Stephenson described his father as a man of 'independent means', and elsewhere as a wealthy businessman and heroic British soldier who had founded the nearby lumber mill and been killed in the Boer War.[4]

Most of this was untrue. Stephenson's father never served with the British Army, and rather than running the local mill he had merely worked there as a labourer for a few years. Each of us can become clumsy when reaching into our past, but this was no slip. In the months before the release of the biography containing most of these exaggerations, Stephenson tried to block the book's publication in just one country – Iceland – where, of course, there were people who knew the truth about his background.

Why did Bill Stephenson run away from his past? The wall he built around his upbringing had less to do with vanity or pride than a desire on his part to cover up the secret at the heart of his childhood, which was only revealed many years after his death, as we shall see.

War was Stephenson's way out of Winnipeg. Aged twenty, he joined the Canadian Expeditionary Force and in 1917 was sent over to France. On the Western Front he was gassed and wounded, and after a long convalescence in Britain he secured a transfer to the Royal Flying Corps. In the months that followed he underwent a metamorphosis. This hitherto quiet and apparently shy young man became an intrepid and fearless flying ace. In the cockpit of a Sopwith

Camel he was transformed, and by the end of the war had notched up an impressive fourteen 'kills' and been awarded the Military Cross, the Croix de Guerre and the Distinguished Flying Cross for his 'conspicuous gallantry' and for showing 'the greatest courage and energy in engaging every kind of target'.[5] He was also commissioned as an officer, and at the same time his relationship with Britain was galvanized. Still a proud Canadian, Stephenson had come to see himself also as a loyal Briton. He had fought for King and Country, and for the rest of his life, wherever he lived, he would insist on having a portrait of the reigning monarch hung over the fireplace.

Captain W. S. Stephenson, MC, DFC, as he now was, returned to Winnipeg as a war hero. At once he set about becoming an entrepreneur, launching a company which sold a new type of can-opener that he claimed to have invented himself (but had not). Soon he was selling other household goods and was earning enough to move out of the red-light district. Captain Stephenson was riding high, until his business fell apart in 1922 and he was declared bankrupt.

Stephenson left Winnipeg in a hurry and moved to London, where he reinvented himself and his past, married an American heiress, joined the General Radio Company and by the end of the decade had made a fortune developing, marketing and selling radio sets. By the mid-1930s, Bill Stephenson was a respectable Canadian millionaire with his own investment fund, but one who preferred not to speak about his past.

It was around this time that my grandparents came to know him. Harold and Alice Hemming were also Canadians who had moved to London. Although Harold came to Britain when he was much younger, Alice had spent most of her life until then in Canada and perhaps had more in common with Stephenson than her husband. Although she was more gregarious and outspoken than Stephenson, they were similar in age and both had been living in poverty in different parts of Winnipeg at the start of the war. Alice and her family later moved to Vancouver, where she became a journalist at the *Vancouver Sun*. But like Stephenson she never forgot the privations of her childhood.

By 1936, the Hemmings and their two children were regular guests at Stephenson's tiny weekend cottage in Buckinghamshire, just outside London. Harold and Alice's diaries give a fleeting taste of the atmosphere there. In winter they would all go foraging for mushrooms, in summer they played with the children in the woods or among the wildflowers. Alice is often sleeping in the sun, or chatting to Bill's wife, Mary. Harold, a banker, is playing around with his new toy, a 'movie camera', or he is talking shop with Bill – the two of them worked together on several business deals including the financing of the Earls Court Exhibition Centre. On one visit, they all went to a nearby waterfall and Bill got soaked and spent the afternoon wandering around in his wife's pink trousers.[6] The mood was relaxed and informal, but occasionally glamorous. At lunch Harold and Alice might find themselves sitting next to wealthy Americans, Canadian writers, English grandees, or the former heavyweight boxing champion of the world Gene Tunney. At one meal, Alice got on so well with the pilot next to her that when it was time to go home she and Harold agreed to have a race. He would drive, Alice and the pilot would fly, which they did, flying to Hendon Aerodrome in north London, where Alice caught a taxi home (and won).

But by the time Stephenson pulled my three-year-old Dad out of his pond, as he did in September 1938, just days before the Munich Crisis, Harold and Alice's visits to the cottage were less frequent and the atmosphere appears to have changed. What my grandparents did not mention in their diaries – because they would not have known – is that by this point in Stephenson's life he was gravitating towards the world of intelligence.

Most of Stephenson's wealth was then tied up in his investment fund, British Pacific Trust, which owned stakes in companies operating across northern Europe. They produced everything from cement and aeroplanes to film sets. As Stephenson's business portfolio expanded, so did his need for better information about the territories in which he had investments. To give him an edge, he came to rely on a loose network of friends, acquaintances and paid informants to tell him about the economic situation in countries such as Sweden and Germany. One of these may have been Harold, whose work for an American stock brokerage frequently took him to Berlin, and who would, according to his diary, always see Stephenson after each of these trips.

Around this time, Stephenson took the unusual step of giving this network a name. He began to refer to it as 'The British Industrial Secret Service'. Given that this operation was small, private, unofficial, and had nothing to do with the British government, it is hard to think of a more peculiar or provocative title.[7] Calling it this made no sense, unless, of course, Stephenson had some deeper desire to be involved in the world of espionage and wanted to pique the curiosity of Britain's actual secret intelligence service.

The first government official to take an interest in his network was Desmond Morton, later described as 'Churchill's Man of Mystery'. Morton was impressed by the quality of Stephenson's 'product', meaning the intelligence his network produced, and by the start of 1939 he was circulating it among his friends and colleagues, including a Conservative backbencher calling for rearmament, Winston Churchill. Another Conservative backbencher to see some of these reports was Sir Ralph Glyn, who decided to introduce Stephenson to MI6.

'He is a Canadian with a quiet manner, and evidently knows a great deal about Continental affairs and industrial matters,' ran the official account of Stephenson's first encounter with MI6, in the summer of 1939, with war fast approaching.[8] The meeting was a success. Stephenson came across as discreet, motivated, and shrewd, and MI6 offered to provide him with assistance and some funding. In return, he would name his sources and share the intelligence they provided. Stephenson agreed.

Just days before the outbreak of the Second World War, this businessman of few words had his foot in the door at MI6.

Although it was unusual for a British intelligence agency to take on a private network like Stephenson's, and his path into MI6 was not typical, there were precedents. It is easy to see why MI6 wanted to work with him. By September 1939 there was an overwhelming demand within Whitehall for better intelligence on Nazi Germany and her neighbours: Stephenson's network was already in position, it was deniable, and it was cheap.

In the days after German forces began to advance into Poland, in September 1939, Bill Stephenson was sent out to Sweden by the head of MI6, Admiral Sir Hugh Sinclair, known to his staff as 'C', with the task of overseeing his small network of agents. But soon this Canadian businessman had plans to do much more, and in the weeks after arriving in Stockholm he began to badger his boss for more funds to expand his network.

'C' refused. Feeling frustrated, Stephenson began to work instead with an offshoot of MI6 called Section D, which specialized in sabotage and 'dirty tricks'. By the end of 1939, he had teamed up with a small group of Section D personnel in southern Sweden. Together they hatched a plan to destroy or disable some port-loading equipment. Given how much iron ore went from Sweden to Germany, this could put a dent in the Nazi war machine. But the new 'C', Colonel Stewart Menzies, installed after the unexpected death of Sinclair, did not approve. They were all stood down.

By April 1940, Stephenson's relationship with MI6 had lost its lustre. He was beginning to think about other ways to support the British war effort, to do his bit as he had done during the last war, when 'C' came to him with an unexpected proposal. It had nothing to do with Sweden, undercover agents, or setting explosives. The new 'C' wanted him to go to the United States and meet the head of the FBI, J. Edgar Hoover.

The relationship between British and American intelligence had by then frozen over. The senior MI6 officer in the US, Sir James Paget, well-meaning but ineffective, had been banned by his American hosts from communicating with anyone in the US government outside the State Department. There was no sign of an imminent thaw, until 'C' heard about a remark which had been made by the Director of the FBI.

Hoover was relaxing in Miami Beach when he mentioned to a British friend that he liked the idea of 'more direct contact' with London.[9] This made its way rapidly to 'C', who remembered that Bill Stephenson had an unlikely friend in common with Hoover – the former boxing champion of the world, Gene Tunney. The two had met at the end of the last war, in France, where they had seen each other box. 'He was an excellent boxer,' Tunney recalled of Stephenson, who was a flyweight, 'quick as a dash of lightning'.[10]

Stephenson told 'C' he would be happy to help, without really knowing what this might entail. He contacted his friend Tunney, who arranged the meeting. Stephenson then took a plane to Paris, a train to Genoa, a ship to New York, a train to Washington DC, and on 16 April 1940 was shown into Hoover's cavernous public office in the Justice Department building.

The walls were canary yellow. Down one side of the space was a run of double-height windows, each framed by gold-pleated drapes, and at the far end a desk of oceanic proportions, its polished lacquer surface like a reflecting pool. Behind it sat a short, wide-eyed man with a permanently quizzical look on his face.

Once the humble filing clerk John Hoover, the meticulously named J. Edgar Hoover had run the Federal Bureau of Investigation and its similarly named predecessor for more than fifteen years. He was methodical and fast, and quick to judge. Right away, Stephenson needed to make a good impression. He had to act the part of the seasoned MI6 professional, even if he was not.

Stephenson's task was to open up a channel of communication

between the FBI and MI6. Relying on the same quiet authority which had so impressed MI6 in that first meeting, he made his case to Hoover. The two men warmed to each other. Almost identical in height and age, both with an initially watchful manner, they kept talking for most of the day.[11] 'Long Washington conference completely successful,' Stephenson cabled 'C' that night, adding that Hoover had sent 'assurances of goodwill and of desire to assist far beyond confines of officialdom'.[12]

There was just one stumbling block. The State Department wanted a monopoly on the American relationship with British intelligence, and had forbidden Hoover from working with MI6. So the FBI director asked the White House for permission to go behind the back of the State Department.

One of Roosevelt's secretaries, General Edwin 'Pa' Watson, reported 'no objection from the White House to such a confidential relationship'.[13]

This was a breakthrough, better than anything 'C' could have hoped for. The president of the United States had not only approved of this new and secret relationship between MI6 and the FBI, he welcomed it, and was 'a little amused', he let Hoover know, 'at the way in which you side-tracked the State Department'.[14] Stephenson had completed his MI6 mission and was due to return to London when Hoover asked to see him one last time. In that meeting, he asked Stephenson to become the personal liaison between the head of MI6 and himself.

It may not have been a job Stephenson had imagined himself having, nor was it a job that had ever existed, but he liked the idea.

Stephenson cabled 'C'. 'I like the suggestion,' came the reply, 'but it is considered you should return to London first of all for consultation and instruction.'[15]

In the days that followed, as Stephenson travelled back to Britain, and with German forces advancing deeper into France, 'C' took a risk. He barely knew Bill Stephenson. Nor did any of his colleagues.

Here was a Canadian businessman who did not fit the mould of a typical MI6 officer, but evidently Hoover liked him, and in only a few days he had achieved what the existing MI6 Head of Station, Paget, had failed to do over many months. Rather than appoint Stephenson as a go-between with the FBI, 'C' went further. He decided to have Stephenson replace Paget and run all MI6 operations in the United States. It was as if a theatre director had given an amateur thespian a cameo in his latest production, and on the strength of one admirable performance had decided that he should play the lead.

At a meeting in London, Stephenson agreed to take the job. He was soon on his way back across the Atlantic on the *Britannic*. But as the ship made its way towards New York, the job he had been given changed shape. Stephenson was still playing the lead, but with opening night only days away the production had been moved to a much bigger venue and he had been given many more lines.

The evacuation from Dunkirk had just finished. Britain was now in dire need of weapons and munitions, as well as ships, food and a regular supply of industrial raw materials. Much of Europe had recently become inaccessible, leaving Britain more dependent than ever on the United States. In Whitehall there was a sudden, jolting realization that without the backing of the American people the flow of US supplies might slow down or just stop, and that this could leave them unable to fight.

Britain's ability to wage war rested on the thoughts and feelings of ordinary Americans. A recent Gallup poll suggested ominously that roughly half of the American people did not think the British should be allowed to buy American planes on credit.[16] Much more had to be done to persuade them that Hitler was a threat to their national security and, no less important, that Britain was worth saving. Although tentative efforts were being made in the open to improve the way Britain was seen in America, there also needed to be an influence campaign behind the scenes.

Who should run it? The obvious candidate was a former MI6 officer called Sir William Wiseman, who had performed espionage miracles during the last war befriending, influencing and spying on President Woodrow Wilson. Wiseman was later hailed by one MI6 officer as 'the most successful "agent of influence" the British ever had'.[17] Since the outbreak of war Wiseman had been lobbying to go out to the United States again. But the problem with Wiseman's plan, it transpired, was Wiseman. 'C' vetoed the idea of using him, possibly because he was too well known.

A debate followed between civil servants in the Foreign Office, the Ministry of Information, MI6 and the British embassy in Washington about who to send instead. Two days before the fall of Paris, as newly declassified files show, one British official within this quickening exchange came up with an unusual solution.

Why not give the job of running this influence campaign to the new MI6 man in New York, Bill Stephenson? Provided he 'is a really competent and suitable person and additional appointments are made to his staff', he should be able to carry out the task.[18] In other neutral countries the responsibility for 'a whole range of covert activities' had fallen to MI6, so why not this one?[19] 'Being less well known than Sir William [Wiseman], he should attract far less publicity.'[20]

Stephenson was unaware of this exchange. As these messages flew back and forth between an archipelago of desks in London and Washington, his ship continued to chug across the Atlantic. Without either asking for this position or being given the chance to turn it down, this first-time spymaster with no experience of running an MI6 station, let alone manipulating public opinion on a nationwide scale, had been given a job of burgeoning responsibility. The first he heard about this was after the *Britannic* arrived in Manhattan, as it did on 21 June 1940, and he introduced himself to his new staff at the local MI6 station.

Stephenson took one look at his new domain, a gloomy suite of rooms on Exchange Place, Lower Manhattan, and decided never to return. Instead he moved his threadbare staff to a different office. He might have chosen a slightly larger or less depressing set-up in the same block. Instead his new charges, no more than ten MI6 employees, were told to report to Hampshire House, overlooking Central Park, where they were led up to a penthouse apartment, one of the most lavish and expensive residences anywhere in New York, which would now double up as both the MI6 station for the United States and Stephenson's home.

His staff could hardly believe their eyes. Their new workplace had featured in a recent issue of *House and Garden*, whose readers were told breathlessly that 'the ceiling is pink, the floor black and white marble', and the lights were 'concealed in the fruit and flower clusters'; its enormous doors were finished in a 'maroon lacquer' with 'chunky white moldings' and scattered around the stately two-storey drawing room were 'carved Georgian banquettes in white, upholstered and tufted in crimson velvet'.[1] It looked like the set of a Fred Astaire musical. An early visitor to the new MI6 office was the actor and singer Noel Coward, who was lined up at one point to work for Stephenson, and who remembered feeling decidedly at home in here amid 'the outsize chintz flowers crawling over the walls'. Few intelligence headquarters have ever been so luxuriously decorated, or so garishly.[2]

The MI6 staff felt as if they had entered a new world, and in a different sense the same was true for Bill Stephenson. Arriving in New York from London was like stepping through the proverbial looking glass. He had left a nation caught up in a defining moment of collective sacrifice, and was now in a city geared to the pursuit of pleasure: a noisy, stifling metropolis where the business of spending money could feel like an art-form in itself. Until then Stephenson had always lived frugally and within his means, but moving to New York had a liberating effect on him. He never took a salary from MI6, and from the moment he arrived in Manhattan he poured his own money into this operation.

As well as moving his office to an exclusive apartment, he splurged on state-of-the-art machines.[3] Drawing on his background in radio, he soon had the latest telegraphic equipment installed in his MI6 station, including what one employee called 'an ingenious teleprinter known as the telekrypton',[4] and a 'secret cipher bureau'.[5] Some of this was approved by 'C' and paid for by the British government, much of it was not. 'C's predecessor, Sinclair, had complained about Stephenson's 'ludicrous ideas on finance', adding, 'I have – even in war time – to consider the taxpayer', an opinion no doubt shared by the new head of MI6.[6] Already it was clear that his man in New York liked to do things his own way.

Stephenson also began to take on more staff. Having inherited just an assistant, a cashier, a principal, a coding clerk, and a handful of secretaries, he soon had a stream of new recruits on their way from Britain.

His existing members of staff were intrigued not only by their colourful new surroundings but by their boss. One employee later recalled the day 'this little Canadian fellow arrived, and no one knew

who he was'.[7] They eyed him with a potent mix of curiosity and suspicion. Slowly, they tried to get the measure of him. They watched
him. They tried to place him. They learned that this compact, wiry
man liked to keep fit, and would start each day with a hundred
skips followed by 'lots of cold coffee'.[8] He had a distinctive gait, one
remembered. 'It was as though he had little springs at the balls of his
feet, even when he walked across his office to shake hands with you.'[9]

They also came to know at a distance the other occupant of
this apartment, Stephenson's wife, Mary, the daughter of a wealthy
tobacco farmer from Springfield, Tennessee. Bill referred to her as
'my old Dutch'.[10] They never had children. Mary was sometimes sub-
missive around her husband, and one friend wondered if 'she was
frightened of him', but he concluded that 'he loved her and they had
a very, very good marriage, I think.'[11]

But for the MI6 staff in New York the sharpest insight to their
new boss came from a remark he made early on. At the time there
was a feeling among some of the MI6 old hands that their American
hosts were essentially 'a bunch of salesmen', as one put it, and 'the
disquieting thing was that they were all rich'.

'That's all bullshit,' Stephenson told them one day, in his quiet voice
with a light Canadian accent. 'They're our friends. They'll help us.
And we need them if we're going to win.'[12]

You can imagine the unnatural silence that must have followed,
and that for several seconds very little would have moved in this art-
fully upholstered apartment high above Central Park. It was not just
the message that was unusual, but the language. The way Stephenson
spoke, his background, his manner, his decision not to take a salary,
all of these set him apart.

None of this should have mattered to his new staff, but what was
worrying, and might hinder the British war effort, was the possibility that Bill Stephenson did not really know what he was doing.
Early on, he had breezily told his staff that he had been given 'a

fairly free hand' by 'C', which suggested that London did not know either.[13]

'Stephenson gave me absolutely no guidance,' one early recruit complained, 'didn't say, here is a job, get on with it – precisely nothing. There was no organization, no orders. Everybody there had to be a self-starter.'[14]

Several weeks in, Bill Stephenson was struggling to reinvent himself as a senior MI6 officer. With some of his staff wondering why he had even been given this job, he turned his attention outwards. To get the British influence campaign going, he needed a fuller sense of what he was up against. More than anything else, he had to understand why so many Americans were passionately against going to war.

4

Fourteen months before Stephenson's ship arrived in Manhattan, another ocean-going liner docked on the same side of the island. It was met by a mob of photographers held back by a line of police. The night was becoming cold by the time the gangplanks went up and the passengers disembarked, all except one. The photographers advanced quietly along the dock. Some made it onto the ship, including one who broke into the cabin of this last passenger and took a picture, before being wrestled to the ground and removed.

At last, the man they had come to see emerged from the cabin. He was surrounded by a scrum of policemen. The cast of his face was thin with boyish, hollowed-out features. He looked 'rather grim and purposeful', one newspaper noted.[1] The *New York Times* reported his 'mouth was set in a firm line'.[2]

Around him was bedlam. 'The photographers ran in front of us and behind us,' he later wrote, 'jamming the way, being pushed aside by the police yelling, falling over each other on the deck.'[3] Amid the shoves and the cries of pain, the tumult of men moments away from getting what they had come for, was the pop of camera flashguns and the burst of light into the night, followed by the smash of burnt-out bulbs as they fell to the ground.

He had not heard those sounds for months, and no doubt they

released a flood of unhappy memories. Some of the men shouted out questions – why had he come back, how long would he stay, what was he doing here?

As usual, he did not answer. It was one of his rules.

Remaining 'characteristically silent', this determined-looking figure climbed into a waiting car which accelerated into the night.[4] After more than three years away, Charles Lindbergh, America's most famous son, had come home.

Now he had work to do.

Lindbergh was by then a global icon. In 1927 he had captured the world's imagination by becoming the first to fly solo across the Atlantic. At the time this seemed to be the ultimate triumph of man and machine over nature, like landing on the Moon for a later generation. His flight had come just after several technological breakthroughs which allowed the imagery and audio of his feat to be shared with a vast international audience. From Manila to Moscow, Shanghai to Santiago, millions of people had seen his plane, 'The Spirit of St Louis', as it came in to land, and had watched this good-looking pilot emerge from the cockpit looking dazed, tired and excited. Aged twenty-five, Charles Lindbergh became the world's first media superstar.

Five years later, Lindbergh's life was upended by tragedy. His one-year-old son, Charles, was snatched from his house while he and his wife were downstairs having dinner. Although the kidnappers had been hoping to secure a ransom for the safe return of the boy, they killed him accidentally during the kidnap. After a long investigation the ringleader was found and later sentenced to death.

All over the world people who had never met Charles Lindbergh felt an almost uncontainable surge of sympathy. As Philip Roth later wrote, Lindbergh's courage in crossing the Atlantic was now 'permeated with a pathos that transformed him into a martyred titan comparable to Lincoln'.[5] The tragedy of his son's death was compounded by Lindbergh's longstanding aversion to the fame which had been thrust upon him. He rarely posed for photographs, signed autographs or gave interviews, which only fuelled his popularity. That shy dignity seemed to echo the modest, homespun values of a bygone era. Shooting to fame in the 1920s, he was an American hero in an otherwise unheroic age. But in reading about the death of Lindbergh's son, many Americans felt at least a brush of guilt, knowing that their interest in his life may have helped turn him and his family into targets for kidnappers.

America's martyred titan never fully recovered from the death of his first child: it is hard to see how anyone could. For the rest of his life this loss remained buried inside him, an implacable wound. He was unable to forgive either the kidnappers for what they had done, or the American press for the way it had treated him before the tragedy and immediately afterwards: once his son's corpse was eventually found and had been prepared for burial, a photographer broke into the morgue, forced open the casket and took a picture.

The Lindberghs then left the country. With his wife Anne and their two young children, Lindbergh started over in the seclusion of the sleepy English village of Sevenoaks Weald. Entombed by grief, the family lived quietly in a tumbledown house that belonged to Vita Sackville-West and her husband Harold Nicolson. Later they moved to an island off the coast of Brittany. They were content in Europe and had no plans to come home, until March 1939, when they heard that Hitler's troops had entered Prague.

In the days that followed, as Nazi forces occupied the rest of Czechoslovakia, Lindbergh decided to cross the Atlantic. He was not the only one. Thousands of European Jews made plans to escape in the days that followed, as did many Americans living in Europe who feared the outbreak of war. On their return they would warn of the threat posed by Hitler. Lindbergh had a different goal in mind. The world's most famous pilot wanted to come home in

order to convince his fellow Americans *not* to go to war with Nazi
Germany.

For years, the press had effectively used Charles Lindbergh to boost
circulation. Now he planned to use them. Reinventing himself as a
political activist would mean wading back into the swamp of celebrity
only four years after he had pulled himself out, and as he told a crew
member on the ship which took him back to the US, 'you have no idea
how unkind the American press has been to me.'[6] But the reluctance
he felt was trumped by his desire, perhaps duty is a better word, to do
what he could to stop the United States from sliding into war. At stake
was 'the welfare of the country', he wrote, and it seemed churlish to hold
back for fear of hurting his own 'personal feelings'.[7]

Less than a month after war had broken out in Europe, Lindbergh
gave his first radio broadcast. The nation was amazed not just by the
sound of his voice, given how rarely he spoke in public, but by what
he had to say. Expecting 'an exciting book of adventure fiction', one
commentator wrote, they were given instead 'a weighty tome on
international politics'.[8] But it was coherent and sincere, and many
found it persuasive.

There was no doubt what Lindbergh wanted. But why had he
embarked on this crusade? What was driving him on? Lindbergh's
answer was simple. He was motivated by a patriotic urge to help his
country. Most people accepted this. Part of Lindbergh's appeal was
that he seemed to come from outside the bubble of Washington DC
and was unlikely to have ulterior political motives. The columnist
Dorothy Thompson wondered whether he was driven instead by a
desire to honour the memory of his father, a congressman who had
led a deeply unpopular campaign against America's involvement in
the last war. Others toyed with a more sinister idea. They wondered
if Charles Lindbergh, that paragon of American endeavour, might
secretly be working for the Nazis.

*

On the evening of Saturday 15 June 1940, the day after victorious
German troops marched into Paris, with Bill Stephenson sailing
towards New York, Lindbergh strode up to the Washington studios
of NBC where he was due to give his fourth broadcast against the
United States' entry into the war. As usual, he arrived at the studios
too early. This was partly because he hated being late, also it was
down to nerves, and for the next ten minutes he paced the block.

Although the capital was witheringly hot that day, NBC insisted
that anyone broadcasting in the evening wear formal clothes. Over-
dressed and anxious, Lindbergh was also worried about being spotted
by a passer-by. One of his tricks was to keep in his pocket at all
times a pair of glasses (without glass) which he could pull on if he
felt in danger of being recognized. This was a defence against what
he hated most about life in the public eye: his lack of control over
who approached him and when. After thirteen years in the spotlight
he had come to crave the certainty of solitude, which only made his
recent foray into politics more unusual.

As Charles Lindbergh pounded the streets of Washington, trying
to avoid eye contact with his fellow pedestrians, life in the city around
him appeared to carry on as normal. Vicars and priests worked
on their Father's Day sermons to give in church the next day, the
new Disney picture *Pinocchio* was playing in the cinemas, the city's
baseball team, the Nationals, was being hammered, as usual, and
out on the Tidal Basin work on the Jefferson Memorial was almost
complete. But there were hints that all was not right. Armed guards
had recently been stationed around Capitol Hill, and across the city
on front porches and lawns one could see Stars and Stripes where
the year before there had been none. The war in Europe may have
been thousands of miles away, but there were moments in the capital,
during the summer of 1940, when it felt closer.

Lindbergh made his way into the sanctuary of the recording booth
deep inside the NBC studios. The clock counted down to the start

of his broadcast. On the desk in front of him was a state-of-the-art ribbon microphone, finished in honeycombed aluminium, and next to it his speech.

All over the country, millions of people congregated around their radio sets, large contraptions usually set up in the smartest room like a futuristic shrine. From Madawaska in Maine to Honolulu, Hawaii, the fact that 'Lucky Lindy' was to deliver a coast-to-coast broadcast on the WEAF-NBC-Red network had been reported as news. Some of those tuning in were Lindbergh fans: others could not stand him. The rest were still making up their minds. Regardless of your position, a speech by Charles Lindbergh was an event.

The red light came on. Lindbergh took a breath and began to speak in his flat, oddly reassuring voice.

'I have asked to speak to you again tonight, because I believe that we, in America, are drifting toward a position of far greater seriousness to our future than even this present war.'

What followed began as a standard riff on the theme of 'isolationism', the principle that the US should stay out of all foreign wars unless they spread to the Americas. Isolationism was similar to the British and French pre-war policy of appeasement, except it had a more obvious logic and stronger historical roots. Britain and France had a record of intervening in foreign wars. The United States did not. Most people would trace this American aversion to intervention back to the Founding Fathers. For John Adams it was 'a first principle and maxim never to be forgotten' that the US should 'maintain an entire neutrality in all future European wars'.[9] George Washington in his 1796 farewell address and Thomas Jefferson in his subsequent inaugural speech warned Americans against entering into 'entangling alliances'.[10]

Another cornerstone of isolationism was the idea that America was fundamentally different to other nations: it was exceptional, and its people's 'manifest destiny' was to settle and develop their nation rather than allow themselves to be dragged into foreign wars. Some also felt that in these darkened times America had a responsibility to rise above the petty European in-fighting and become, for the rest of the world, Winthrop's 'city upon a hill'. Few Americans saw their country as a global superpower. Fewer still saw Britain as a natural ally.

Lindbergh hit most of these notes in his broadcast, and did so with skill. He salted his speech with folksy references to 'the old west' and 'those old pioneers of ours', at one point throwing in a timeless bromide about how 'the red-blooded wisdom of the old west is gone from American politics today'. But at the heart of his speech was a classic isolationist appeal: 'Shall we submerge our future in the end-less wars of the old world? Or shall we build our own defenses and leave European war to European countries?'

This last line had an electric resonance for many of those Ameri-cans who had left Europe themselves, or whose parents had done so, women and men for whom the act of immigration could feel like a psychic break with the past. By turning away from Europe they had turned towards America, and its dream of a new life without the prejudices of the old. Isolationism was an extension of that trium-phant release, a sense that being American was a choice rooted in an ideal and this allowed them to abandon the troubles of the Old World without losing themselves in guilt.

Much of this had been said before, yet towards the end of his broadcast Lindbergh ventured into new territory.

'As far as invasion by air is concerned, it is impossible for any existing air force to attack effectively across the ocean,' he told his millions of listeners. This line had considerable weight coming from a man famous for having crossed that same body of water in an act of epic endurance. 'With our geographical position, nothing but the gross neglect of our military forces, or quarrelling between American countries themselves, could make possible an invasion by foreign armies.'

Those on the other side of the argument saw the Atlantic Ocean as a giant no-man's-land, one that could easily be breached. Here was Lindbergh urging his listeners to think of it as the world's largest moat.

He was right. Only one foreign nation had ever landed its troops on US soil in an offensive action, and that had been Britain during the War of 1812. For most of American history the Atlantic had helped stave off the possibility of a European invasion. Lindbergh's point was valid, but the idea to include it in his speech had not been entirely his.

The red light went off. Lindbergh made his way out of the recording booth, while across the country people began to talk among themselves. Of the millions of different responses to this broadcast one stood out.

In Washington, a pipe-smoking Nazi diplomat reflected on what he had just heard. He was excited by the thought of America staying out of the war, and in the wake of Lindbergh's speech he also experienced a small sense of satisfaction, pride perhaps, at a job well done.

The social life of Hans Thomsen was quieter than it had been for years. Once a popular fixture on the Georgetown diplomatic circuit, he and his glamorous wife, Bebe, had been ostracized since the start of the war. By the summer of 1940 they were used to quiet evenings at home, unless Hans had to work late at the German embassy, where he was chargé d'affaires. For reasons that he kept to himself, lately this had been happening a lot.

Less than two years earlier, the Nazi regime had orchestrated Kristallnacht, a state-sponsored pogrom in which paramilitaries throughout Germany attacked Jewish property, killing dozens of Jewish men and women, and arresting thousands more, most of whom were sent to concentration camps. Roosevelt had responded by ordering home his ambassador to Germany. In retaliation, Hitler had recalled the German ambassador to the United States. This left as the ranking German representative in the US the little-known career diplomat Hans Thomsen.

Fastidiously polite, tall with blond hair and bee-stung lips, Thomsen had been working for the German state long before Hitler ventured into politics. He was not a diehard Nazi, but at the same time he was at pains to show Berlin that he deserved to remain in post, which explains why he was so busy.

By the time Lindbergh walked up to the NBC studio in Washington DC, in June 1940, Hans Thomsen was running an elaborate influence campaign inside the United States. It was wide-ranging, expensive and increasingly bold.

His orders from Berlin were simple: 'to prevent by all means at my disposal the entry of the United States into the war'.[1] Earlier that year, one of Thomsen's undercover agents had persuaded an American publisher to print and distribute Nazi propaganda, including *The German White Paper*, a book containing translations of the so-called 'Warsaw Papers' which appeared to show Roosevelt promising American support to countries facing Nazi aggression.

This was a start. Thomsen had since developed a more daring scheme centred on the congressional 'franking privilege'. This privilege allowed senators and representatives to reproduce and mail out, at no cost to themselves, any item that had appeared in the *Congressional Record*, the official log of speeches made in the house and other material added at the request of members of Congress. Instead of attaching a postage stamp, members could use their personalized frank, designed to look like a reproduction of their signature.

Thomsen's plan – which must, he urged Berlin, 'be treated with the greatest secrecy'[2] – was to approach sitting members of Congress and ask them to insert German or pro-German material into the *Congressional Record*, then have these articles reproduced by the US government – he estimated print runs of up to 1 million – before these politicians used their personal frank to mail them out to a list supplied by the German embassy of 'specially chosen persons'.[3]

This could expose hundreds of thousands of Americans to anti-war material, and do so in a way that conferred congressional authority on everything they read. Thomsen was also excited about what this could mean for the German taxpayer. 'At the very least,' he wrote, 'mail expenses amounting to many tens of thousands of dollars would be saved', or, rather, transferred to the American taxpayer.[4] His plan sounded good in theory, but the problem, surely, would be to find any member of Congress willing to risk their political career by taking part.

Somehow, Hans Thomsen managed it. By June 1940, this unprepossessing diplomat had inducted into his congressional franking scheme 'several Senators and Congressmen',[5] including Republican representative Jacob Thorkelson of Montana.

On 20 June 1940, Thorkelson rose to his feet in the house and asked for parts of a controversial new book, *The German White Paper* – paid for by the German government – to be included in the *Congressional Record*. His request was accepted, the excerpts were added, and this material was later mailed out to tens of thousands of Americans chosen by the German embassy. Two days later, Thorkelson was at it again, this time asking to have added to the *Record* a recent interview with Hitler in which the German Chancellor insisted his country posed no threat to America. In a cable to Berlin, Thomsen happily took credit for having 'induced' Thorkelson to do this.[6]

Why did the congressman cooperate? The word 'induced' suggests bribery, and while there may have been money involved there is no evidence that Thorkelson was paid, nor that he was acting against his will. There was certainly nothing scandalous at that time about an American politician wanting to stay out of the war, or hoping that Germany defeated Britain. In a *Fortune* poll carried out in the same month just under 8 per cent of those surveyed thought the US should enter the war on the side of the British.[7] As the German victories piled up, there was even a chance that support for Hitler would grow. The American people rarely like to back a loser.

'There is scarcely any doubt left that England will be defeated', Thomsen wrote at the time.[8] A senior British diplomat in Washington described simultaneously the sudden 'wave of pessimism sweeping over this country to the effect that Great Britain must now inevitably be defeated, and that there is no use in the United States doing anything more to help it,' adding gloomily that this 'is beginning to affect the President'.[9]

The Nazi influence campaign was becoming bolder by the day. German agents would soon be bribing delegates at the Democratic National Convention, in Chicago, to oppose Roosevelt's nomination. Germany's most senior diplomat in the US was paying so many agents and intermediaries that he no longer risked keeping receipts, knowing that if these fell 'into the hands of the American Secret Service', it would 'mean political ruin and have other grave consequences for our political friends'.[10] Staff at the German embassy continued to feed inflated figures on the strength of the Luftwaffe to their contacts in the US military, assuring them that Britain was doomed. The German military attaché, General Friedrich von Bötticher, was by then such a familiar sight in the US War Department in Washington that he was no longer frisked on entering the building.

German diplomats and undercover agents were now in touch with a wide range of military officers, businessmen and politicians, including one who approached Thomsen shortly after Lindbergh's speech in June 1940 with a risky proposition. He was a prominent isolationist politician, so important that Thomsen kept his name out of cables to Berlin and referred to him only as a 'well-known Republican Congressman'.[11] This particular congressman wanted German help in organizing a 'lightning propaganda campaign' to coincide with the imminent Republican National Convention.[12]

The first part of his plan was simple. Berlin would pay for fifty isolationist congressmen to attend the convention, where they could lobby against going to war. This would cost the Germans just $3,000. The American politician also wanted Berlin to contribute between $60,000 and $80,000 to a series of newspaper advertisements due to appear on the last day of the convention, just as the all-important Republican foreign policy plank was finalized.

Berlin approved both plans. Fifty Republican congressmen were sent to the convention in Philadelphia. Few ever realized that the bill for their travel had been picked up by the Third Reich. Several days later, on 25 June 1940, full-page advertisements appeared in a string of leading newspapers under the headline 'Stop the March to War'.[13]

The timing was perfect. Later that same day the Republican resolutions committee agreed on a foreign policy plank with a heavy isolationist slant. As Thomsen reported to Berlin, parts of this resolution had been lifted 'almost verbatim from the conspicuous full-page advertisements in the American press'.[14] The Nazi intervention in the US political process continued to be precise and effective, and Hans Thomsen was now running what one historian has called 'at the time the most extensive foreign intervention – direct intervention – ever into an American election campaign'.[15]

Who was the Republican congressman working with the Nazis? Thomsen tried to conceal his identity, but he left several clues. In one of his messages he let slip that this unidentified politician was the driving force behind the 'ad hoc Republican Committee' associated with the advertisements. This was the National Committee to Keep America Out of Foreign Wars, run by the well-known Republican congressman Hamilton Fish.

Less than a year before the war, Hamilton Fish had been the main speaker at the German Day celebration at Madison Square Garden. Standing before a backdrop of Stars and Stripes and a single swastika, this brooding figure with a military bearing and a stentorian voice had promised to do everything he could to stop the United States going to war with Germany. Shortly before Hitler ordered the invasion of Poland, Fish was flown to Oslo by the German foreign minister, Joachim Ribbentrop. When questioned in Congress about this trip the congressman was indignant: 'I have no apology to offer for riding in von Ribbentrop's plane, and I have no regrets for doing it either', calling the man who had raised this in the press 'a jackass'.[16]

His response to Berlin's publication of the 'Warsaw Papers' was to call for Roosevelt's impeachment.[17]

All the evidence suggests that Hamilton Fish was the congressman who asked for and received Nazi help at the Republican convention. Like so many American politicians, Fish wanted the US to stay out of the war and he had no desire to fight Germany. The same was true of Senator Ernest Lundeen, of Montana, who was not only in touch with Hans Thomsen. He was also a friend of Charles Lindbergh.

In the days leading up to his NBC broadcast, Lindbergh had met various isolationist politicians in Washington, including Senators Clark, Wheeler and Reynolds, who had persuaded him to give this broadcast in the first place.[18] He also saw Senator Lundeen. They had dinner together shortly before the NBC speech. We do not know exactly what was said, only that hours after their meal Lindbergh scribbled in his diary: 'changed and retyped last page of address'.[19]

This last page included the passage for which his speech was later remembered, about the impossibility of Germany crossing the Atlantic to invade America. Thomsen would later claim 'partial credit' for Lindbergh having included this in his broadcast.[20]

Several days later, Senator Lundeen 'asked and obtained leave' in the Senate for this speech to be included in the *Congressional Record*, after which, no doubt, it was mailed out with the help of the German embassy.[21]

Charles Lindbergh had been fed an idea by a man cooperating with the Nazi influence campaign, and passages from his speeches were being mailed around the country as part of a scheme run from the German embassy. But he was unaware of this. Ingenuous and determined, Lindbergh was stubborn in the trust he placed in those who shared his views. It is unlikely that he suspected Lundeen of working with the Nazis, or indeed that he would have been too concerned if he had found out.

Lindbergh's overriding concern by June 1940 was not whether his friends were in touch with the German embassy, it was how to keep the US out of the war. So far his speeches seemed to be making an impact. By the time he left the NBC studios on 15 June 1940, just half an hour after the broadcast finished, thirty telegrams had arrived. 'All but three were in support of my stand,' he wrote, with satisfaction.[22] An editorial in the *Pittsburgh Press* later praised its 'hard common sense',[23] one in the *Detroit Free Press* admired its 'unanswerable logic'.[24] Although others took issue with what he had said, millions of Americans saw Lindbergh's stance as authentic and level-headed. In Congress, Hamilton Fish declared 'Lindbergh was right', arguing, as the pilot had done, that 'the only reason that we are in danger of becoming involved in this war is because there are powerful elements in America who desire to take part.'[25] He did not elaborate on who or what these elements were.

Like Lindbergh, Hamilton Fish was convinced that the United States was being inveigled into a foreign war. Both had acquired the barrelling righteousness of men who have been wronged, and were becoming bolder and more bullish in what they said. Certainly if either one had heard of the arrival several days after Lindbergh's speech of a new MI6 officer, Bill Stephenson, so soon after Berlin had warned that the British were sending 'a large number of agents' to the Americas 'to arrange incidents' and 'a hostile attitude against Germany in the United States',[26] they would have denounced him in the strongest terms.

The idea of Churchill sending British spies into the country would only confirm each man's darkest fears about a plot against America. Their condemnations would have been angrier and more determined if they had known that this particular MI6 officer would soon be trying to destroy their careers.

Bill Stephenson's first report to MI6 in London had been forwarded to the Foreign Office by his boss, 'C', who had given it an enthusiastic write-up, saying it came from 'my new representative in New York, who has excellent and longstanding contacts and is a very competent observer'.

The Foreign Office did not agree. 'He may be a competent observer,' came the acidic reply, 'but he does not express himself clearly.'[1]

'C' agreed to find out 'exactly what he means'.[2]

Stephenson had moved his operation into the lavish apartment, taken on new employees, installed expensive equipment and had tried to engineer a new ethos in his office. But he was struggling to convince his staff, his superiors, and perhaps himself, that he was right man for the job. He needed a victory, a breakthrough, anything, really, to remove that sense of doubt.

One of the few contacts he had inherited from his MI6 predecessor was Vincent Astor, scion of New York's powerful Astor family, a man both phenomenally wealthy and not at all interested in being rich. Astor was more intrigued by espionage. Recently he had been told about a particular dinner party held in his family's flagship hotel, the Waldorf-Astoria. A group of American businessmen, led by a senior executive from General Motors, had taken a private room to celebrate the recent Nazi victories in Europe. Their guest of honour was the Commercial Counsellor at the German embassy, Dr Westrick. Astor thought this might be of interest to MI6, so he passed it on.

Now Stephenson had to decide how to use this information. His instructions were to protect British supplies from sabotage and to 'organize American public opinion in favour of aid to Britain'.[3] In short, he had to ensure a constant flow of American aid across the Atlantic. A minor German diplomat having dinner with a group of American businessmen appeared to have little to do with this, unless Dr Westrick was part of a wider Nazi campaign to turn American public opinion against Britain.

Stephenson decided to investigate. He began by having Dr West-rick's home monitored. Over the coming weeks British operatives observed his house in suburban Westchester, slowly building up a list of who had visited. Some turned out to be ordinary German-Americans, others were powerful US businessmen, including the chief of Texaco, Torkild Rieber. Stephenson's team also discovered that Dr Westrick had been lent a Texaco company car,[4] and that he had an aristocratic assistant, Baroness Irmingrad von Wagenheim, related to the German Foreign Minister, Joachim Ribbentrop.

It was a suggestive haul of intelligence, but hardly explosive. Stephenson's next step should have been to pass it on to J. Edgar Hoover at the FBI, perhaps with an apology. By having his staff spy on Dr Westrick, Stephenson had gone beyond the terms of their informal agreement. But he knew that if he were to do this the FBI would sit on the information about Dr Westrick and nothing more would come of it. His team had uncovered no evidence of criminality. None of the details in themselves demanded investigation. But piled on top of each other they had a surprising weight. Was Dr Westrick more powerful than his junior position at the embassy suggested?

Stephenson decided to weaponize this intelligence. He instructed a member of staff to turn it into 'a first-class news story'.

Now he needed a trustworthy editor who might be willing to publish it. According to the once classified history of his office, this article about Dr Westrick was passed on to an 'intermediary', never named, who supplied it to a journalist at the *Herald Tribune*.

On the face of it, this was a huge risk. If the journalist twigged that this article had in fact been put together by British spies then that, surely, would become the story. In trying to expose a possible German spy, Stephenson might expose his own nest of spies.

But in fact there was little risk of exposure. The *Herald Tribune* journalist agreed to have this article go out under his own byline because the person who had handed it to him, the 'intermediary', was almost certainly his boss.

Although Ogden Reid's name appeared on the masthead of the *Herald Tribune*, his difficulties with alcohol meant that the actual proprietor in all but name was his wife, Helen Reid, a political progressive, feminist and pronounced Anglophile. Her father-in-law had been US ambassador to Britain, and on her most recent visit she had spent the weekend with her close friend Lord Lothian, now British ambassador in Washington DC. 'I want to be of service in any way that I can,' she had written to the Foreign Secretary, Lord Halifax.[5] When Stephenson put together a list of his press contacts at this time, Helen Reid's name was on it.[6]

On 1 August 1940, the story about Dr Westrick broke in the *Herald Tribune*, as well as the *New York Times* and the following day a piece based on fresh information appeared in the *Baltimore Sun*. Stephenson had probably been put in touch with the proprietors of all three newspapers by the British ambassador.[7]

Millions of Americans were now reading about this German official, variously described in the press as 'Hitler's Special Agent', 'The Disappearing Doktor', or a 'Mystery Nazi Agent'.[8] For an older generation, these stories brought back memories of German agents during the last war. But they also had a contemporary resonance.

Since the fall of France the world had gorged on tales of 'Fifth Columnists' setting up hidden Nazi networks, which had either risen
up in support of the German invasion, or were lying in wait within
neutral countries. Some Americans worried that the Nazis might
have a 'Fifth Column' poised to strike inside the United States, and
these stories only stoked that fear. Dr Westrick came across in the
press as a potent blend of old-school German agent and new-fangled
Fifth Columnist.

Westrick himself tried to make the story go away, telling the
journalists camped outside his house that he was merely a diplomat laying the foundations for better trading relations between
the US and a victorious Germany. This was largely true. Although
some of the businessmen he had spoken to, including a General
Motors executive, had told him they planned to push Roosevelt into
ordering a 'suspension of armaments shipments to Great Britain',
this never materialized.[9] None of the allegations against him indicated criminal behaviour. But the mood in the country was such
that the *idea* of a German spy at large in the United States, in
Westchester, of all places, an oasis of suburban certainty, with a
glamorous assistant related to Ribbentrop, was enough to ignite a
publicity wildfire.

Westrick's assistant, Baroness von Wagenheim, was shocked less
by the allegations about her boss than the one about her age.

'I am not in my middle forties,' she complained to the journalists.
'I am only twenty-eight.'[10] She then agreed to be photographed.

This photograph helped to keep the story going, and so did Stephenson's decision to drip-feed some of his team's juiciest findings
to the *Herald Tribune*. As each of these articles was syndicated,
and Westrick's reaction to them was reported, the scandal gathered
momentum. Soon there began to be calls for him to be deported.

'He met this threat,' one account recalled, 'with true German
subtlety, by playing "God Bless America" and "The Star Spangled

Banner", interminably, on his gramophone.'[11] The *Herald Tribune* continued its daily updates, and by the end of the month the head of Texaco, who had done so much to look after this German diplomat, had been forced to resign, and Dr Westrick himself was told to leave the country.

In the German embassy, Hans Thomsen was incensed. In cables back to Berlin he railed against these 'vicious attacks' on his colleague, complaining that information had been 'presented to the public in totally distorted and exaggerated form'[12] – an odd complaint from a man then running a nationwide influence campaign. He was also angry about the impact this story was having on his work. Previously friendly American businessmen were now severing relations with German companies, or refusing to be seen in public with embassy staff.

One person who was not at all angry about this run of stories was Jay Racusin, the *Herald Tribune* journalist whose name had appeared on each of the articles about Dr Westrick. Racusin was later awarded a silver medal by the National Headliner Club for his alleged investigation of the German spy.

Bill Stephenson had learned the first and most basic lesson of covert propaganda. How to encourage millions of people to listen to your story sympathetically? Disguise where it has come from.

Earlier in 1940 the British ambassador had argued in a speech that 'the truth is never propaganda'.[13] But sometimes, as Churchill would later declare, the truth must be protected by 'a bodyguard of lies'.[14] The story about Dr Westrick was accurate, but lies had been told to ensure that it was seen as such. Stephenson and his team had deceived the American people to make the truth sound truthful.

They had also learned that a good news story is like a fire. To start the blaze, you must light it in more than one place, and you need fresh material on hand to feed in once the flames have caught.

For Stephenson's team in his penthouse suite high above Central

Park this episode was both nerve-wracking and exciting. They had never attempted anything like this under their previous boss. Slowly, their new chief seemed to be finding his feet. His staff were beginning to understand him, even if still they knew little about his past. At all times he kept this fenced off, and only many years afterwards did it become clear why.

Brilliant detective work more than half a century later by a local Winnipeg historian, Bill MacDonald, would unearth the secret at the heart of Stephenson's childhood. Bill Stephenson was not really Bill Stephenson.

In 1897 he was born instead as William Stanger, the eldest son of William and Sarah Stanger. Shortly after his father's death, in late 1901, when he was just four, Bill's mother made the heart-rending decision to give up her eldest son. As a widow, she could not afford the cost of raising all three children. So he was passed on to their close friends in Point Douglas, the Stephensons. His mother and two siblings left town altogether, and he never saw them again.

Aged four, Stephenson, as he now was, had effectively been orphaned. In quick succession his father had died, his two siblings had been taken away from him, and his mother had abandoned him. His new parents were Vigfus and Kristina Stephenson, his new siblings Gudlauger, Johinna, Gudmindur, and Julianna, all of Icelandic stock like his mother. Once the eldest of three, he was now the youngest of five.

Although it was not uncommon at the time for Icelanders to foster their friends' children like this, it is hard to think of a more punishing sequence to inflict on a four-year-old, and undoubtedly this left a mark. Growing up, Bill Stephenson was remembered for being unnaturally quiet. As a teenager he rarely spoke, and was known instead for his love of boxing and his photographic memory. Years later one colleague called him 'a very, very private man'.[15] Of those who were a little closer, one remarked that 'he never talked about his past'.[16] A Canadian friend remembered that 'if I got on the subject of his early upbringing in Winnipeg, he would close up like a clam. Just change the subject. Obviously didn't want to discuss it at all. I couldn't understand this, because he was so forthcoming in everything else. He would talk about anything without hesitation. Not Winnipeg.'[17]

Just as he did not want to talk about Winnipeg, for most of his adult life Stephenson would never go back there. But this was about more than having lost his original family. When he left Winnipeg in 1922, he did so under a cloud. His new business venture had failed. He was bankrupt and he owed money to ninety-seven creditors, many of them friends or relations within the Icelandic community including his adoptive father, Vigfus. Unable to pay them all back, he ran away. Having been given up by his first family, Stephenson cut himself off from his second family.

Why does any of this matter? It changes our understanding of who Bill Stephenson was, what he needed in life, and the risks he was willing to take. His earliest years had loaded him down under a backpack of trauma, one he refused to share with anyone. From an early age he had been schooled in the art of keeping secrets, such as the identity of his biological parents. By the time he arrived in London he had lost his family twice over, making him a man without a past who had surprisingly little to lose.

He was also someone who needed to feel part of a family. After angling for a position inside MI6, the country's most exclusive club, he had been welcomed into the fold. Now he was part of an elite tribe. He felt respected and powerful, and no doubt he relished his new sense of belonging. Stephenson's difficult past matters because it made his position within MI6 more valuable to him than those around him may have realized. He was unlikely to take any risks which might endanger it, and was even more determined to succeed.

'I speak to you today as I would speak to close friends,' Charles Lindbergh told a crowd of forty thousand strangers, and tens of millions listening at home. It was 4 August 1940. The first story about Dr Westrick had appeared three days earlier. Lindbergh was in Chicago on a scorching day to address a 'monster' anti-war rally at Soldier Field, a neoclassical arena perched like a beached liner on the shores of Lake Michigan. Before him was a vast crowd of people, many of them wearing white shirts and blouses, and some with dark parasols which poked up from the audience like mushrooms.[1]

This was the first time Lindbergh had addressed an anti-war rally, but he had been here before, in what must have felt like a different life. Thirteen years earlier, shortly after his legendary transatlantic crossing, he had given a short speech in the same arena on the future of aviation. He had looked jaunty and piratical that day in a leather jacket with just one button done up. Now he wore a sombre suit, and there was a new intensity to his voice.

'American opinion is now definitely and overwhelmingly against our involvement,' he told his audience, and 'since we have decided against entering the war in Europe, it is time for us to consider the relationship we will have with Europe after this war is over.' After this neat rhetorical shimmy – making the argument for neutrality by telling his audience the argument had been already been won – he took a more radical step. He suggested that Nazi aggression was justified. In Britain 'the rich had become too rich', he told them, in central Europe 'the poor had become too poor' and it had been obvious to him, during his time in Europe, this 'would have to change, either by agreement or by war'.

This was a daring shift. Having hovered for months over the question of which side he wanted to win, Lindbergh had just come down on Hitler's side, and was now urging his listeners to do the same and imagine the war from a Nazi point of view. He wanted them to consider with an open mind the benefits of a 'Europe dominated by Germany', and to ignore press 'accusations of aggression and barbarism on the part of Germany'.

Hans Thomsen was ecstatic. He would soon rhapsodize about 'the spiritual and, particularly, the moral superiority and purity of this man'.[2] One of his colleagues had recently described Lindbergh's speeches as 'the highest and most effective form of propaganda'.[3]

Having made the case for Nazi expansion, Lindbergh struck a more familiar isolationist chord. He called for stronger American defences and none of 'the foreign entanglements and favoritisms that [George] Washington warned us against'. He also mentioned 'interests in this country and abroad who will do their utmost to draw us into the war', telling his listeners to be 'continuously on guard', without going into this further.

Elsewhere his speech was peppered with forelock-tugging lines about how he was no expert in 'this era of experts', just an ordinary citizen saying it as he saw it. 'I am told that one must not stand too strongly against the trend of the times, and that, to be effective, what one says must meet with general approval,' he volunteered. 'I prefer to say what I believe, or not to speak at all.' Nor was he doing this to be liked. 'I would far rather have your respect for the sincerity of what I say, than attempt to win your applause' – a line which was met with loud applause.

It may not have been a stream of golden words and at no point did he lead his audience up to a memorable climax, but he had crafted his speech well and delivered it with conviction.

This was not entirely surprising. Although Lindbergh itched to be seen as a political outsider, he was anything but. For ten years, his father had been an outspoken Republican congressman. Charles Lindbergh had grown up observing him address political rallies, and as a teenager had lived through his father's doomed crusade against America's involvement in the last war, by the end of which he was a political outcast.

Lindbergh understood the hatred that politics could inspire, but in the moments after finishing his speech in Chicago, as he looked out over the crowd and thought perhaps of the millions listening at home, he sensed nothing but support from the audience. It seemed that his address had been a success. The atmosphere by the time he had finished was charged and elemental. 'The crowd seemed to want to applaud at every opportunity,' he wrote in his diary, 'which is rather disconcerting when one is not used to it.'[4] There had been rousing shouts of 'You tell 'em, Lindy!'[5] As one journalist noted, during each ovation the aviator's face broke into 'a youthful smile'.[6] For the first time since his return to the public eye, Lindbergh seemed to be enjoying himself.

The only danger was that he may have gone too far, and too soon. It was hard to say how many of those listening at home would accept, as he urged them to, the idea of a Europe dominated by Hitler. There was also his family to consider.

After each of his broadcasts Lindbergh received hundreds of messages. Most were supportive, some took issue with what he had said, which he did not mind, but what bothered him were the letters, cables and calls to his house which contained anonymous threats against him, his wife or his children.

Several weeks before giving this speech a woman had called up to warn that his pregnant wife, Anne, was in danger. 'I would rather live in the front line trenches than have the constant worry of safeguarding my family against criminal stealth,' Lindbergh wrote that night. 'It has caused me more worry during the last eight years than anything else I have encountered in life,' he continued. 'One of the worst parts about these threats is the effect they have on one's home. They create an atmosphere in which it is impossible to bring up a family normally.'[7] Beneath the surface of his life, faint but impossible to forget, was the memory of his son's kidnap.

The bolder Lindbergh became in his broadcasts, the more of these threats he received. But he was not about to step out of the limelight. He was now the country's leading spokesman for the isolationist cause, the only campaigner capable of consistently reaching middle-of-the-road Americans and reinforcing their desire to stay out of war. His Chicago speech was set to be a major step in that direction, although he could not be sure of its impact until he had seen the next day's newspapers.

That night, after dinner, he went to stay with one of the few men outside the capital whose fame rivalled his own: Henry Ford, the renowned industrialist and tycoon, who had once been ranked by fellow Americans as the third greatest person of all time – after Jesus and Napoleon. Like Lindbergh, this celebrity businessman was bitterly opposed to the prospect of war with Nazi Germany. Unlike Lindbergh, Ford was directly in touch with the German embassy. One of the German diplomats he had recently spoken to was Dr Westrick, shortly before he was forced to leave the country. Ford had passed on a suggestion for how Hitler could improve the way ordinary Americans saw Nazi Germany.[8]

The following morning, America's two best-known isolationists sat down for breakfast. It was probably at around this time that Lindbergh saw the morning papers.

Lindbergh's speech was front-page news, as he had hoped, but so was another speech arguing directly against what he had said. Most editors had given this rival broadcast more space than Lindbergh's. The acclaimed pilot had been moments away from a touchdown, only to be sent flying by a tackle from a player he had not seen coming.

The player in question was the elderly General John J. Pershing, Commander-in-Chief of the American Expeditionary Force during the last war, an iconic figure for many Americans. Several hours after Lindbergh's, he had given a nationwide radio address on the subject of the European war. This was in spite of his having officially retired from public life some years previously.

General Pershing focused in his broadcast on the threat posed by Hitler. It was time 'to face the truth without flinching', he told the nation, in a rasping delivery which sounded as if it came from beyond the grave.[9] He urged the American people to back the British, and to send them more supplies.

Hans Thomsen could not understand what had just happened. He was in contact with 'the circle around Lindbergh',[10] and had heard in advance about this Chicago speech. He had been eagerly awaiting its impact on the political debate, only for that to be demolished by Pershing's riposte.

The ageing American general's timing had been perfect. So good, in fact, that Thomsen became suspicious. He was convinced that Pershing had been put up to this. He was right.

The people mainly responsible for General Pershing's speech on that warm evening in early August 1940 belonged to a secretive group known to its members as the 'Century Group'. Today, the Century Group sounds like a phantom dreamed up by a conspiracy theorist. Most of the two dozen members of this informal clique were enormously wealthy, highly educated and well-connected East Coasters. They were New Yorkers who read the *New Yorker*, remarkably successful in their chosen fields and generally used to having things their own way. Named the Century Group after the New York private club the Century Association to which many of them belonged, the members of this group included the future head of the CIA Allen Dulles, the screenwriter of *Prisoner of Zenda* John Balderston, future White House speechwriter Robert Sherwood, CBS commentator Elmer Davis, Pulitzer-Prize-winning author Herbert Agar, the founder of Viking Press Harold Guinzburg, the film producer Walter Wanger, and, most influential of them all, Henry Luce, publisher of the magazines *Time*, *Life* and *Fortune*.

On paper, at least, the Century Group was phenomenally powerful. Its members were also highly motivated. Most had served their country during the last war and they had come together in the days after Dunkirk, early June 1940, around a shared understanding that

Nazi Germany posed a serious threat to the United States. 'In a sense Judgment Day is approaching for all of us,' one of them explained. 'We have only a short interval left in which to prepare.'[1] They had agreed to do everything in their power to take on Hitler, and that the best way to do this was by backing Britain and campaigning to bring their country into the war.

But for all their ideals, their wealth and their dazzling connections, within weeks of coming together the Century Group was starting to fall apart. Its first public offering, an expensive newspaper advertisement urging Americans to back Britain, had been a flop.

Nobody seemed to be interested. Many of those who responded to this advertisement did so only to complain about its belligerent tone. The energy and sense of purpose was leaching out of the Century Group when one of its members had the idea of meeting the British ambassador, Philip Kerr, 11th Marquess of Lothian, known to his staff as Lord Lothian.

Lothian relished his life in the United States. Despite his aristocratic heritage, American values appealed at once to his progressive, open and often rebellious nature. He was an avid student of American life, and had grasped early on in his diplomatic posting the importance in American politics of public opinion, a realization that influenced almost every move he made as ambassador.

When meeting the Washington press corps for the first time, in 1939, Lothian made a point of wearing a creased suit rather than the traditional top hat and tails. During the photo-call he also managed to grab a stray kitten and pose with it for the photographers. Lothian wanted to rebrand the British as approachable, honest and open, and friendly to kittens. Following the outbreak of war he refused to sanction any British propaganda in the United States, reminding Foreign Office colleagues in London that 'No Propaganda' is 'our watch word'[2] and 'anything which looks like British propaganda designed to influence American policy creates a cold fury in the American mind.'[3]

But in May 1940, as the European situation deteriorated, Lothian changed his tack. There was only so much he could do by posing with kittens. He began by meeting a leading interventionist, William Allen White, briefly acting as an intermediary between him and Churchill. Then on 4 July, of all days, the British ambassador secretly met a member of the Century Group.

This was Dr Henry van Dusen, a distinguished theology professor, who asked Lothian for assurances that Britain would never sue for peace with Germany. Van Dusen also wanted full details of how bad the British military and economic situation had become, how many ships they had left and which supplies were needed most urgently.

Lothian might have told him to mind his own business. Instead he agreed to everything. A British embassy despatch rider would soon arrive at the office of another Century Group member, Whitney Shepardson, to deliver an oversized envelope bearing Lothian's elaborate wax seal. Inside were the shocking details of Britain's military losses including a carefully guarded secret: of the Royal Navy's 176 destroyers at the start of the war just 68 were now 'fit for service in home waters'.[4] The British were losing almost a destroyer a day. They desperately needed more destroyers. As Churchill wrote to Lothian: 'there is nothing that America can do at this moment that would be of greater help than to send fifty destroyers, except sending a hundred.'[5]

'Please keep the source of this information confidential,' Lothian told the Century Group, in a letter never before published. 'Provided the use of the substance of it is likely to lead to the need being met I would take a chance on publicity,' adding, in a flash of exasperation, 'why America sits by and watches its own front door being taken while all top people realise that if it is taken this year America itself is doomed, and that it can save that front door for the matter of 100 destroyers or so, is a mystery to me!!'[6]

What Lothian had just done was technically illegal: without authority he had shared sensitive and classified information with a

group of private American citizens. But this gambit worked in the
sense that it kept the Century Group alive. Lothian's intervention
was like a shot in the arm, and in the days that followed the Century
Group leaders set up their headquarters in New York and sketched
out plans for 'awakening America to the danger'.[7] Others went to the
White House to press the president on the idea of a destroyer transfer.

Roosevelt had already risked much to help the British. In the last two
months he had authorized two secretive arms deals, the first for 324
Curtis P-40s and 81 Grumman fighter planes, the next involving a
mountain of US Army munitions including 87,500 machine guns,
25,000 automatic rifles, 500,000 rifles and 895 75mm field artillery
guns, as well as mortars and heavy bombers. He did this in spite of a
series of laws passed during the 1930s, known as the Neutrality Acts,
which had been designed to stop him, or anyone else, from selling
arms to warring nations like Britain. The premise underpinning these
laws was that arms dealers had helped to drag the country into the
last war, so by making it harder for Americans to profit from war
there would be less incentive to enter future conflicts.

But within this knot of Neutrality Acts were several loopholes,
which Roosevelt managed to exploit. For example, he knew that
under the Neutrality Acts aeroplanes could not be transported
mechanically to a belligerent nation. His solution was to have US
pilots fly the planes he wanted to sell up to the Canadian border,
where they landed, turned off their engines and wheeled the planes
over the border into Canadian territory, before starting up their
engines again and continuing on their way.

Today legal scholars are 'generally agreed' that these two
Anglo-American arms deals were not only unlawful but constituted
grounds for impeachment.[8] Roosevelt was potentially risking his
presidency to help the British. But for Churchill it was not enough.

Over the last two months, the British prime minister had repeatedly pressed the US president to authorize the transfer to the Royal Navy of 'forty or fifty' ageing US destroyers.⁹ Roosevelt had refused, telling him this would have to go through Congress, which was bound to vote against it.

On 1 August 1940 three Century Group members saw Roosevelt in the White House. They made the case to him, as Churchill had done, for transferring forty or fifty US destroyers to the British. The president's response was the same as it had been to the prime minister: the destroyer transfer was impossible because it would never get through Congress.

One Century Group member then had an idea. He proposed asking the elderly General Pershing to give a nationwide speech in support of sending aid to Britain, including a transfer of fifty destroyers. Roosevelt agreed that this could help, but he wanted to keep his hands clean. If it ever leaked out that the Century Group was behind Pershing's broadcast, the president warned them, 'and you say the idea came from me, I shall call you a liar'.¹⁰

The Century Group not only came up with the idea for Pershing's speech, its members also obtained Roosevelt's secret backing, they persuaded Pershing to give the speech – which was not easy given how many of his fellow veterans were diehard isolationists – and then secured radio time. Finally they asked one of their members, Herbert Agar, to work with the journalist Walter Lippmann on the text of the speech itself. The Century Group also got their timing right. They ensured that Pershing was heard several hours after Lindbergh, and with enough time for newspaper editors to include both speeches side-by-side in the next day's morning editions.

The Century Group had been behind this speech, but without Lothian's support the group would have fallen apart. Similar to the Dr Westrick exposé, this episode involved Britons working behind the scenes with Americans. Both interventions were Anglo-American collaborations in which British officials, such as Lothian and Stephenson, had worked with influential and wealthy Americans, like Vincent Astor and Helen Reid or the well-connected members of the Century Group. Britain could not win the war single-handed, and nor could they bring the US into the war on their own. In order to succeed, Lothian and Stephenson would need to master the art of covert collaboration, and do so soon. Time was starting to run out.

Several days after General Pershing and Charles Lindbergh gave their speeches, in early August 1940, the Battle of Britain entered a new phase. The Luftwaffe began to target the RAF directly. For those living in Britain it felt as if the invasion could begin at any moment. The mood across the country was a heady mix of excitement and gritty determination. War was everywhere. It had permeated every facet of daily life, changing the way people shopped and worked, how they travelled, what they ate, and even when and where they slept, just as it had given many of them roles they had never in peacetime imagined themselves capable of performing.

One such Briton was the Oscar-nominated screenwriter Eric Maschwitz, who found himself in the early days of the Battle of Britain racing around Yorkshire in a car loaded up with Molotov cocktails. Tall and easy-going, Maschwitz was the type of person at his happiest when making jokes at his own expense. The son of a Jewish Lithuanian émigré and his much younger Australian wife, Maschwitz had recently been working in Los Angeles for MGM where he had co-authored the script for *Goodbye, Mr. Chips*, fallen in love repeatedly and written songs about the experience, including 'These Foolish Things', which had been recorded by Billie Holiday. Now he was in uniform, in Yorkshire, preparing for the German invasion of his country. He had gone from Beverly Hills in California to Beverley in East Yorkshire. The worlds of film, theatre and music could not have felt more distant.

Until then, Maschwitz's war had played out like a hastily written comedy. It began with our apparently hapless hero trying to persuade the War Office to take him on. 'Nobody appeared to have any use for a myopic lyric-writer of 38,' he complained.[1] Sitting in the bath as Chamberlain announced the outbreak of war, he felt 'as useless as any man can feel who has made a mess of his peacetime life and can't even get into a war!'[2]

But he did not give up, and eventually landed a job in censorship. Here he worked under a man who 'loved music and the theatre and could never quite get over his bewilderment at finding the author of *Balalaika* [one of Maschwitz's hit musicals] working under him (at £6 a week)'.[3]

Shortly before starting this job, Maschwitz had also taken the time to write to an elderly admiral he had met several times, one who had 'the face of a faintly amused frog; out of uniform he was so oddly indistinguishable from other little men with the faces of faintly amused frogs that I had always had difficulty in remembering exactly what he was like! Still, he *was* an admiral, and admirals could get things done'.[4] Without really understanding what he had set in motion, Eric Maschwitz had just contacted the then head of MI6, Admiral Sir Hugh Sinclair, also known as 'C'.

The lyricist was soon summoned to London and given a job working for Section D, the MI6 offshoot which specialized in political warfare and sabotage. 'I never had a desk of my own and seemed to be continually standing up,' he complained, but he did at least get to meet 'the strangest assortment of men and women imaginable'.[5] One of these was almost certainly Bill Stephenson, who was working with Section D in Sweden at around this time.

Needing a stock response for when one of his theatrical friends asked what he was doing, and not wanting to reveal he was working for Section D, Maschwitz began to say he was writing songs for a forthcoming revue show. This was not true, but after a while he wrote the songs anyway. Once he had them down on paper, and he thought one or two of them might be good, he decided to stage the revue. Which is why, two days after the German army began its assault on Denmark and Norway, Eric Maschwitz's new revue show, *New Faces*, opened at the Comedy Theatre.

The timing was not ideal, but *New Faces* was a hit, mainly because it contained a catchy new song by Maschwitz called 'A Nightingale Sang in Berkeley Square'. As recording artists began to enquire about the rights, its composer was told to take a course in explosives.

'This was a severe test for somebody who had never cared particularly for "bangs",' he recalled. Nor did his teachers inspire much confidence. When he arrived for his first day of instruction he could not help but notice 'with some misgivings that the Chief Instructor had had part of his jaw blown away, while his Sergeant Major was short of three fingers on one hand'.[6]

During his first live exercise Maschwitz lit the fuse on an explosive device and ran away, straight into a tree. The blast nearly killed him.

Several days after he had finished the course, a telephone call came in to the Comedy Theatre for 2nd Lieutenant Maschwitz. He was told he must leave for Calais the next morning. His job would be to demolish British supplies before they fell into German hands, which is what would probably then happen to him. Maschwitz did what many people would do in a situation like this. He went on an all-night bender, reporting for duty the next day with 'battle dress, a "tin hat", a revolver – and a fiercesome hangover'.[7] But the situation in France had deteriorated to such an extent that the operation was called off.

The enthusiastic lyricist was then sent away from the capital and from his friends in theatre to East Yorkshire, where he began to feel more useful. He was now a recruiting officer for the Auxiliary Units, an underground network of military personnel and civilians preparing to mount a guerrilla campaign against the occupying German forces in the event of a successful Nazi invasion. His new job involved driving around in a car full of explosives and either showing these off to prospective recruits, or building up hidden arsenals across the Yorkshire countryside. Maschwitz soon had a small army of would-be resistance fighters 'who had buried in their gardens, under hayricks and manure heaps, the wherewithal with which to cause the invader quite a lot of trouble'.

Overhead the Battle of Britain was becoming frantic. The gaps between sorties were shorter than ever, planes were becoming scarce, pilots were starting to run on empty. Everyone was readying themselves for the invasion. 'We worked like fiends,' Maschwitz remembered, 'ate and slept like new-born babes and with the rest of the population did not for a moment believe that, even supposing that the Germans should have the cheek to appear off those shelving beaches, they would have a dog's chance of getting ashore.'[8]

In truth, if German troops had made landfall at least some would have been able to fight their way inland. The key to Britain's survival was to prevent that from happening. This meant winning in the air and at sea. The Royal Air Force needed more pilots and planes, and the Royal Navy needed more destroyers. This was where the United States came in.

If President Roosevelt was to push for the destroyer transfer that Churchill was clamouring for, he had to be certain that Britain would stand firm and these ships were unlikely to be captured by the Germans. Although nobody was suggesting that Britain had the military might to defeat Nazi Germany and take Berlin, the question was whether she could resist an invasion. How would ordinary civilians like Eric Maschwitz, with no experience of war, react when British cities began to be flattened by the Luftwaffe, or when German troops landed on British beaches?

These were the kinds of questions Roosevelt had asked Colonel William J. Donovan, a tigger-ish lawyer whom he had sent to London several weeks earlier. In early August 1940, after a whirlwind tour, Donovan began the long journey back to the United States where he would report to the White House on what he had seen. Donovan did not meet Eric Maschwitz on this trip, but their paths would soon cross.

Known as 'Wild Bill' to most US newspaper editors, Bill to his friends, Donovan had been sent out to Britain as an unofficial White House representative. On his return to Washington DC, in the early days of August 1940, he saw a number of US government officials, passing on requests for greater collaboration from the Royal Navy, the RAF and MI6.[1] He also met a remarkably friendly Canadian called Bill Stephenson.

Within two days of Donovan's return to Washington, Stephenson had begun his charm offensive. To look at, the two Bills made an odd couple. Donovan was a bear of a man, big-spirited and broad, his presence enough to fill any room. Stephenson was over a decade younger, more circumspect, and compact. Yet from the moment they met, the high-powered lawyer and the man from MI6 had a rapport.

Both had grown up in poverty near the US-Canadian border, Donovan in a tough Irish neighbourhood in Buffalo, New York, Stephenson in a tough Icelandic neighbourhood in Winnipeg. Each had volunteered at the first opportunity in the First World War, risen through the ranks, and emerged as a war hero. Donovan was thirty-four when he arrived on the Western Front and was soon commanding the legendary 'Fighting 69th', New York City's Irish

regiment. Known to his troops as 'Wild Bill' for his manic enthu-
siasm when drilling them, Donovan had an almost unsettling lack of
fear. He once told his wife that when being shot at he felt as excited
as 'a youngster at Halloween'.[2] By the end of the war he had been
awarded the Congressional Medal of Honor, the Purple Heart and
the Distinguished Service Cross, making him one of America's most
decorated soldiers.

In different ways, both Bills had been transformed by their experience of the last war, and each became a self-made millionaire in
the years that followed. Donovan built up a prestigious law practice,
Stephenson concentrated on technology and his investment fund.
By the start of the Second World War both were enjoying the kind
of gilded existence that must have seemed unattainably remote
when growing up. They lived in opulent homes, were driven around
by chauffeurs and dined in gratuitously expensive restaurants in
New York and London. Yet beneath the sheen of success, each one
hankered secretly after something else. Stephenson wanted to enter
the world of intelligence. Donovan had long ago set his sights on
political office.

Unfortunately for him, he kept missing the target. In 1922 Donovan
ran for lieutenant governor of New York and lost. Several years later
he was passed over as Attorney General. In 1926 he was mooted as a
candidate for New York governor, but nothing came of it. Two years
on and he was mentioned in the *New York Times* as a possible Republican Vice-Presidential pick, but this failed to materialize. Instead
Donovan worked on Herbert Hoover's campaign, and was assured
by the presidential candidate that he would become his Attorney
General if he won, and although Hoover was victorious he reneged
on this offer.[3] Four years on, Donovan stood for Governor of New
York and again was defeated.

Bill Donovan was a talented military commander and a fine lawyer,
but he lacked a political nose. Nor was he a natural performer. Up

on stage, his charm and wit seemed to drain out of him and in his efforts to sound statesmanlike and serious he came across as wooden and dull.

But in the summer of 1940, finally, Donovan's luck appeared to have turned. 'I saw the President very recently,' he told a British friend excitedly on 20 June 1940. 'He asked me whether I would like to be Secretary for War. I said that there was nothing I would like more. Keep it under your hat, of course, till it's officially announced, but I thought you'd like to know.'[4] Donovan's dream of a political career had at last come true. This was what he had been stumbling towards for almost two decades. He was on a high, until, at the end of that conversation, he heard on the radio that the new Secretary of War had been announced. It was not him. The president had changed his mind and chosen instead Henry Stimson.

In the days that followed, Bill Donovan experienced perhaps the lowest ebb of his life. It was not just that he had failed again to attain political office. He was also learning to live with the death of his beloved daughter, Patricia, who had died several months earlier in a car crash. 'His hair seemed to turn white almost overnight,' one biographer recorded.[5] Shortly after being passed over as Secretary of War, this grieving father had been asked to go to London on behalf of the White House. Indeed he was given this task partly to take his mind off the death of his daughter.

In the days before Donovan left, in July 1940, Bill Stephenson heard about this coming trip. Although he had not yet met Donovan, he urged 'C' to make a fuss of him when he arrived, telling his boss that Donovan was 'personally representing President'[6] – he was not – and was a 'key man' – which he might yet be.[7]

It would be wrong to say that during Bill Donovan's seventeen days in Britain he was treated like royalty. His experience was better than that. In a trip stage-managed by MI6, he had an audience with King George VI and the Queen, as well as the Prime Minister,

'C', the Director of MI5, the Director of Naval Intelligence, and a galaxy of top civil servants and senior officers from the Army, the Royal Navy and the RAF, all of whom had been instructed to give full and frank accounts of the British economic, military and supply situation. 'We showed him a great deal,' wrote the Secretary for Air, Sir Archibald Sinclair, 'and took him very largely into our confidence.'[8] Donovan was also swept out of London to see factories and military bases, he was put up in Claridge's, and was assigned a team of officials to look after him and provide detailed answers to any question he might have.

'Wild Bill' was being wooed. It was neither subtle nor complex. Just relentless. 'C' had ensured that Donovan was given intelligence and access of the highest order, and that he was feted and flattered, listened to, and loaded with secrets in a bid to make him feel trusted and important.

In his recent bestseller *How to Win Friends and Influence People*, Dale Carnegie had described how 'the big secret of dealing with people' boiled down to one basic truth: all of us want to feel important.[9] By the end of his stay in London Donovan could hardly have felt more appreciated.

We tend to think of 'agents of influence' as people who lobby on behalf of a foreign state, and are aware of what they are doing. Perhaps they have been blackmailed, they are in it for the money, or theirs is an ideological crusade. At the very least they are conscious of the unwritten contract into which they have entered. But it is also possible to have an 'unconscious' agent of influence, one who does a similar job for another nation without realizing it. By showering someone with hospitality, flattering them, providing access, friendship and intelligence or lucrative business deals, a foreign state can leave an individual feeling a binding sense of gratitude and debt towards that nation. The individual who has been targeted might find themselves fighting that nation's corner in a future political discussion, without for a moment thinking they themselves have become that nefarious thing an 'agent of influence'.

By lavishing so much attention and intelligence on Bill Donovan, the head of MI6 had taken a risk. His target was a proud Irish-American with no inherited affection for the British Empire. He had been sent to London on a fact-finding mission for the US government, and there was no guarantee that Donovan would keep the secrets he had been given.

But his ploy appeared to have worked. In one of Donovan's first conversations with Stephenson, shortly after his return to Washington, the American told his new friend that while he had been warned beforehand the British might be '"difficult", secretive and patronising' – which in peacetime they might have been – his experience had been 'exactly the opposite'.[10] He was 'emotionally convinced' that Britain could hold firm,[11] and was now energetically spreading the word in Washington that it was not too late 'for American aid, both material and economic, to exercise a decisive effect on the war'.[12] Donovan had arrived in London as a grieving father and a failed politician, feeling overlooked and unimportant. His reception changed forever the way he felt about Britain and the British, and it probably made him more amenable to a friendship with Stephenson.

In the days that followed, Donovan lobbied hard for the destroyer transfer to Britain. But Stephenson wanted more. In particular, he wanted his new friend to help persuade Congress to back the new military conscription bill.

Unimaginable today, by 1940 the US army was smaller than that of Bulgaria. This was testament to the country's historic aversion to having a large standing army. Few Americans wanted a government so powerful it could vote to send their sons to fight overseas. In some parts of the country the low-level hostility to the military was such that army officers preferred to wear civilian clothing in public. In 1939, after the outbreak of the European war, there had been numerous anti-war marches led by students. Many young Americans had vowed never to serve in the armed forces.

The military was unpopular, and so was the prospect of conscription. In spite of this, earlier that summer the Burke-Wadsworth Selective Service Training Bill had been introduced to Congress, in the hope of securing a peacetime draft for the first time in American history. So far, this had met a wall of resistance.

But for the British as well as the American interventionists it was essential that the bill passed into law. There was little point in the United States entering the war if her armed forces were unable to make an impact. When Donovan met 'C' in London they had discussed the conscription bill and what he could do to help it through Congress.[13] Donovan had already lobbied in support of it around Washington. Now Stephenson urged him to take the argument to the nation.

'While it is absolutely true that if you want to fight you've got to be strong,' Donovan announced, in a radio broadcast carried coast-to-coast on the Mutual Broadcasting System, 'it is equally true that if you want peace – you've got to be stronger still – and it is because I am for peace that I am for conscription.'[14] Donovan's talk went down well. 'We have been keeping up the fight,' he wrote to one of the British officials he had met in London, 'and I really believe that we will probably have the [conscription] bill passed and in effect within the next month.'[15]

Two days after his radio broadcast, Donovan moved on to print, co-authoring four articles about the dangers of Nazi Fifth Columnists. These were syndicated nationwide and read by millions of Americans. In the last of these pieces, Donovan described the jaw-dropping scale of Germany's global programme for sabotage and propaganda. It was costing Berlin '$200 million' a year, he revealed. 'As matters now stand, it is conceivable that the United States possesses the finest Nazi-schooled "fifth column" in the world, one which in case of war with Germany could be our undoing.'[16]

This was potentially devastating. In reality, the German 'Fifth Column' in the United States amounted to no more than a handful of agents, many of them incompetent. Donovan's articles were littered with exaggerations and half-baked rumours. Almost all of these had been fed to him by Bill Stephenson.[17]

The new MI6 officer had been passing Donovan what journalists at the time would call 'wrongos', or just 'fake news'.[18] It is hard to say whether Donovan believed everything he was given by Stephenson, who told him it came from classified reports. But Stephenson himself would have known that much of this information was unsubstantiated.

This marked a new direction for him. Stephenson's story on Dr Westrick had been full of innuendo but it was accurate. Now the MI6 man was starting to get his hands dirty, and perhaps rediscover aspects of himself which he preferred to forget.

On his return to Canada after the end of the First World War, Stephenson had patented a revolutionary can-opener he called 'Kleen Kut'. As he explained at length in an interview with a local newspaper, during the war his plane had been shot down, he was captured by the Germans and taken to a prisoner-of-war camp. In there he had dreamed up 'all sorts of mechanical devices', he explained, including this ingenious can-opener.[19]

Kleen Kut was an instant success, Stephenson's first breakthrough as an entrepreneur. But it was built on a small deception. While he had indeed been shot down and held as a prisoner-of-war, Stephenson had then stolen from a German staff kitchen an unusual looking can-opener. He later realized that owing to the date and location of its manufacture the German inventor would have been unable to file a worldwide patent. So he took the can-opener back to

Canada and filed the patent in his own name, passing off the design as his own.

Although Stephenson had not broken any laws, he was clearly embarrassed by this episode and later had it removed from a biography. His reaction to what he had done, as much as the act itself, hints at a version of himself that he was uncomfortable with. After less than two months in his new incarnation as the MI6 Head of Station in '48-LAND' he was starting to grasp that there were times when he had to embrace that side of himself: to treat fanciful or tendentious rumours as if they were hard-boiled facts, and even be willing to mislead people he liked, including Bill Donovan.

During August 1940, Donovan made the case for conscription and the destroyer transfer in the press, on the radio and in person to officials in Washington DC, but his most telling contribution came at sea.

On 9 August 1940, 'Wild Bill' stepped onto the presidential yacht, the *Potomac*, where he was scheduled to spend a day and a night with Roosevelt. They were escorted throughout by a lone destroyer, a constant reminder on the horizon of the main item on Donovan's agenda.

The president had not come out in support of either conscription or the destroyer transfer. The reason was simple. He did not think the country was ready, and polls suggested he was right. 'In earlier New Deal times, and in a period of less anxious foreign relations, "a way around the law" might be attempted to avoid asking Congressional sanction,' a commentator had written in the *New York Times*.[20] 'But that will hardly be risked now.' From some quarters he was being urged to give up on Britain, notably by his ambassador to Britain, Joe Kennedy, father of the future president, who had told Roosevelt only the week before that the RAF would be obliterated by the Luftwaffe, and that a British surrender was 'inevitable'.[21] His source on the size and power of the Luftwaffe? Charles Lindbergh. Kennedy's advice on sending aid to Britain was unequivocal: there was no point. Now Donovan had to persuade the president otherwise.

Their fishing trip did not start well. Roosevelt was initially distracted and unreceptive, either taking messages from his secretary or fussing over his rods as he tried to hook a striped bass. When Donovan did get the chance to speak, the president crowded him out with long monologues.

It was not the first time these two had failed to connect. Long ago they had been in the same class at Columbia Law School but had barely spoken to each other. One a Republican, the other a Democrat, they were about as different as two high-achieving young Americans could be. Donovan was the brilliant footballer from a humble background; Roosevelt the privileged dandy apparently incapable of taking his studies seriously. Although their relationship had since improved, and during the 1930s Roosevelt had sent Donovan on several European fact-finding missions, there were times when these two struggled to find the measure of one another.

As the day wore on, Roosevelt tired and his guest became bolder. By the afternoon Donovan felt that he was landing more of his verbal blows. By nightfall, he was sure he had convinced the president of Britain's 'excellent prospects of pulling through'.[22]

The next morning, Donovan disembarked in Boston. As he alighted from the presidential yacht, a stack of that day's newspapers went in the other direction, including the latest edition of the *New York Times*. Taking up almost half of the editorial page in that day's paper was a letter signed by four well-known lawyers. 'No Legal Bar Seen to Transfer of Destroyers' was the headline.[23] In impressive detail the authors argued that the president did not actually need congressional authority for the destroyer transfer.

This changed everything. The lawyers suggested that the law

blocking the transfer could only apply if the ships had been built specifically for foreign use, which, of course, these ageing destroyers had not. The letter was signed by four lawyers but it had been written by just one, Dean Acheson, a former member of Roosevelt's administration and now key player in the Century Group.

Although Acheson's legal reasoning was hopeful at times, or just wrong, his timing was exquisite. The president read this letter after Bill Donovan had assured him repeatedly that Britain could hold out if she had enough destroyers. In the hours that followed, Roosevelt came round to the idea of authorizing this destroyer transfer without going through Congress.

By that point, public opinion was on the move. A Gallup poll conducted the month before suggested only 50 per cent of the population supported the destroyer transfer.[24] But in a survey carried out just after the *New York Times* letter and Donovan's radio address, and with Pershing's speech still fresh in many people's minds, the figure had crept up towards 60 per cent.[25]

Leadership is often seen as the art of knowing when to lead and when to follow. Roosevelt was beginning to master a different form: the art of leading by appearing to follow. He had asked the Century Group to make the case for the destroyer transfer to the public, which they had successfully done. Now he could respond in public to this apparently organic shift in the national mood by approving a policy he had already agreed to.

In the days after his fishing trip with Donovan, Roosevelt reached an agreement in principle with Churchill on the transfer of fifty destroyers to the Royal Navy. In return, the United States would receive ninety-nine-year leases on naval and air bases in the Caribbean, Bermuda and Newfoundland. It was a lopsided bargain, very much weighted towards the US, but Churchill was in no position to hold out for a better arrangement. What had originally been described as a 'gift' or 'transfer' was now a 'deal', which also made it easier to sell to the American people.

'I think the trick has been done,' Lord Lothian wrote at around this time. 'At least the President told me on the telephone this morning that he thought it was. Donovan helped a lot'.[26]

Just one obstacle remained.

During a hot and stormy convention in Philadelphia, two months earlier, the Republican party had chosen as its presidential candidate a lawyer called Wendell Willkie. Anyone who told you at the time that they had seen this coming was almost certainly lying. Willkie was the unlikeliest presidential nominee in the history of the GOP. He was a dishevelled former Democrat and utility company president without any political experience. But he had charisma. As Holly Golightly puts it in Truman Capote's *Breakfast at Tiffany's*, set in 1943, 'if I were free to choose from everybody alive, just snap my fingers and say come here you,' one of the two men she would have had in an instant was Wendell Willkie.[1]

Here was a politician with sex appeal. But in the weeks after his nomination, some Republicans began to worry that they had fallen for the wrong man, and not least after they heard his acceptance speech. On a cripplingly hot day in Elwood, Indiana, the new leader of the Republican party Wendell Willkie had said 'the loss of the British fleet would greatly weaken our defense', and described the prospect of a Europe dominated by Germany as 'a calamity to us.'[2] He also declared that, in his opinion, 'some form of selective service is the only democratic way to secure the trained and competent manpower we need for national defense.'

None of this went down well with the party faithful. The Republican foreign policy plank agreed upon at the national convention was defiantly isolationist, partly due to the hard work of Hamilton Fish and Hans Thomsen. Most Republicans wanted nothing to do with the British fleet, the European war or military conscription. Willkie had trampled over all that, seemingly oblivious to these core Republican beliefs.

In mitigation, he had not formally come out in support of either measure and he might yet go either way. But some of his advisers saw this speech as a missed opportunity. Roosevelt was vulnerable on foreign policy. They wanted their candidate to take a tough isolationist stance, and galvanize the country's anti-war feeling behind him. Instead he seemed intent on giving the president a pass.

Willkie's early refusal to go after Roosevelt on foreign policy inspired whispers that hardened later into conspiracy theories about where his loyalties might lie. C. Nelson Sparks's bestselling *One Man – Wendell Willkie*, published in 1943, argued that Willkie was actually a creature of the British ambassador and a small group of influential East Coasters including Helen Reid of the *Herald Tribune*. Later came the more sensational accusation that MI6 had somehow rigged the Republican National Convention in June 1940 to get Willkie nominated; in other words, that the leader of the Republican party was working either with or for Bill Stephenson.

This last claim was made by the historian Thomas Mahl in his book *Desperate Deception*, published in 1999, and is still repeated today.

Is there anything to it? The MI6 plot described by Mahl is certainly elaborate. It begins in May 1940 with a meeting of the Committee on Arrangements for the Republican Convention. During this session the seventy-year-old chairman of the committee, Ralph E. Williams, had a stroke and died several days later. According to Mahl this was not a natural death: instead Williams was assassinated by MI6.

His evidence seems thin, and appears to be based mainly on a quote from a former member of a separate British agency about how his organization *may* have been responsible for targeted wartime assassinations. According to Mahl, the reason MI6 wanted to bump off this elderly Republican was that they knew he would be replaced by Sam Pryor, Willkie's campaign manager and, he goes on, an MI6 agent.

Pryor certainly played a pivotal role in the Republican convention, and he worked hard to secure Willkie's election. There were times when he may have used his position as chair of the Committee on Arrangements to improve his candidate's chances of victory. But was he also working for the British?

Mahl's evidence is unconvincing. Pryor must have been a British agent, he argues, because once the US entered the war he helped the British build several airports in South America; in the years after the war his job at Pan Am Airlines included liaising with the CIA; and, finally, as a boy Sam Pryor had 'adolescent fantasies' of being a spy.[3]

Another problem with Mahl's argument is to do with the dates. Stephenson arrived in New York just four days before the start of the Republican National Convention, and several weeks *after* the death of Ralph E. Williams. The office he inherited was tiny, understaffed and directionless. In short, MI6 was unable at the time to interfere in the Republican convention and there is no evidence that they actually did.

For all that, the relationship between Willkie and the British *was* closer than many people realized.

Just days after his controversial acceptance speech, in August 1940, Willkie sent a letter to the British ambassador that would not surface for many years. 'I have had a personal message from Willkie,' Lord Lothian reported to London, 'to say that he was personally in favour of doing everything possible to see that Great Britain did not get beaten in the war'. Willkie also told the British that 'he would not oppose the transfer of destroyers'.[4] Realizing how it might look if this letter ever appeared in the press, the Republican leader was 'most insistent' his message only be shown to Churchill and the British Foreign Secretary, and 'should not in any circumstances be allowed to leak out'.[5]

This was just the start of a secret relationship between Willkie and the British.

The new leader of the Republican party was also closer than he cared to admit to the Century Group. One of its members, the editorial writer at the *Herald Tribune*, Geoffrey Parsons, drafted the foreign policy section of Willkie's acceptance speech. Throughout August 1940, other Century Group members urged the Republican to come out in support of the destroyers-for-bases deal, or at least refrain from attacking it.

In late August 1940, Willkie finally agreed. He would not use this against the president. A Century Group member called up the White House to pass on the news. The final obstacle to the destroyer transfer had been removed.

On Monday 3 September 1940, the destroyers-for-bases deal was announced. The next day the first three US destroyers set off for Britain. This sent a message to the world, and in particular to Nazi Germany. 'The British Empire and the United States will have to be somewhat mixed up together in some of their affairs,' Churchill had told Parliament a little earlier, before his speech took a more lyrical turn. 'I could not stop it if I wished; no one can stop it. Like the Mississippi, it just keeps rolling along. Let it roll. Let it roll on full flood,' he intoned, 'to broader lands and better days.'[1] That afternoon the prime minister could be heard singing 'Ol' Man River' to himself.[2]

Britain's chances of holding out against Nazi Germany remained poor, but they were better than they had been for months. The news of this deal almost certainly influenced Hitler's decision, less than a fortnight later, to postpone the German invasion of Britain.

'Give yourself fifty pats on back sometime,' Stephenson wrote to 'C'. 'Without Colonel [Donovan], it could not possibly have happened at this time.'[3] Another British official hailed Donovan as 'a firm friend in the Republican camp' now 'proving of immense value'.[4] For the journalist Walter Lippmann, Donovan 'almost single-handed overcame the unmitigated defeatism which was paralyzing Washington'.[5]

At least some of the credit for the destroyers-for-bases deal also belonged to the head of MI6 in London and his New York represent- ative. Between them, 'C' and Stephenson had built up Bill Donovan, flattered him, befriended him, showered him with intelligence, and done everything in their power to make him feel important. Ste- phenson had urged Donovan to give radio broadcasts, write articles and to pressure the president. He had also fed him questionable intelligence in an attempt to swing American opinion.

The day after the first of these fifty destroyers left the United States, the British received more good news. On 5 September 1940, after a remarkable shift in public opinion on the conscription bill, with those in favour leaping from just under 50 per cent in early June[6] to nearly 70 per cent in late August,[7] Congress approved the Burke-Wadsworth bill. The US Army was about to go on a growth spurt.

These two campaigns, one focused on the destroyers-for-bases deal, the other on the conscription bill, had much in common. Although most of the work had been carried out by American interventionists, their efforts had been galvanized by the British. Just as MI6 worked on 'Wild Bill' Donovan, Lord Lothian had kept the Century Group going as it was set to fall apart. This marked the start of a new kind of Anglo-American collaboration. Informal, loose and at times hard to pin down, it was centred on a small band of Americans and Britons with many friends in common. They were publishers, editors, government officials, intelligence officers, or well-connected lawyers. Few were being paid for their work. Nor were they doing this to get ahead. Instead they were bound together by the single, deadening realization that nothing was more important in their lives at that moment than defeating Hitler.

With the first destroyers on their way to Britain and the conscrip- tion bill passed by Congress, they had momentum behind them. Although there was a long way to go, it seemed that the country might perhaps be starting to move towards intervention. But by the end of that week a very different picture had emerged.

'Dictator Roosevelt Commits Act of War,' was the response to the destroyer-for-bases-deal in the *St Louis Post-Dispatch*. 'If Roosevelt gets away with this, we may as well say good-by to our liberties and make up our mind that henceforth we live under a dictatorship.'[8] The isolationist congressman Hamilton Fish described the deal as 'virtually an act of war', a sentiment shared by many of his colleagues on the Hill.[9] Even Churchill was worried by the effect of the president's announcement, fearing that it could lead to 'the German Government declaring war'.[10]

Roosevelt also feared that he might have gone too far. The president's secretary recalled him saying 'the deal could result in his impeachment'.[11] Already several congressmen were calling for this. His Attorney General, Robert Jackson, later described Roosevelt's tendency 'to think in terms of right and wrong, instead of terms of legal and illegal. Because he thought that his motives were always good for the things that he wanted to do, he found difficulty in thinking there could be legal limitations on them'.[12] There was no doubt in Roosevelt's mind that giving Britain all possible aid was right. By approving the secret transfer of arms and planes to Britain earlier in the summer he had already crossed a line. In bypassing Congress to push through the destroyers-for-bases deal he may have done so again. Of course if he was not impeached, he might be punished instead at the coming presidential election, now less than two months away.

Several days later, the Luftwaffe launched a new type of attack on London. 'This was no nuisance or insomnia raid. This was business,' reported the *New York Times*: 'hordes of German bombers could be seen high overhead until at one point they looked like swarming bees,' and 'time after time the ground shook beneath this office as though London was experiencing an earthquake'.[13]

The Blitz had begun. After the momentary euphoria of victory in the Battle of Britain and the news of the destroyer deal, the British were again on the back foot.

Meanwhile in the United States the isolationist movement was on the cusp of a major transformation. On the same day that the House approved the conscription bill, a press conference was called in Washington to launch a new isolationist group.

It was called the America First Committee. Right away, it appeared to be different to any other anti-war group. It was youthful, dynamic and well-funded, and it had backing across the isolationist spectrum, including the support of Charles Lindbergh. The America First Committee was better organized and more motivated than anything that Bill Stephenson had come up against so far. In the battle for the hearts and minds of the American people, the British and their interventionist allies suddenly had a new and more potent enemy.

PART TWO

SPYMASTER

7 SEPTEMBER 1940

Days Britain at war – 370
Allied shipping losses in the Atlantic (to date) – 2,448,609 tons
Aircraft lost by RAF in past month – 792[1]

28 SEPTEMBER – 5 OCTOBER 1940

Gallup Survey: If you were asked to vote today on the question
of the United States entering the war against Germany and
Italy, how would you vote — to go into the war or to stay out
of the war?
Go in – 15.6%[2]

Charles Lindbergh did not like committees. He felt the 'idea of forming committees to get action' was 'one of the greatest of American fallacies'. They were 'cumbersome and slow-moving and controversial'.[1] But he liked America First.

Lindbergh was deeply impressed by the young man in charge of the new America First Committee, Yale law student R. Douglas Stuart, calling him 'a fine type of young fellow'.[2] Within weeks of the launch of what was soon known as just 'America First', Lindbergh was urging his fellow isolationists to support it.[3] He recognized the role America First could play in slowing the flow of aid to Britain and keeping the United States out of the war. He also liked the name of this new group, and probably had a keener sense of what it implied than its youthful leader may have done.

As a political slogan, 'America First' had first come to life in the late nineteenth century when Republicans in some parts of the country used it to protest against rising immigration from China, Ireland and parts of Eastern Europe. During the 1916 presidential election both candidates promised to put 'America first'. By the time the United States entered the First World War 'America first' was a jingoistic battle cry, like 'Rule Britannia', 'Deutschland über Alles', or someone today shouting 'U! S! A!'

But in the years after the war its meaning began to shift. During the 1920s 'America First' morphed from being a political slogan into more of an ideal. Echoing earlier nativist movements such as the nineteenth-century Know-Nothings, 'America First' became shorthand for rugged patriotism, individualism and a prickly attitude to the rest of the world. If you heard a 1920s politician declare that he stood for 'America first', you could be sure he supported tough protectionist tariffs and an isolationist foreign policy, and had an icy suspicion towards international bodies like the World Court or the League of Nations.

'America First' also hinted at a lingering anxiety about the country's ethnic breakdown. At the time many believed that being a 'true' or 'hundred per cent' American was less about character, outlook or values, but the colour of your skin and where your parents were from. Eugenic theories of 'scientific racism' and 'Nordicism' had seeped into the mainstream. Nordicism was a version of white supremacism which held that people from northern Europe were biologically superior to everyone else, a set of ideas behind countless books including the 1916 bestseller *The Passing of the Great Race* by Madison Grant, and the popular film of the same year *Birth of A Nation*, the first motion picture to be shown in the White House. 'My only regret is that it is all so terribly true,' President Wilson reportedly said after watching it.[4]

As the 1920s wore on, and 'America first' was adopted as a slogan by the Ku Klux Klan, a growing number of Americans concluded that 'Nordic' people really were better than others, and that these were the type of people who should be encouraged to come to America. The clearest expression of this was the 1924 Immigration Act, or Johnson-Reed Act, in which Congress imposed national quotas on immigration which reflected their racial sense of how the United States should look. One of the many European admirers of the new quota system was a young Adolf Hitler.[5]

This new law reduced to a splutter the flow of arrivals from southern and eastern Europe, ended altogether the stream of migrants from Asian countries, and encouraged a flood of newcomers from Germany, Denmark, Sweden, Britain, and, of course, Norway. 'We should have more people from Norway,' was the sentiment, the same words used ninety-four years later by the US President Donald Trump, who promised repeatedly to put 'America first'.[6]

When the law student R. Douglas Stuart had the idea in 1940 of forming a nationwide isolationist alliance he did not focus much on the name. Nor did any of his fellow Yalies in the group, including Potter Stewart, Sargent Shriver and Gerald Ford, who would go on to become respectively a US Supreme Court justice, founding director of the Peace Corps and 38th President of the United States. It was only after speaking to some of the country's leading isolationists that Stuart decided on a name. '"Defend America First" will be our theme,' he wrote in August 1940, after a conversation with his boyhood hero, Charles Lindbergh.[7] Several weeks later that was shortened to 'America First'.

The America First Committee got off to a blistering start, thanks to a combination of hard work and good management as well as luck, pharaonic ambition, and a hitherto untapped desire among so many isolationists to come together as a single movement. By the end of September 1940 America First was operating out of a large headquarters in Chicago. Money was pouring in. Talented publicists were on retainer. Its advertisements were being seen in newspapers throughout the country, and already the committee's aims and outlook were being discussed and explained on the radio.

In a Gallup poll released several months earlier, in July 1940, less than 13 per cent of those surveyed said they would 'vote to go into the war, if a vote came up in the next two weeks'.[8] Right away, America First harnessed this nationwide aversion to war. Soon thousands of Americans were applying to join its local chapters, and it acquired a platform of prominent supporters. Its new chairman was General Robert E. Wood, US Acting Quartermaster General in the last war, its committee now included a series of powerful labour leaders, businessmen, clergymen, several scientists, and Henry Ford, who had been personally brought in by Lindbergh.

Although Lindbergh was active behind the scenes of America First, he had not formally agreed to join. Instead he spent the weeks after the destroyers-for-bases deal sequestered away with his family. On most days he was out walking his dog, playing with his children, reading and writing, or gearing up for the birth of his fourth child, due any day now. When he did listen to the news or pick up a newspaper, he felt a glow of optimism. America was out of the war, and there were few signs that this might be about to change.

On 27 September 1940 there was more good news for Lindbergh and America First. The Axis powers had signed the Tripartite Pact. Under this new treaty, if one of Germany, Italy or Japan was attacked by the United States the others would automatically come to their aid, a move designed to box in the US fleet and further reduce the chances of America entering the war. Lindbergh welcomed this, and saw it as another opportunity to attack the president, telling the press this pact was the result of Roosevelt's 'blundering diplomacy'.[9]

This comment appeared in many newspapers, including one delivered to the Department of Justice, in Washington DC, where a government employee reached for his scissors, cut it out, and added it to the growing FBI file on Charles A. Lindbergh.

Over the past year J. Edgar Hoover's department had received a stream of complaints about Lindbergh. Most had come from members of the public who suspected him of being a German spy. One was adamant that the superstar pilot was part of a 'German propaganda unit' primed to 'cooperate with the Nazi regime'.[10] Others reported the names of extremist organizations using his name in their literature who might also be working with him.

The FBI investigated each of these leads, but found nothing. The right-wing groups they were warned about merely admired Lindbergh. Nor was there any evidence of his being a German spy. But the suspicion did not go away, and it was not confined to the FBI.

'I felt that it could not have been better put if it had been written by Goebbels himself,' Roosevelt said after reading one of Lindbergh's recent speeches.[11] 'I am absolutely convinced that Lindbergh is a Nazi,' he added, but he needed proof.[12]

So did Bill Stephenson.

The most unusual part of Bill Stephenson's new walk to work came at the end. His MI6 station was no longer based in his luxurious apartment high above Central Park. Instead his daily commute began as he rode the lift down to the lobby of Hampshire House and crossed the chessboard marble floor, his shoes making a neat *clickety-click* sound. Stephenson looked like a businessman off to a meeting. His suit was expensive without being ostentatious, his manner neat and contained, face full of undescribed purpose. By the entrance there might have been a quick exchange of greetings with the doormen before he stepped out onto Central Park South.

This was like leaving the safety of the womb. Exiting the building, he was jumped upon by the heat, the haze, the din of the street and the pungent smell of droppings from the horses pulling carriages up and down the street. Out of Hampshire House he went right, and at the end of the block either he turned down Sixth Avenue, or, more likely, kept going for another block to cut across the southern side of Grand Army Plaza, past the Pulitzer Fountain, before striking out onto Fifth Avenue.

Here the view stretched majestically to the horizon, the skyscrapers on each side of him forming a sleek canyon. To his left was a river of cabs, and on his right a parade of shop windows, office blocks and stern-looking bank façades. On he went, past the bootblacks and the food vendors, invisible at times among the secretaries, labourers, businessmen and tourists, until after about five minutes the blackened entrance to St Patrick's Cathedral came into view on the other side of the street. At this, Stephenson wheeled to the right, past the 'Atlas' statue, by Lee Lawrie and Rene Paul Chambellan, and through a revolving door taking him into the hushed edifice of the Rockefeller Center's International Building.

With its veined green marble and bronze mouldings, and a ceiling picked out with squares of copper leaf, this lobby had the cautious, low-lit atmosphere of a mausoleum. The MI6 officer continued to the lifts at the far end, usually full at that time of day, and rode up to the 35th floor where he padded down a corridor to an office marked 'British Passport Control'.

The set-up inside was small and humdrum. Not surprisingly, on account of the Blitz, few people were applying for British visas. There were one or two passport officials and administrative staff at work, but that was it.

At least it appeared to be. The British Passport Control office also contained a door, an unremarkable piece of joinery which looked as if it might lead into a kitchenette or storeroom. Instead it gave onto a hidden annex, a vast office filled with desks, filing cabinets, telephones, unexplained machines, and a flurry of people all working for MI6.

Several weeks earlier, American and British military officials had agreed in London that 'the time had now come' for a full and ongoing exchange of intelligence.[1] On the same day the House voted in favour of conscription, 5 September 1940, Roosevelt had quietly signed a presidential order allowing British officials to see reports from the State Department and US consulates. A torrent of classified information would now flow between the two countries, and it was decided that this should be processed by Stephenson's office. No matter how many crimson-tufted banquettes he moved out of the way, his apartment would be unable to cope. Stephenson needed more staff and a much larger office.

Remembering that a co-director in his London investment firm, the elderly Lord Southborough, had been involved in the development of the International Building in the Rockefeller Center, Stephenson approached him, and soon secured an office for a peppercorn rent.

Next, he went on a recruitment drive. Advertisements for 'reliable young women' available for secretarial duties in New York appeared in newspapers across Canada, including Stephenson's hometown of Winnipeg.[2] A sudden influx of secretaries from Britain, speaking in a variety of accents, might attract unwelcome attention. Instead a stream of Canadian recruits arrived in Manhattan, and by the end of the year Stephenson had close to one hundred employees in his new Rockefeller Center office, many of them Canadian secretaries.

Secrecy remained vital. With more staff and a more public location for his office, there was a much greater risk of exposure. One of his precautions was to insist that the new secretaries live together, either at the Barbizon Hotel or in the Beekman Tower. Each day they were bussed into work en masse. If one of these secretaries had a medical problem she was required to see an office-approved doctor, including one who was the brother of the MI6 office manager.

It was a cosseted existence, but when interviewed many years later none of these former secretaries resented it. Instead they reminisced happily about the excitement of their work, the camaraderie they felt towards each other, and the thrill of leaving Canada for the first time to live in the most glamorous city on earth. They talked about Radio City Music Hall, seeing the Rockettes and the 'Fifth Avenue parades' go past their office, or 'the glamour night spots' such as 'the Stork

Club, El Morocco, the St. Regis Iridium Room with an ice show, the Rainbow Room', drinking cheap 'thirty-five cent martinis', seeing 'movie classics at the Museum of Modern Art', enjoying 'the beautiful stores and store windows' such as 'Saks, Lord and Taylor, Altman's Bergdorf' or just gawping at 'the gorgeous jewels in the window of Van Cleef and Arpel's and Cartier'.[3]

As the new secretaries settled into their work, Stephenson carried on with his. He needed to find more ways to change American public opinion. Soon he was sending 'C' in London an array of suggestions. Most were passed on to the Foreign Office for approval. All were turned down.

'The NY representative of "C" should be told to refrain from sending in ideas of this kind', was a typical response to one of Stephenson's plans.[4]

'Our American friends desire guidance,' Stephenson wrote to 'C' shortly after, a reference to the Century Group, 'as to what requirements they may assist to fulfil.'[5] There was no reply. Two weeks later, uncertainty creeping in, Stephenson tried again, asking 'C' for 'guidance as to general lines of policy and requirements'.[6] Again he was told to do nothing. After the excitement of the summer, the British campaign to bring the US into the war had entered a new and more hesitant phase.

'I started from scratch,' Stephenson later said of this period. 'I had no experience. I was a businessman and in the early days of the job, I got plenty of bangs on the head.'[7] Most of these came from either the Foreign Office or 'C'. Others were delivered by the man who was rapidly becoming Stephenson's guide to the American political system and a mentor of sorts: the British ambassador Lord Lothian.

Stephenson liked Lothian. He found him 'sympathetic and helpful', keen to work with MI6, and 'thoroughly familiar with the local political scene'.[8] But it was clear now that Lothian wanted him to rein in his activities. On his watch there would be no more hidden propaganda, no deceit, and absolutely no meddling by the British in the coming US presidential election.

Stephenson was learning to hold back, and the same was true for Bill Donovan and the Century Group. The mood among the band of Britons and Americans who had campaigned so energetically for the destroyers-for-bases deal and the conscription act was starting to sour. The wide-eyed optimism that had driven them on over the summer and characterised their interactions was replaced by a creeping sense of powerlessness.

The reason for this new approach was simple: with US elections taking place within less than two months, the mood across the country had become jittery and more suspicious. The American people had become, as one US columnist put it, probably 'the most propaganda-conscious people on earth. We are strongly allergic to it, over-skeptical about it, and shy away sharply from anything which emits even faintly the fragrance of propaganda.'[9] They were particularly on guard against anything which smelt like British interference. 'BEWARE THE BRITISH SERPENT!' ran the top line on an anonymous poster that had begun to be plastered up around the country after the start of the war. 'Once more,' it went on, 'a boa constrictor – "Perfidious Albion" – is crawling across the American landscape, spewing forth its unctuous lies.'[10]

By 1940, many Americans firmly believed that during the First World War a conspiracy of Wall Street bankers, Anglophile arms dealers and British spies had tricked them into entering the war. This narrative worked partly because it felt so familiar, and fed into a more established fear of powerful East Coasters colluding with the British. This theory about why the country had entered the last war had become so popular and credible that in 1934 it led to a senate committee investigation.

Even if this committee found no evidence of a conspiracy, the underlying suspicion remained about there having been a British plot to bring the country into the last war. Such is the power of a long-running investigation. A Gallup poll in 1937 found that 70 per cent of the American people thought the nation's involvement in the last war had been a mistake. Millions of Americans believed they had been duped by the British. They did not want to fall for the same trick twice.

The British ambassador Lord Lothian was acutely aware of this. He wanted to give the American people a different and more sympathetic vision of Britain. Just weeks after Stephenson had moved his MI6 office into the International Building of the Rockefeller Center, Lothian set up the new British Press Service (BPS) in the neighbouring RCA Building (better known today as '30 Rock'). This new British organization 'would avoid secret service-style whispering campaigns', Lothian insisted. Instead it would provide American journalists with accurate, reliable and up-to-date information on the British war effort.[11]

This was not a bluff. The ambassador was convinced that the best way to win over the American people was by being consistently friendly, truthful and direct. In London, many civil servants agreed. The BBC had recently broadened its Empire Service to include parts of the United States and was using American broadcasters as well as Britons with regional accents such as J. B. Priestley. Like Lothian, they wanted to make the British sound less fusty. A volunteer American RAF pilot who had fought heroically in the Battle of Britain was being lined up to visit politicians in Washington. There were plans for a newsletter by A. A. Milne, author of the *Winnie the Pooh* books, aimed at British children who had been evacuated to the US. The Ministry of Information commissioned the scriptwriter Michael Powell to make a pro-intervention film for an American audience.

These were just some of the initiatives now coming out of London, each one sensible, progressive and guaranteed not to offend.

Together they achieved almost nothing. Hollywood studios were scared of putting out any film which could be labelled interventionist, partly for fear of an anti-Semitic backlash against Jewish movie exec-utives, so Powell's film, *The Invaders*, was not released until after the US had entered the war. The A. A. Milne newsletter was cancelled after a ship containing child evacuees was sunk. The American RAF pilot was injured and died before he could cross the Atlantic. As for the BBC broadcasting into the US, the renowned CBS broadcaster Ed Murrow would point out that in a nation of more than 130 million people these broadcasts reached just '5,000 class people', if that, and most of them were already pro-British.

Lothian was also starting to put his faith in the Blitz, hoping that reports by the likes of Ed Murrow might inspire the American people to call for war. Churchill felt the same. 'The bombing of Oxford, Cov-entry and Canterbury, will cause such a wave of indignation in the United States that they'll come into the war!' he declared in private.[12] The Blitz had lit 'a fire in British hearts, here and all over the world', was how he worded it in public, a blaze which would 'burn with a steady and consuming flame until the last vestiges of Nazi tyranny have been burned out of Europe, and until the Old World – and the New – can join hands to rebuild the temples of man's freedom and man's honour'.[13] Newspaper reports and radio broadcasts gave Americans a taste of life during the Blitz; newsreel footage filled in some of the gaps. Slowly the reality of what was happening in London percolated into the American consciousness.

The British were also pinning their hopes on the outcome of the presidential election. Increasingly they were convinced that if Roose-velt won he would be free to lead his country into the war.

None of this, however, offered immediate relief. Like Lothian and Churchill, in the weeks leading up to the US presidential election Bill Stephenson was left to watch, wait and hope. In the meantime, America First continued to grow in strength.

It had been an eventful morning for Charles Lindbergh. After putting his life in the hands of an experimental Russian inventor, America's leading isolationist took a break for lunch. It was 9 October 1940. He had just survived a test flight in his friend Igor Sikorsky's prototype of a helicopter. As the machine juddered up into the blank autumn sky, swaying slightly as Sikorsky manoeuvred it over a treeless field in Connecticut, Lindbergh was for a moment removed from the news cycle – the war, America First and the coming election. It was a welcome break, even if it did not last long.

After their test flight, Lindbergh and Sikorsky went for lunch at a roadside inn. 'While we were eating,' Lindbergh recalled, to their surprise 'Willkie drove by, in an open car with a large motorcycle police escort. I caught a quick glimpse of him as he flashed by the window.'

The sound of this motorcade as it arrowed past, the flashing lights, and the way Lindbergh's fellow diners turned without thinking towards the eye of this storm took him back to the days after his transatlantic crossing when he had been the one travelling around with police outriders, his every move a news story in the making. Now he had come to know a different type of fame, one he was starting to appreciate. For the first time in his life, Lindbergh was starting to feel that he had harnessed his celebrity to a cause he believed in, and that he was using the press to his advantage. 'He is more than welcome to it all,' Lindbergh concluded as Willkie's car sped out of sight.[1]

No doubt this interruption turned the lunchtime conversation back to the election, now less than a month away. Lindbergh did not think the result would have a major impact on the isolationist campaign, as both candidates seemed to be either agnostic on the question of war or were leaning towards intervention. But of the two he preferred Willkie. The Republican party had at least come out against intervention, and in time they might persuade their candidate to do the same.

Lindbergh had been disappointed by Willkie's performance so far. In the weeks after his nomination a Gallup poll put him just one percentage point behind Roosevelt.[2] But in a more recent poll, published three days before Lindbergh went up in the helicopter, the president was twelve points ahead. Although Willkie was attacking Roosevelt for trying to secure an unprecedented third term as president, and for the excesses of the New Deal, he held back on the one subject uppermost in many people's minds: the war. On foreign policy it was often hard to tell the two candidates apart. Or as Lindbergh later said, in a slightly unusual comparison: it was as 'if Hitler had run against Goering'.[3]

Lindbergh and his friends in America First were increasingly frustrated by Wendell Willkie. The isolationist Senator Arthur Vandenberg, a defeated candidate for the Republican nomination, went out to see him on the campaign trail and confronted him about his stance on the war.

Willkie now faced a choice. He could stick to his original position, one that he and his closest aides believed in, or abandon his principles, bow to the conservative elements in his party and take up a more isolationist stance. He chose expediency.

With just one month to go until the election, this charming

Hoosier with come-to-bed eyes reinvented himself as a moderate isolationist. To the delight of Lindbergh and those in America First, Willkie was now accusing Roosevelt of wanting to go to war and of having struck a secret deal with the British to enter the conflict.

The polls started to move. With the election drawing close, Willkie was eating into Roosevelt's lead. Soon he had cut it in half. By the middle of October 1940, with just three weeks to go, the Republicans had the momentum every political party dreams of at this stage in an election. Polls also showed a steady growth in the number of Americans who felt it was wrong for a president to stay in office for a third term.[4]

'Panicked' might be too strong a word to describe Roosevelt's state of mind. But he was worried, and so were those around him.

'I have said this before, but I shall say it again, and again and again. Your boys are not going to be sent into any foreign wars,' he promised in his last major campaign speech, just a week before the election. 'We will not send our army, navy or air forces to fight in foreign lands.' His White House speechwriters were in despair. One of them, Sam Rosenman, had urged the president to finish that last sentence with the words 'except in case of attack'. Roosevelt had refused, arguing the phrase was redundant. Although he had distanced himself from intervention, promising there was 'no secret treaty, no secret obligation, no secret understanding' with any foreign government – in other words the British – this line would haunt him.[5]

Another man busy giving speeches in the days before the election was Charles Lindbergh. Arguing passionately against going to war, he also tore into Roosevelt and his administration.

The last of these speeches was hosted by the Yale University chapter of America First, one of the organization's many new chapters that had sprung up around the country. Those running America First were now 'having a hard time to keep up with the growth', as one told Lindbergh.[6] The group was expanding exponentially. The optimism was infectious. Anything seemed possible, and soon the leadership of America First had plans to send Lindbergh on a flying tour of the nation to promote the group.

'The propaganda was clever,' a member of Stephenson's staff wrote, 'and was calculated to obtain the support of the greatest possible number of groups and cliques. It appealed to pacifists, haters of Roosevelt, haters of Great Britain,' as well as 'admirers of Germany, American imperialists, devotees of big business, and to those who hated Europe, who regarded that continent as a corrupt and backward region which stood for all the things from which the Pilgrim Fathers and their successors had fled.'[7] On top of all this, there was the draw of Lindbergh himself.

Even as he veered away from mainstream thought, attacking the White House or urging his fellow Americans to think of Nazi Germany as the victim, the superstar pilot remained credible and likeable. According to a *Fortune* poll taken just before the election, almost a third of Americans thought 'Lucky Lindy' was 'unselfishly and patriotically' trying 'to straighten out the nation's thinking on the war'. Less than 3 per cent thought that he was 'unpatriotic' and might be 'deliberately working in the interests of Germany'.[8]

The dramatic growth of America First, the swing towards Willkie, a run of angry speeches from Lindbergh: this was the stuff of dreams for Hans Thomsen in the German embassy, and a welcome distraction from the other concern in his life.

Several days before the election, Thomsen had been told about a German agent working for the Abwehr, or Nazi military intelligence, who had recently been despatched to the United States. The problem with this agent was not that he was on the verge of committing an act of sabotage or interfering in one of Thomsen's schemes, but that he was inept. This bungling spy had recently broken the most basic protocol by wandering into the German consulate in New York, asking to speak to the consul and telling the receptionist that he was an undercover German agent.

Earlier that year, Thomsen had learned that the Abwehr was sending a stream of saboteurs into the United States. He knew how badly this could play out with the American public. During the last war German sabotage operations – notably the 1916 munitions explosion on Black Tom Island which had caused millions of dollars' worth of damage, even affecting the nearby Statue of Liberty – had helped turn the country against Germany before it entered the war. 'It is absolutely necessary', Thomsen cabled Berlin in March 1940, for all 'confidential agents' not gathering information to be withdrawn from America 'in the interest of keeping the USA out of the war'.[9] Instead they kept coming. Next he heard of an Abwehr agent in New Haven offering explosives training to American citizens. 'I cannot warn too urgently against this method,' he pleaded, even offering to pay himself for this agent to be sent home.[10] Thomsen knew the exposure of just one German saboteur could damage relations between the two nations. But so could the release of the 'Potocki Report'.

On 3 November 1940, two days before the American people went to the polls, the *New York Enquirer* ran an explosive lead story. The newspaper that would later become the *National Enquirer* had obtained a report by the former Polish ambassador to the US, Jerzy Potocki, which became known as the 'Potocki Report'. It described a pre-war conversation between Potocki and the US ambassador to France, William Bullitt, in which the American diplomat had reportedly said the US would enter the war.

The story itself was not new, but the public had never seen a detailed account of the conversation. For the isolationists, this was proof of their basic charge against Roosevelt – that he had already agreed to go to war.

An equally sensational story, if anyone could get hold of it, was about how the *Enquirer* had acquired this damning report. It had come to them from Berlin, via Hans Thomsen, who had initially tried to feed it to several isolationist newspapers in the Midwest. They had turned him down, partly because the story felt old, also because they thought 'it would be unpatriotic and treasonable for Americans to use Nazi propaganda material'.[11] For the same reasons the Republican party election committee would not touch it.

The *Enquirer* had no such scruples. Its publisher, William Griffin, conceded to one of Thomsen's agents that running this story might lead to 'harassing interrogations' and 'punitive measures'. But nonetheless he would go ahead with it. The $7,000 he was reportedly paid by the German chargé d'affaires may have helped to stiffen his resolve.

Hans Thomsen understood the risks involved. His arrangement with Griffin constituted, by his own admission, 'interference in American internal politics' and was a 'direct personal attack by us on Roosevelt and his foreign policy' that might lead to a 'rupture' in diplomatic relations. One historian has described this episode as 'one of the most massive interferences in American domestic affairs in history'.[12] But Thomsen felt it was a risk worth taking. If the publication of this report could swing the electoral outcome in New York, a state which might, he hoped, hold 'a decisive role in the presidential election', then the Germans would succeed in one of their long-term aims: Roosevelt would no longer be president.[13]

On the evening of the election, 5 November 1940, Charles Lindbergh and his wife went to an apartment in New York on the Upper East Side for an election party. 'The Democrats I know are very worried,' he noted beforehand. Some of his Republican friends were predicting a big win for Willkie, who had 'been gaining rapidly in popularity during the last several weeks'.[14]

But as the results began to come in, the mood in the party flattened. Giddy anticipation was replaced by disbelief, resignation, anger and the inevitable search for scapegoats. Willkie had performed well in the popular vote, securing over 22 million votes, an improvement on his predecessor Alf Landon's showing four years earlier, but Roosevelt had won more than 27 million votes. Willkie had done well, but not well enough. He was consistently in second place, and in the electoral college won 82 votes to Roosevelt's 449. The Republicans had lost by a landslide.

As the dinner party wore on and the extent of the defeat became clear, the guests continued to drink. 'We discussed the campaign, the war, and the future of America and Europe,' Lindbergh recalled, and at one point late in the night he made a provocative remark, one that he would not have risked in public or among people he did not trust.

'I said that I did not believe a political system based on universal franchise would work in the United States, and that we would eventually have to restrict our franchise.' There is no record in Lindbergh's diaries of the immediate reaction to this. But nobody changed the subject.

Who should be denied the vote? Lindbergh suggested African-Americans. 'Everyone there agreed.'[15]

Having broached one taboo, the conversation moved swiftly on to another. A fellow guest brought up what he or she called 'the Jewish problem'.

At this point in the discussion Lindbergh remembered himself as the voice of restraint, warning the dinner party that this question must be handled 'with intelligence and moderation'. 'Personally, I am afraid that it will get out of hand, and I think that would be a tragedy. We are not a moderate people, once we get started, and an anti-Jewish movement might be considerably worse here than in Germany. I think it is essential to try to prevent such a movement from starting, but how is it to be done?'[16]

That question would have to wait. In the early hours the last of the guests staggered out into a crisp New York night, still trying to make sense of the defeat.

Roosevelt was victorious, but it had been a hard-fought and bitter victory. The opposition had told the American people repeatedly and at great expense that their president was a warmonger, an opportunist, a secret ally of the British, and a power-hungry dictator. According to a *Fortune* poll published just after the election only one in four Americans thought Roosevelt could be trusted with the decision of whether to go to war.[17] 'There is now in the United States a convinced and active minority group,' wrote Ted Roosevelt, the president's cousin and one of his many opponents,[18] and that group 'knows what it is about and knows it is fighting'. They were battling to stay out of the war, and none of them were struggling harder than Lindbergh and America First.

Charles Lindbergh was now so important to Berlin that the Nazi press had been told he must 'be passed over in silence'.[19] Any hint of contact between him and the Nazi regime might destroy his credibility. At the same time this celebrity pilot was seen by the British as such a threat that Lothian warned London, in a similar fashion, that 'Lindbergh must not be attacked by us'.[20] The British and Germans both knew that any hint of either support or disapproval directed at Lindbergh and America First would have the opposite effect on the American people. They also understood that their popularity could change the shape of the war, and that Britain was unable to defeat Hitler without American help.

The isolationist movement within the United States was now the greatest single obstacle to America's entry into the global conflict. Lindbergh and America First had never been so powerful. They were riding high, and there seemed to be nothing the British could do to stop them.

Soon after the presidential election, the British ambassador Lord Lothian returned from a trip to London. At LaGuardia airport he approached a group of waiting journalists and was reported to have said:

'Well boys, Britain's bust. It's your money we want!'[1]

The members of the press, not to mention his aides, were astonished.

'Oh yes,' Lothian said, when questioned. 'It's the truth, and they might as well know it.'[2]

The story ran nationwide. The question of aid to Britain was again front-page news.

In London, Lothian had seen the devastation wreaked by the Luftwaffe. He had also been shown the confidential details of the country's dire economic situation. Even by the most optimistic Treasury projection, the British government would soon be unable to pay for US supplies with cash. Under the terms of the Neutrality Acts, this was the only way they could pay for them. Unless something changed, within a matter of months the country would exhaust certain key supplies.

Shortly after announcing that Britain was running out of money, Lothian went to the White House to see the president. Rather than be sympathetic to the British ambassador, given his country's plight, Roosevelt was furious. Even Thomsen, at the German Embassy, heard about how angry he was at the way Lothian had used the press to force the issue of aid to Britain. Roosevelt 'made no secret of his annoyance over the English propaganda pressure. He did not wish to be put under pressure by the English. He had assured the American people that he would not lead them into the war and he intended to keep his word.'[3]

Lothian knew what he was doing when he made that remark at LaGuardia. He understood that it was not the role of an ambassador to bring up a matter like this with the press. But he had rarely been bound by tradition. As the grandson of the lay head of the Catholic Church in Britain, the Duke of Norfolk, Lothian had earlier broken with centuries of family tradition by becoming a Christian Scientist. His recent decision to rein in Stephenson's activities was driven less by a desire to abide by the rules than by pragmatism. Frequently he acted without Foreign Office approval. Now he had broken precedent to force Roosevelt into a public response on the question of aid for Britain, and it was not clear that this had worked.

Lothian left the Oval Office feeling both chastened and tired. A fellow diplomat had noticed how in recent weeks the ambassador would frequently drop 'off to sleep for a brief spell in the middle of one of his sentences'.[4] The buildings he passed on the drive back from the White House looked cold and funereal in the wintry light. The future seemed bleak. While the Blitz had brought out a compassionate response from the bulk of the American people, it had not triggered the wave of indignation he and others had hoped for. One colleague who arrived in the US at this time noted how the Americans he met, 'from the highest to the lowest, were tremendously kind to us, and universally felt the deepest sympathy for the English and the greatest admiration for the way they were "taking it", but on the question of how much help the US should give, or whether the country should even go to war, 'opinions differed very widely'.[5]

Even Lothian's new British Press Service, which he had hoped would change the way Americans thought about Britain, was floundering. 'Feel I'm beating the air on this job,' wrote the man appointed to run it. 'All time low of blueness reached,' his diary went. 'A bloody awful, ghastly day. Every bleeding thing went wrong.'[6]

Lord Lothian, the rebellious aristocrat who had grown into himself as British ambassador, excelling where so many had thought he would flounder, appeared to have done all he could to bring the United States into the war. Over the coming days he drafted a letter for Churchill to send to Roosevelt, setting out Britain's grim financial situation and pleading for more American support. The prime minister was reluctant to send this, but Lothian insisted. He also began to compose a speech to the American people, his most direct yet.

'The issue now depends largely on what you decide to do,' he wrote, as if removing himself from the process. 'Nobody can share that responsibility with you.'[7] After that he came down with a minor infection.

The most successful agents in the long and storied history of intelligence often have a mercurial ability to disappear in a crowd, or to be forgotten almost as soon as they have been seen. Colonel William J. Donovan was not one of these people. Having tried to leave the country quietly, even changing his name to 'O'Connell' on a travel document, he had been spotted by a journalist in Baltimore as he made his way onto a seaplane bound for Bermuda, a regular stop on the way to Europe.

'Donovan on Mystery Trip' ran a triumphant headline.[1] '"Wild Bill" Leaves on Secret Journey', was another.[2] 'Departs Incognito', was a sub-heading on the front page of the *New York Times*, a rather hopeful assertion given how many millions of Americans now knew about his trip.

He had at least concealed his final destination:[3] 'Wild Bill' was 'believed to be en route to Europe',[4] suggested one newspaper, another thought he was on a 'secret mission tied to France'.[5] A more enterprising journalist contacted the airline to learn the names of Donovan's travelling companions.

'Mystery surrounding the departure from Baltimore today of Col. William J. (Wild Bill) Donovan, famed World War hero, deepened tonight,' began a follow-up report, 'when it was learned three

Englishmen accompanied him.' One was a British embassy official, Charles Des Graz. The other two were unknown to the press. 'Edwin Herbert of London,' the report continued, and 'William Stephenson, British citizen returning from a brief visit to New York.'[6]

No more was written about these last three because no more was known. None of the journalists was aware that the first two worked for British Imperial Censorship in Bermuda, or that the last, an MI6 officer, had not only initiated Donovan's trip, but saw it as the first step in a daring plan to bring the United States into the war.

After months of biding his time, following Lothian's lead, Stephenson had arrived at a bold realization. He needed there to be a new kind of American intelligence agency, one that could become 'a counterpart' to his own MI6 operation. He had understood the limitations of working exclusively with the FBI.[7]

By that stage of the war Stephenson was passing on to the FBI 'all the intelligence from secret sources that he was able to obtain', and in return, Hoover, the FBI Director, 'could hardly have been more cooperative'.[8] Stephenson would later recommend him for an honorary knighthood – which he received – hailing Hoover as the unofficial 'patron' of his MI6 office in those early days.[9] Stephenson's staff provided the FBI with expertise in areas where they were weak, such as counter-espionage and security intelligence, and supplied the Americans with intelligence from territories outside FBI jurisdiction. But there was only so much their offices could do together.

Hoover was worried about the public finding out about this ongoing collaboration with MI6, telling Stephenson he feared 'a major political scandal with every isolationist and non-interventionist in the country after his scalp'.[10] Nor was he likely, in Stephenson's opinion, to take part in any covert efforts to bring the United States into the war.

Stephenson had begun to dream about what he could achieve if there was a different kind of US intelligence agency to work with,

one that specialized in 'clandestine, subversive, and offensive operations', and was run by someone sympathetic to the British cause.[11]
Although US naval and military intelligence departments had been
set up in the 1880s, and in 1908 the Justice Department had created
a Bureau of Investigation, by the start of the Second World War the
United States did not have a centralized intelligence agency, let alone
one that dealt in the type of aggressive overseas activities which Stephenson had in mind.

The longer Stephenson toyed with this idea, the more he came to
admire its possibilities. As he imagined it, the only way 'Germany
would be provoked into a war with the United States' was through
'direct aggression'.[12] If such an American agency existed, it might be
able to wage an undercover war against Hitler, a secret campaign of
provocation, antagonizing the German leader into a declaration of
war against the United States. Rather than wait for Congress to vote
for war, why not provoke Hitler instead?

It was an attractive idea, but by early December 1940 the chances
of the White House setting up a new intelligence agency with a brief
to carry out special operations overseas seemed to be almost non-ex-
istent. Another problem was that the man Stephenson envisaged
running this new agency, Bill Donovan, was unsure if he wanted
anything to do with it.

'Wild Bill' had recently been telling friends he wanted to get back into
uniform, and how he hoped to spend the winter training up an infantry
division. Donovan had always seen politics as the peacetime substitute
for the military. Being a spy chief did not come into his thinking.

But Stephenson kept at him. The MI6 man 'continually pressed'
Donovan with 'his view that some extension of American intelligence
organisation was going to be required', and that he was the man to
take charge of it.[13]

Usually Stephenson did this over long martini suppers at the St.
Regis Hotel, or the exclusive 21 Club. One can imagine the pair of

them sitting across from each other at one of the club's circular tables, small enough to bring them into a conspiratorial scrum. Stephenson talked up 'the need for the United States to have a worldwide intelligence service like Great Britain's',[14] and stressed that Donovan was the ideal man to run it. Slowly, carefully, Stephenson was starting to outline the idea of the CIA.

In most photographs of 'Wild Bill' his mouth is set in the uneasy start of a smile, as if waiting to hear a punchline. This is probably how he looked as Stephenson made his case. Eventually he warmed to the idea. At last, he stopped saying no,[15] and in late 1940, according to Stephenson, he 'agreed in principle'.[16]

'Well, I don't know anything about this Bill,' Donovan was reported as saying. To which Stephenson replied: 'Well you better go to London, and I'll put you in touch with the people who are running these things in London. They'll tell you everything you want to know.'[17]

Donovan had not exactly committed himself, but he was open to exploring the idea further. This would mean another trip to London, so he went to see his old friend Frank Knox, the Navy Secretary, who agreed to the trip and soon had Roosevelt's approval. Over the next few days Donovan's mission expanded. After London, he would tour the Mediterranean to make a strategic assessment. At least, that was the official remit. As Donovan explained in private, he had also been told by Roosevelt 'to impress on everyone the resolution of the American Government and people to see the British through'. He would tour the capitals of neutral Europe promising that the United States was willing to 'provide all possible assistance' to those who resisted 'Nazi aggression'.[18]

This was almost exactly what the isolationists had accused the White House of doing before the start of the war, as laid out in the 'Potocki Report'. Roosevelt must have known that Donovan's trip would be seen in Berlin as a provocation. Perhaps that was the point.

With Donovan preparing for the trip, Stephenson wrote to his colleagues in London describing 'Wild Bill' as 'presently the *strongest* friend whom we have here', urging 'C' to 'repeat his good work of last occasion'.[19] Lothian also wrote to London about Donovan, hailing him as a man 'with a great deal of influence both with the Service Departments and the administration', and one who was 'on the inside of all pro-British activities'.[20]

These messages had a different tone to those which had preceded Donovan's last trip to London, five months earlier. Back then, this enthusiastic American had been a figure to fuss over and flatter in the hope that he might become sympathetic to Britain's plight. By December 1940, Stephenson's messages suggest a more serious relationship. He told 'C' that Donovan had a 'controlling influence' over the Navy Secretary, Frank Knox, a 'strong influence' on Henry Stimson, War Secretary, and 'friendly advisory influence' on the Secretary of State and the president,[21] and that he was in a 'unique position to advance our aims here'.[22] He also implied that Donovan had agreed 'to combat forces of appeasement here [the isolationists]'.[23] 'Much can be achieved here more quickly than by any other means', he went on, if Donovan was 'directed' by the British 'as to his future course of action in the mutual interests'.[24]

That word 'directed' does not in itself show that Donovan had agreed to work for the British. This patriotic American had not been overcome, either, by a sudden love of Britain. He was pro-British only 'from a practical American standpoint', seeing that 'only Britain is between Hitler and America'.[25] Donovan also had much to gain by getting close to the British, and would later describe that country as not only America's 'shield' but also its 'laboratory', a place where experiments in warfare were being made from which the United States could benefit.[26] Yet by agreeing to coordinate with an MI6 officer on a British political objective, Donovan was a whisker away from being a British agent of influence. He would argue that he was working in the interests of his country. Others might have been less generous.

Soon after leaving Baltimore, the seaplane carrying Stephenson and Donovan arrived in Bermuda where it was delayed by bad weather. Six days later, the two men were still in Bermuda, waiting for the storm to pass, when they heard the news.

Lord Lothian had died.

On his death certificate the cause of death was given as uremic poisoning, or kidney failure. But really he had died as a result of his religious beliefs. As a Christian Scientist, Lothian believed that illnesses should be treated with prayer, not medicine. He had always been a curious blend of rigidity and rebellion. After leaving the Catholic church to become a Christian Scientist, he was not about to abandon the consequences of this earlier decision. Just after Stephenson and Donovan left the country, Lothian came down with a kidney infection that was easily treatable, but he refused to seek help. As his situation deteriorated, those around him might have stepped in to save his life however his secretary, deputy and even his driver were Christian Scientists, and as such they blocked attempts to have him seen by a doctor.

One colleague described Lothian's death, on 12 December 1940, as 'an appalling tragedy for Britain'.[27] Lothian was the country's leading spokesman in the United States. He was trusted, admired and popular. Stephenson described his death as 'a great shock'.[28] He had learned a lot from Lothian about the American political system and the intricacies of public opinion. Just when they needed him most, the British had lost the cornerstone of their campaign to bring the country into the war. The entire edifice seemed to have collapsed, and in the days that followed it was hard to see how it could ever be rebuilt.

18

With loss comes a momentary sense of weightlessness, as Eric Maschwitz had begun to discover. By Christmas Day 1940, the Hollywood screenwriter had lost most of his belongings and nearly been killed. First a German incendiary bomb had obliterated his top-floor flat in Covent Garden, the heart of London's Theatreland, and with it his treasured collection of first editions. He had salvaged what he could and stored it in the basement of a nearby theatre, only for that building to take a direct hit.[1] Ten minutes earlier, Maschwitz had been up on the roof helping to put out incendiaries. The explosion had knocked him to the ground, but he emerged with no injuries other than a sliver of copper bomb casing lodged in his back.

This was the closest Maschwitz had come to being killed by the Luftwaffe. Many were less fortunate. In the first month of the Blitz more than five thousand British civilians were killed, with many more injured. Hundreds of thousands of homes had been damaged or destroyed, from Maschwitz's cramped flat through to Buckingham Palace and 10 Downing Street. Most inhabitants of the country's major cities were now used to emerging from their shelters each morning to see what had changed, which buildings had gone and who was missing.

Everyone, it seemed, was on the move. Either they had been posted overseas or to some distant part of the country, evacuated, or, like Maschwitz, bombed out of their home. This nationwide transience brought out in some a pronounced desire to carry on as before, and to mark special occasions as they had done in peacetime, which sometimes led to air raid warnings being ignored.

When Eric Maschwitz's parents heard that their son was coming home to Birmingham to see his touring revue show *New Faces*, his father, a gregarious retiree who loved to play the host, insisted the cast come for dinner after the performance. There was much to celebrate. The show was going well, and so was his son's hit song, 'A Nightingale Sang in Berkeley Square', which had just been released in the US in a recording by Glenn Miller. Several days before Christmas 1940, it would enter the new Billboard chart at No. 5.[2]

With Maschwitz and the cast enjoying themselves in his parents' house, the air raid siren started up. In a small act of defiance everyone stayed put. Just before Eric's Australian mother could bring out the food, a bomb hit the house next door. 'The blast' threw 'most of us off our chairs', Maschwitz recalled, including his co-writer, Jack Strachey, who was blown 'into an open cupboard where we had difficulty locating him! Lights were out, windows gone, the ceiling collapsed. When candles were brought, we discovered my good Papa standing in front of the fire, apparently so unmoved by the fracas that he had not spilled one drop from the full glass in his hand.'[3]

Maschwitz returned to London and his dreary new job ordering in radio-sets for the army, having recently left Section D and his resistance fighters in Yorkshire. On Christmas Day itself, or shortly before, he received the news. Despite his father's apparent sangfroid, the shock of the bomb landing next door had 'tragically made its mark upon a man of over 80', and 'as a result of that eventful evening, he was paralysed by a stroke.'[4]

The effect on Maschwitz of losing his possessions and his home, and having a parent crippled all as a result of the Blitz was similar to how people all over the world respond to aerial bombing raids. The experience left him with a powerful need for revenge, a new hatred for the enemy and an extraordinary feeling of camaraderie towards those going through the same thing. As Maschwitz remembered it, London was now a 'gallant background of bombed buildings and brave hearts'.[5] But good morale among the British was having an unexpected effect on the chances of America coming into the war.

A short British propaganda film then playing in the United States was called *London Can Take It*, which seemed to be a fair account of the situation. But few Americans concluded on seeing it that their country needed to come to Britain's aid. As one observer pointed out, the effect of films such as this one saying 'London can take it' was like showing a 'painting of a noble stag bleeding to death on a Scottish moor, but mutely asking no one to be sorry for it, because it is still "Monarch of the Glen".'[6]

Most Americans agreed London *could* take it, and there was probably no need for the US to rush to the rescue. Britain's resilience was standing in the way of her salvation. While many Americans felt a profound sympathy for the British, nowhere in the story of the Blitz was there a sense that the events in London endangered them.

British propaganda policy was failing. The Ministry of Information had not produced a coherent message that combined fear with hope, giving a sense of not just how bad the situation would be if the United States did not act, but a glimpse of the glorious future if it did. Nor were they doing enough to attack or undermine the rival message being put out by Berlin and the isolationists. Reports of the Blitz were not having the effect that Churchill and others had hoped for, and it was hard to see how they could.

On 16 December 1940, four days after Lothian's death, the two Bills arrived in London, each with a list of people to see. Donovan's most important meeting came two days after his arrival when he had lunch alone with Churchill at 10 Downing Street. As far as we know, they discussed the situation in the Mediterranean.

Stephenson pursued a different agenda. He spent the following days making proposals about his American activities to 'C' and other senior figures in British intelligence, but it is hard to map his movements during this brief visit. One of the few times we know exactly where he was, with whom, and roughly what he was doing, was on the evening of Boxing Day 1940 when he was having dinner at Claridge's with a major in the Royal Artillery: my grandfather, Harold.

Although Bill Stephenson got on well with my grandmother, Alice, and had tried unsuccessfully after the start of the war to recruit her to his short-lived network in Sweden, he was also close to Harold. Here were two Canadians in their forties who had both fought in the last war, had frequently worked together on business deals and were bound forever by one having saved the life of the other man's son. They trusted each other, and there is a chance that as dinner progressed Stephenson told Harold about his work in New York.

We may never know. We do know, however, that there were no air raids that night and from Claridge's the pair of them sailed on to the bar in the basement of the Mount Royal Hotel where there was music and dancing into the early hours. All over London that night other underground parties were taking place, sometimes in tube stations, custom-built air-raid shelters, bars or basements, all with a carnival atmosphere. 'The regular shelterers in the London Tube stations entertained themselves in family parties that often overlapped and intermingled,' The Times reported the next day. 'Hospitality was exchanged between group and group. Girls in party frocks whirled on the platforms to dance music.'[7] Many of those celebrating, like Stephenson, like my grandfather, like Eric Maschwitz, were miles away from their families, which made these occasions freer than usual and tinged with sadness. Everyone was dancing as much to enjoy themselves as to forget.

The next morning, Bill Donovan went to start his Mediterranean tour. The day after, Bill Stephenson left for New York. Both had a new sense of purpose.

'We found that the English are coping with the situation in a very intelligent manner,' declared James Deasy, a Battalion Chief of the New York City Fire Department, to the journalists assembled before him in the seaplane terminal overlooking Bowery Bay. It was 14 January 1941, a windswept, mean-looking day in New York. Deasy had returned from London, where he had been learning how to extinguish airborne incendiary devices. 'To say that England is going to fold up is a joke,' he went on, 'That bunch will never give up.'[1]

As the fireman regaled his audience with tales of London during the Blitz, just behind him, forgettable and small, fellow passenger Bill Stephenson made his way to the immigration desk, where he gave his occupation as 'British diplomatic courier'. Either that day or the next, the FBI was informed of his arrival. The following week he went to see them.

As Stephenson explained to his friends in the FBI, he had been busy in London. According to their account of this conversation, Stephenson had arranged to be placed in charge of 'all British intelligence activities in the Western Hemisphere'.[2] Having inherited an office so small he could run it out of his own apartment, Stephenson was now in control of a large MI6 station which covered both Americas, he was also responsible for the Imperial Censorship station in Bermuda, the North American activities of MI5, Britain's domestic security service, and the British Purchasing Commission (BPC), the body which bought war materiel from American manufacturers and ensured it arrived in Britain on time and in good condition. Stephenson explained all this to the FBI in good faith, but he held back the most controversial change to his organization.

Six months earlier, the British had established the Special Operations Executive (SOE). Nicknamed the 'Ministry of Ungentlemanly Warfare', SOE immediately began to wage a shadow war against Nazi Germany using 'sabotage, secret subversive propaganda, the encouragement of civil resistance in occupied areas, the stirring up of insurrection', while also coordinating other 'underground warfare'.[3] It operated mainly in occupied Europe and adjacent neutral territories, specializing in guerrilla warfare and 'dirty tricks'. Its agents were expert at blending into the civilian population, and they were trained to kill. So it would have come as something of a surprise to the FBI if Stephenson had revealed that he was about to open an SOE station in New York. Which is why he kept it to himself.

In London, Stephenson had met the head of SOE, Frank Nelson, and they had agreed that the Canadian should 'assume control' of all SOE activities in the Americas. 'No provision for staff was made at this time,' ran the official record of this conversation, 'and it was left to G' – Stephenson's new SOE codename – 'to explore his way and make whatever recommendations to London that he saw fit.'[4]

Stephenson was now 'our man in New York' for MI6 as well as SOE, but he had not been given a free hand. He was told that his activities must not, under any circumstance, interfere with American politics. That was essential. The Foreign Office also insisted that this new SOE office in New York should avoid 'subversive activities of any kind'.[5] Instead Stephenson was permitted to look into broadcasting propaganda back into occupied Europe, or finding European refugees to be sent back into their home countries as SOE agents. That was it.

Perhaps sensing these instructions might not be followed to the letter, the head of SOE sent out a trusted officer to help run this new American office. But when Colonel G. G. Vickers, VC, arrived in New York he was in for a shock.

Stephenson explained to the colonel that unfortunately his job had already been taken by one of his staff. Vickers was confused. Stephenson replied that he was 'determined to keep the organisation under his own control', adding, perhaps in a more forgiving voice, that he was not saying this to be 'uncooperative', but was worried about security. He then launched into a meandering speech about 'the dangerous circumstances in which his organisation was working', adding cryptically at one point, 'the use of knives and poison was not unknown'.

Vickers must have sensed this was simply an attempt to get him out of the way. But it worked. Rather than stand his ground, the colonel wrote back to London saying they should follow Stephenson's rec-ommendations, going on to praise his 'efficiency' and 'power of quick decision'.[6] 'The New York organisation should never be asked to act except on an important and definite issue, and all detailed planning should be left to them,' was the official conclusion in London, a com-plete reversal of the instructions Stephenson had been given several weeks earlier.[7] Just two days after arriving in New York, Colonel Vickers cabled London asking for permission to come home, 'as there was little more he could usefully do'.[8]

With Vickers out of the way, Stephenson was now running the American offices of MI6, MI5, SOE, BPC, and BIC in Bermuda. Suddenly he had more power than ever, perhaps more than he was ready for. He was beginning to feel a greater sense of autonomy, a shift reflected in the way he had the different offices under his control interact with one another. Rather than insist on their being separated by 'watertight compartments', as was the norm, he arranged for them to pool intelligence and work more closely together.[9] Today this sounds like common sense. At the time, in the guarded, fractious and sometimes insular world of British intelligence, it was unusual.

Stephenson also decided on a new cover name for his rapidly expanding intelligence machine. Until then the name on the door had been 'British Passport Control Office'. From late January 1941, this office began to be known as 'British Security Coordination' (BSC).[10] If anyone asked, BSC was responsible for the security of British supplies before they were shipped across the Atlantic: a forgettable task which would hopefully deflect further enquiries.

But Stephenson's biggest breakthrough in the weeks after his return concerned the White House. One of Stephenson's most trusted American contacts was Vincent Astor, who had tipped him off about Dr Westrick the year before. Astor was also close to the president, and in early February 1941 he became the 'personal liaison' between Stephenson and the White House.[11] No longer would the MI6 officer have to go through the FBI if he wanted to pass information to Roosevelt.

'C' monitored these changes from his desk in London and sensed trouble ahead. With Stephenson running a much larger office, with better access to the White House and much greater reach, it was almost inevitable that he would feel a lighter connection to London. 'C' told him to 'remember that the old Firm has constant and imperative needs',[12] a gentle reminder that he had been sent to New York by MI6, he worked for MI6, and he continued to answer to the head of MI6.

Stephenson did not resent this. In the days that followed there were no signs of him launching any wild schemes, flexing his muscles, or reacting in a way that might allow 'C' to think he was moving out of his orbit. Stephenson had put together a team of many talents and had consolidated his power, but he had not put it to the test. His efforts to bring the US into the war continued to be steeped in restraint. By the start of February 1941, perhaps the most surprising thing about Stephenson's rapidly expanding organization was just how little impact it was having on American public opinion.

Also surprising was how few American officials knew of its existence. But that was about to change.

Adolf Berle did not like spies. More than most US government officials he loathed secrets, intelligence-gathering, spy chiefs, and the 'paranoid' world these people inhabited.[1] Another of Berle's pet hates was the British.

'Feeble and foolish', he once called them, 'terribly slow on the up-take', and full of 'obtuseness' and 'rank impertinence'.[2] Yet what really set him off, if it was not spies or the British, was the idea of foreigners peddling propaganda inside the United States. A team of British spies spreading covert propaganda within America was the apotheosis of everything he disliked in life. Others felt the same, but Berle was in a position to act on it.

Adolf Berle had been a child prodigy, before going on to be the youngest ever graduate from Harvard Law School at the age of twenty-one. Later he was a key Roosevelt aide in the early stages of the New Deal, and knew the president well enough to address him in letters 'Dear Caesar' (a practice Roosevelt begged him to stop). By January 1941, as an Assistant Secretary of State, this precise and orderly bureaucrat ran the committee Roosevelt had set up to bring together the nation's bickering intelligence chiefs.

Berle may not have liked the secret world, but running this committee made him one of the most powerful figures within it. In the months that followed, if there was ever a hint of the British trying to influence American public opinion, or so much as thinking about running spies inside the US, Berle would push for an investigation. One Foreign Office official described him as 'very anti-British'; another replied, 'we might start a BERLE file.'[3] Berle would have been flattered.

Underlying his suspicion of Britain and the British was the fear he had that the American government might repeat some of its mistakes from the aftermath of the First World War. Berle had been part of the US delegation at the Paris Peace Conference in 1919, and had come away frustrated and angry. 'We came so [far] into the English camp that we became virtually an adjunct to the British war machine,' he complained. The British 'kept that position after the war was over, and the result of that was that we got not one single thing that we really desired in the ensuing peace. This time it seems to me that the thing should be the other way around.'[4]

But increasingly he felt as if he was on his own. Berle worried that his colleagues were ready to do everything they could to help Britain, a country he saw as America's oldest enemy. He bemoaned his countrymen's apparent lack of political nous, seeing himself as a Cassandra figure whose role was to warn against British influence.

On hearing a speech by Charles Lindbergh, in October 1940, Berle conceded 'of course this is Berlin stuff, pure and simple', and yet, he went on, 'if he means we ought not to get too deep into English intrigue, I agree with him, for I have a good working notion that when this mess is over, we shall find that the British were no more truthful with us now than they were in 1917.'[5]

So Berle was understandably suspicious when in February 1941 he heard about a new British agency in New York called British Security Coordination. According to the British embassy it prevented sabotage against British supplies. Berle asked colleagues at the State Department to find out more, and their investigation suggested otherwise.

Although they were unable to discover where this new British agency was based, they had at least found out the name of the man in charge: Stephenson.

The most curious thing about Stephenson, as Berle discovered, was that none of the American officials working on counter-sabotage had ever heard of him. Berle was also told that Stephenson, whoever he was, had undercover officers and agents working for him throughout the United States. As the State Department report concluded, this new British agency was cloaked in 'the utmost secrecy'.[6]

Berle decided to find out more.

In the past, when Charles Lindbergh spoke out against the war, whether it was in a radio booth or at an outdoor rally, he read from a script. This was a man who longed to be in control, and to know what was coming before it arrived. But on 23 January 1941, that was set to change.

Lindbergh was in Washington DC to give evidence to the House Foreign Relations Committee. As usual, he arrived too early on what was a blustery, grey-looking day. To kill time, he took a brisk walk around Capitol Hill, past the buildings and monuments he had seen as a boy in the days when his father had been a congressman, before returning to the new House Office Building, known today as the Longworth Building, where he found hundreds of his supporters waiting for him.

The question of whether the United States should enter the war had been largely in the background over the last twelve months. The conscription bill, the destroyers-for-bases deal, and the massive increase in defence spending had brought it briefly to the fore, and in the closing weeks of the election it had been on many people's minds. But otherwise this question appeared to be settled. The US was staying out. Roosevelt had said as much on the campaign trail.

In January 1941 this changed, abruptly, when the president introduced his 'Lend-Lease' bill. Now the question of whether to go to war was the single most important political issue in the United States, and would remain as such for the rest of the year.

The 'Great Debate' had begun.

Roosevelt's Lend-Lease bill was divisive, unusual and counter-intuitive, and that was if you asked his supporters. It was the president's ingenious response to Britain's fragile financial position, which had been laid out to him in a letter signed by Churchill but drafted by Lothian. The president read this message repeatedly during a Caribbean cruise in the days leading up to Christmas. 'Then one evening,' recalled Harry Hopkins, Roosevelt's aide, 'he suddenly came out with it – the whole program. He didn't seem to have any clear idea how it could be done legally. But there wasn't a doubt in his mind that he'd find a way to do it.'[1]

Roosevelt's idea was inspired, and so was the way he presented it. In a White House press conference shortly before Christmas he asked the journalists to imagine a homeowner who finds that their neighbour's house is on fire. Naturally, the president explained, they would lend their neighbour a garden hose if they had one. They would not first ask their neighbour for $15 to cover the cost of the hose. 'If the hose were returned undamaged,' he went on, 'he would expect the thanks of the neighbour; if it were damaged, he would expect the neighbour to replace it.' In the same sense, the president wanted the United States to lend war materiel to Britain, and after the war this could be returned undamaged or replaced in kind. 'There would not be too much formality,' the president assured them, trying to make a radical idea sound folksy and simple, 'and as long as he got back the hose or its equivalent he would be satisfied.'[2]

He followed up in late December 1940 with one of his 'fireside chats', in which he addressed the nation informally over the radio, one of his many successful innovations as president. 'There is danger ahead,' he warned, 'we cannot escape danger, or the fear of danger, by crawling into bed and pulling the covers over our heads.' If London fell, 'all of us, in all the Americas, would be living at the point of a gun'. The United States had to become 'the great arsenal of democracy'.[3]

The president's argument was that by giving more aid to Britain, the United States would *improve* its chances of staying out of the war. The isolationists saw this as mere sophistry. For them, Lend-Lease was just another step towards intervention. By empowering the president to decide which countries received military aid, how much, when, and the manner in which they had to pay it back, all without going to Congress, Lend-Lease also took the nation closer to an imperial presidency.

In late January 1941, thirteen days after the text of this controversial bill had been released, Lindbergh prepared to testify against it before the House Foreign Affairs Committee. His supporters flooded the gallery, giving the room 'the atmosphere of a gala occasion'. The man they had come to see was dressed entirely in blue – light blue shirt, blue suit with a herringbone pattern, dark blue knitted tie – and as he walked in he seemed to project an unassailable certainty. 'He went about the business of testifying with the air of a veteran,' wrote one impressed reporter. 'There was no trace of shyness in his manner as he instructed the photographers to get their pictures at once and not to set off any flashlight bulbs while he was testifying.'[4]

Beneath this was a man who wanted to be elsewhere. Lindbergh hated the way the room had been 'flooded with brilliant lights for the motion picture cameras', and resented the presence of 'two or three dozen "still" photographers gathered around the table where I was to sit – almost all the things I dislike, and which represent to me the worst of American life in this period.'[5]

None of this affected his performance. Over four and a half hours, Lindbergh answered questions and spoke engagingly and well about the prospect of Lend-Lease and whether the United States should participate in the war. Germany was simply too strong, he argued. She could not be defeated even by an alliance of Anglo-American forces. One of the congressmen asked if he thought Germany was sure to win. 'She already controls the continent,' he replied, adding that in Britain 'there is famine and a total upset of normal life.'[6] Rather than help one belligerent or the other, he argued, the White House should do everything in its power to end the war.

'To my amazement,' Lindbergh wrote, 'I found that the crowd was with me. They clapped on several occasions!' So did the committee, which rose to applaud him at the end of his marathon session. Among those looking on in admiration was the congressman who had invited him to testify, Hamilton Fish.

Lindbergh's testimony was widely reported and his answers raised tricky questions in the debate over whether to enact Lend-Lease. His performance was a boost to the isolationist cause. America First continued to grow at a monstrous rate, and would soon have as many as 800,000 members and more than four hundred chapters nationwide. Hundreds of other isolationist groups also sprang up in the weeks after Roosevelt introduced the Lend-Lease bill.[7] Americans all over the country were now staging meetings, organizing petitions, paying for advertisements in their local newspapers, or going door to door with badges, bumper stickers and posters, many of them urging people to contact their representatives in Washington and register their opposition to Lend-Lease. Congressional offices on the Hill were being swamped with letters and phone-calls, most of them protesting against the proposed legislation.

Only a handful of those involved in this vast campaign had any idea that the Nazis were involved as well. Hans Thomsen reported to Berlin that he was busy 'promoting the organization of the isolationist opposition',[8] and had 'good relations' with 'isolationist committees', including America First, and was able to 'support them in various

ways'.[9] He was not secretly running the American isolationist movement, as some would later imagine. Rather than being the director
of this ensemble piece, Thomsen was more like a wealthy investor
who liked to attend rehearsals and offer advice.

As well as helping America First, Thomsen was using undercover
agents to 'induce as large a number as possible of the American voters
to write to the congressmen and senators of their districts letters of
protest', all at 'considerable expense'.[10] He had helped coordinate a
women's march on Washington, was in touch with isolationist senators
and was working 'with the Irish-American press and Irish-American
leaders', in particular the *New York Enquirer*, to have them put out
more pro-Nazi stories. At the same time, agents of his offered support to the radio celebrity Father Charles E. Coughlin. As many as
40 million listeners tuned in each Sunday to hear Coughlin's CBS
broadcasts, each one an unlikely blend of organ music, Bible stories,
easy-going homilies and tirades against Jews.[11]

But the biggest breakthrough for Thomsen, Coughlin, America
First and all those doggedly campaigning against intervention and
Lend-Lease was an interview which appeared in the press shortly
before Christmas. A leading interventionist, the newspaper editor
William Allen White, had switched sides. 'The Yanks are not coming,'
White said in that interview. All that mattered now, he explained, was
'to keep this country out of the war'.[12]

This was a major scalp for the isolationists. Lindbergh wondered
if it was now time 'to welcome him to the camp of the "isolationists"'.
In any case, Lindbergh concluded, 'the anti-war sentiment seems to
be gaining, at least momentarily, in this country'.[13] A few weeks later
he was sounding more optimistic than ever. 'I think we still have a
good fighting chance to stay out.'[14]

Opposition to the Lend-Lease bill had never been so strong. All
over the country Americans seemed to be following White's lead by
moving away from intervention and putting their weight behind the

isolationist cause. The anti-war movement was flourishing, and so was the Nazi influence campaign.

Meanwhile the mood in Whitehall was becoming desperate. 'We do not know how long Congress will debate your proposals,' Churchill reminded Roosevelt, 'and we are fighting for our lives.'[15]

If ever there had been a time for Stephenson and his office to inter-
vene in the debate over Lend-Lease, surely this was it. But first he had
to meet the new British ambassador, who was due to arrive in Washington DC the day after Lindbergh's testimony against Lend-Lease.

Almost as soon as Lord Lothian's death was announced the
speculation began as to who would replace him. The new British
ambassador to the United States had to be accessible, enthusiastic,
and a natural in front of a newsreel camera, as well as being modern
and progressive, with an obvious liking for America and Americans.
Stephenson hoped the new ambassador would also be someone who
could become an ally, a diplomat alive to the possibilities of covert
work rather than afraid of them.

Instead Churchill sent over Lord Halifax, his cadaverous former
Foreign Secretary. As one British official in New York put it: 'Halifax
is Ambassador. Christ.'[1]

Edward Wood, 3rd Viscount Halifax, was enormously tall and
no less aloof. One official who worked under him in the British
embassy thought he was also 'a curiously lazy man'.[2] Although Halifax had an impressive political pedigree, and had once been seen
as a future prime minister, Roosevelt confessed in private to being
'bitterly opposed' to Halifax's appointment as British ambassador 'as

he had hoped for a man of the people'.[3] The president's worry was that Halifax might bring out the other side in America's love-hate relationship with Britain.

While many Americans admired the British, they were also suspicious of them. They appreciated Britain's written culture and its tradition of parliamentary democracy, the language and religion shared by the two countries and the many years of commercial ties, but they bridled at the injustice of the British Empire, gave hearty thanks each year for victory in the War of Independence, and for all the friendly Britons they may have met in their lives they continued to see the British as being indecisive, snooty and stiff, the qualities least attractive to any American – then and now.

Halifax seemed to embody an American caricature of the Englishman abroad. He had been sent to Washington not because he longed to have the job or had good American connections, but so that Churchill could get him out of the way. Since the death of the former prime minister Neville Chamberlain, in October 1940, Halifax had been the principal voice of appeasement. Posting him to Washington gave Churchill greater control over his cabinet.

But for everything stacked up against Halifax, some of which he could do nothing about – such as his height, his education, or who his parents had been – he was intelligent and astute and there was every chance he would find a way to make a good impression on the American people.

One of Halifax's first meetings on arrival in the US was with Bill Stephenson. It became immediately clear that the new British ambassador and his MI6 counterpart were 'two men as different as day and night', as one close to them explained.[4] Although they never fell out, they never really got on either. Stephenson worked with Halifax 'amicably', 'but neither so intimately nor so informally as he had done with Lothian'.[5] There was no mystery to this. Lothian understood the importance of combining overt and covert propaganda, Halifax did not. He 'remained nervous and apprehensive on the subject of British Secret Service activities in the United States'.[6] Lothian had gone, and even after the arrival of Halifax it seemed that he had not been replaced.

But Stephenson did not see this as an opportunity to do as he liked. He continued to follow his instructions from London to hold back. Although Churchill wanted to do more, saying in private 'the first thing is to get the United States into the war',[7] with the Lend-Lease bill still working its way through Congress, the Foreign Office would not sanction any action which could lead to a negative story in the American press about British interference.

On 8 February 1941, the House voted by a margin of 260 to 165 in favour of Lend-Lease. Now the bill had to pass through the Senate. The debate that followed has been described as 'one of the most heated in American history'.[8] As it became angrier and darker the mood in the isolationist camp brightened. Again Lindbergh testified, this time before the Senate Foreign Relations Committee, and again this had the effect of hardening the nationwide opposition to Lend-Lease.

At around the same time a rumour began to flit around the capital about another well-known personality who might appear before the same committee. Several days later it was confirmed, and less than a week after Lindbergh had testified for a second time, Wendell Willkie, still leader of the Republican party, settled down in the marble-clad splendour of the Caucus room inside what is now the Russell Senate Office Building, to give his opinion on the Lend-Lease bill.

'His hair freshly trimmed but still drooping over one eye, his voice throaty and hoarse as ever, smoking endless cigarettes and always ready with an answer,' Willkie was, one reporter wrote, 'the same aggressive, unyielding battler that he proved to be in the Presidential campaign.'[9] He may have lost the election several months earlier, but he remained popular and relevant. Willkie's predecessor

as Republican presidential candidate, Alf Landon, had been sent
6,000 letters of support in the wake of his 1936 defeat. Willkie had
received 100,000.[10] Almost all were from Americans who had come
to know him from his speeches on the campaign trail, including those
in which he accused Roosevelt of colluding with the British and had
called for the country to stay out of the war.

Some of these fans would have been surprised, then, by what he
now said to the Senate Foreign Relations Committee. Rather than
attack Lend-Lease, Willkie urged the country to support it, and to
back the White House. 'He is my president now,' Willkie said of
Roosevelt, insisting that the US should give Britain its fullest support.
'Millions of them will die before they give up that island,' he said of
the British. 'When the going gets tough they'll force that bunch of
robbers to give up.' When challenged about his earlier isolationist
remarks in the run-up to the election, Willkie dismissed them as
'campaign speeches'.[11]

'Aid Britain or War in 60 Days – Willkie', ran one of the next
day's headlines. 'Willkie Plea May Speed Aid to Britain', and 'Give
Britain 10 Destroyers a Month – Willkie'.[12] His emphatic support
for the president, Lend-Lease and the British was relayed across the
country as major news. But the greatest impact of his testimony was
on the committee he had addressed. The undecideds were swayed.
The following day this committee voted 15–8 in favour of the bill.
One month later, after marathon filibustering by the bill's opponents,
Lend-Lease was approved in the Senate by 60 votes to 31.

Willkie's testimony was the pivotal moment in the Lend-Lease
debate. But it came at some personal cost, turning Willkie into even
more of a pariah figure for diehard Republicans.

So why did he do it? The main reason was the simplest: in his
opinion the best way to protect the United States was by ensuring
Britain's survival. But there was more to it than that.

*

One of the items discussed by the Century Group when they met for dinner after the presidential election in November 1940 was 'Mr. Willkie's new project'.[13] Correspondence between key members of this group, including the president's speechwriter Robert Sherwood, makes it clear what this 'new project' was.

The Century Group wanted Willkie as the national spokesman for intervention. They saw him as a counterweight to Lindbergh, and they were not alone. Bill Donovan's friend Frank Knox, Secretary of the Navy, was also keen to have Willkie speak out in favour of intervention. One Century Group member had already approached Willkie, but had been rebuffed.[14] So they tried another tactic.

A different member of the Century Group, the publisher Harold Guinzburg, teamed up with one of Roosevelt's closest advisers, Felix Frankfurter, and together they spoke to Willkie's mistress.

This was Irita van Doren, literary editor at the *Herald Tribune*, who had been having an affair with Willkie for several years, and was by then his political mentor and adviser as much as lover. Although their affair was something of an open secret in Washington, it had never been exposed in the press.

In the conversation that followed, Guinzburg and Frankfurter suggested to van Doren that her paramour should go on a tour of Britain, as a prelude to coming out in support of intervention. There is no record of how van Doren reacted, only that she passed this on to Willkie. Several days later the leader of the Republican party agreed to visit London and campaign for intervention.[15]

Why did Frankfurter and Guinzburg approach van Doren? Perhaps they thought their message would have more weight coming from her. She was someone Willkie looked up to and whose opinion he respected. But there was also in this the lightest hint of a threat.

Roosevelt had long known about Willkie's affair with van Doren but had chosen not to bring it up during the election. Even as his opponent was gaining on him in the polls, the president refused to take advantage. Each time Willkie and his estranged wife appeared at rallies standing happily next to each other, Roosevelt had bit his tongue. Admittedly it would have been unusual to expose this relationship, in an age when politicians' private lives remained largely private, but it was not unheard of. Now the election was over, Roosevelt perhaps wanted to remind Willkie of the card he had up his sleeve.

Less than a fortnight after Willkie had been told, via his mistress, that he should visit Britain, he formally came out in support of Lend-Lease. Willkie was then seen going to the White House where he spoke with the president and the Secretary of State, Cordell Hull, a conversation which took place in private. It was the first time since the election these former rivals had met. Roosevelt's son later recalled hearing 'great bursts of laughter' coming from the room, and he assumed the encounter between his father and Willkie had gone well.[16] But this meeting was off-the-record and he never found out what was said.

Certainly it would have come as a surprise to the president's son, or anyone else, that two days after this confidential session in the Oval Office a detailed report of what had been discussed was on the desk of 'C' in MI6 Headquarters in London.

On 20 January 1941, the day after Roosevelt spoke to Willkie in private, half a million Americans gathered in Washington DC for the presidential inauguration. Under gloriously clear blue skies, with planes flying overhead in tight formation and flags down each of the capital's main streets, they watched the re-elected president remove his top hat and take a solemn vow to preserve, protect and defend the US constitution. The man so many millions of Americans had hoped to see taking that oath instead of him, Wendell Willkie, was not in the capital that day.

While Roosevelt was out in the open, his opponent was behind closed doors having a meeting that did not appear in his diary. It is easy to see why. On the day of Roosevelt's inauguration, the leader of the Republican party was in New York having 'a full confidential discussion', in an undisclosed location, with, of all people, Bill Stephenson.[17]

Willkie had recently been slammed in a *Chicago Tribune* editorial as a 'fifth columnist', a presidential candidate who had never understood the values of the Republican party and should not have run for office.[18] The idea that while Roosevelt was taking his oath Willkie was in conclave with a British spy was so improbable, so offensive, it would have been dismissed by many Americans as 'fake news'. But this meeting took place, as we know from Stephenson's detailed account which was passed on to 'C' and forwarded to a Foreign Office official, before being filed in a Foreign Office archive where it remained until 2013, when at last it was declassified and released to the National Archives.

As the record shows, Stephenson began the discussion by asking Wendell Willkie about his meeting in the White House. Willkie might have batted this away, telling the MI6 man it was confidential. Instead he provided such a detailed account that there was too much for Stephenson to fit into his report.

'Only item of interest to us,' Stephenson told 'C', was Roosevelt's anger at Halifax's appointment. The president had said he wanted someone more in keeping with the political shift to the left already under way in Britain, rather than a fox-hunting Old Etonian. 'Willkie remarked to me that all this came strangely' from someone like Roosevelt who had himself been 'born in the purple'.[19] Willkie also told Stephenson, 'very much off record and strictly between ourselves', that if Britain was going to adopt socialism after the war, 'I feel deep down that it would be difficult to put one's whole heart into this struggle'.[20]

The Republican then confided that Roosevelt had agreed to put a two-year limit on Lend-Lease in return for his support. He also gave Stephenson a long account of what the Secretary of State had said, including his take on the international situation. After this he moved on to his forthcoming trip to Britain.

What does this tell us about Willkie's relationship with the British? The answer depends, really, on whether the leader of the Republican party knew that Stephenson was working for MI6.

The wording of Stephenson's report suggests that if he did not already, then soon he would. The first clue is in Stephenson's assertion that Willkie was 'quite prepared to have his programme arranged by us' during his forthcoming tour of Britain.

'Us.'

Either Willkie took 'us' to mean the British in general, or it was a more specific 'us', an 'us' that implied MI6. A line further down appears to clear this up. Stephenson asked 'C' to 'take possession of arrangements' as soon as Willkie arrived in Britain, 'just as you did in Donovan's case', and to impress upon Willkie exactly who was looking after him, in order to improve Stephenson's standing with Willkie.

'You will appreciate how potentially valuable it will be to me,' he wrote, 'if he [Willkie] returns feeling my Chief was responsible for making things easy for him.'[21]

If Willkie did not already know that Stephenson was working for MI6, by the end of his British trip, at the very latest, he would have done.

What makes this exchange so interesting is that Wendell Willkie would later emerge as a voluble critic of the British Empire. At no point in his career does he come across as beholden to the British. Instead he seems to have decided shortly before securing the Republican nomination in 1940 that his country should come into the war, and in the meantime he was willing to almost do everything possible to help Britain. The last few weeks of the election campaign had been an aberration.

By the start of 1941 Willkie's aim was to stop Hitler, and if that involved confiding in a senior MI6 officer such as Stephenson, or agreeing to help Roosevelt, he was willing to do this.

During Willkie's time in Britain, MI6 did more than look after him. They also ensured that he was able to take part in the Lend-Lease debate. After Willkie mentioned to Stephenson that he was 'toying' with the idea of visiting the Mediterranean after Britain, Stephenson urged 'C' to talk him out of this, telling him 'it is of greatest importance he should return here within a month to assist in pushing through Lease Lend Bill'.[22]

Willkie never made it to the Mediterranean. Instead the Republican leader toured Britain, met the King and Queen, trade union leaders, politicians of every different stripe, thousands of ordinary British people, and Churchill, who, contrary to what he had been told, turned out not to be an alcoholic. As Willkie later explained, he knew this because when they met 'he did not have as much as I had'.[23] His visit was then cut short when the US Secretary of State asked him to testify before the Senate Foreign Relations Committee. Seeing that he was not in the Mediterranean, Willkie was able to race back in time to give his decisive testimony.

Today the Lend-Lease Act is seen as one of Roosevelt's great political achievements. The idea had been his, he was the one who presented it to the American people and steered it through stormy congressional waters. But by his own admission much of the credit lay elsewhere. 'We might not have had Lend Lease,' Roosevelt insisted, 'or Selective Service [conscription] or a lot of other things if it hadn't been for Wendell Willkie. He was a godsend to this country when we needed him most.'[24] Or as one aide to the Secretary of State put it, 'there's no question that Willkie was the real hero.'[25]

Stephenson's new friend had also been a godsend to the British. Willkie's trip to Britain, and his passionate support of Lend-Lease helped to guarantee that Britain would have an almost limitless supply of war materiel.

Lend-Lease was also, in the words of a *New York Post* columnist, at last, 'a straight sock in the eye for our homegrown pro-fascists. [. . .]

What can Father Coughlin and Colonel Lindbergh be thinking? They must be stunned. They thought they had us figured. They thought they knew how a democracy would behave. It ought to be a stumblebum, always indecisive, always pulling back from danger until the crisis comes. Look what we did!'[26]

But there was still much to do.

Public opinion on the war remained overwhelmingly against the US entering the war. In the days that followed the final congressional vote on Lend-Lease, some of the key players in the 'Great Debate', including Lindbergh, Roosevelt and Willkie, as well as Stephenson, Donovan and Thomsen, took stock of the situation and weighed their next move. It had always been clear to those on both sides of the divide what they wanted. Over the weeks ahead they would have to decide how far they were willing to go to achieve it.

In late March 1941, Stephenson heard some important news from his liaison with the White House, Vincent Astor. The president had 'stated categorically' he would 'act to bring USA in very shortly'.[1] Something was about to happen. Nobody was sure what.

There were other signs that Roosevelt was willing to do more than before to bring the United States into the war. As well as Lend-Lease, there was now increased military cooperation. Senior American officers had recently met their British counterparts to hammer out a shared strategy, the 'ABC-1' policy, for how to respond if the United States went to war against Japan and Germany. The president had also sent Bill Donovan on a tour of the Mediterranean with instructions to urge neutral leaders in Bulgaria, Yugoslavia, Turkey and Spain to resist Nazi aggression, a trip that had not gone unnoticed in Berlin.

'If Germany sent a military expert on such a trip to Central and South America, how they would howl!' exclaimed one Nazi newspaper, with some justification, before describing Donovan's trip as an 'impudent act' by Roosevelt.[2]

The German reaction was even angrier when they discovered what Donovan had been up to in Yugoslavia.

After meeting the pro-Nazi Yugoslav regent, Prince Paul, Donovan had seen the leader of the opposition, General Dušan Simović, an avowed anti-Fascist. Donovan confided in Simović that – in his opinion – Britain was able to hold out and the United States would come into the war eventually. On 27 March 1941, emboldened by his conversation with 'Wild Bill', Simović launched a successful military coup.[3] Prince Paul was ousted. Now Yugoslavia was controlled by an anti-Fascist government. Hitler had to commit troops to a land invasion, which began on 6 April 1941. This cost Germany money, men and above all time, and may have delayed the attack on the Soviet Union.

Several days after the German invasion of Yugoslavia, Roosevelt made his boldest foreign policy move since the start of the war. Shortly after telling Astor he was going to 'act to bring USA in',[4] he ordered American troops to occupy Greenland and for the US Navy to start patrolling a vast sweep of the Atlantic all the way east to the twenty-fifth meridian. This would place US warships inside an area described by Hitler only the month before as a combat zone.

Roosevelt told the public this was a defensive measure designed to protect American interests, but that was misleading. Several days after this announcement, the British ambassador, Halifax, had a rare lunch at the White House, and reported afterwards that the president 'expected' these new patrolling arrangements to 'lead to an incident'. He also mentioned that from the way Roosevelt had spoken about it, this 'would not be at all unwelcome'.[5]

The Interior Secretary, Harold Ickes, also referred to 'the President's scarcely concealed desire that there might be an incident which would justify our declaring a state of war against Germany'.[6] On the other side of the Atlantic, the US ambassador to London was, Churchill wrote, 'longing for Germany to commit some overt act that would relieve the President of his election and pre-election declaration regarding keeping out of the war'.[7] Roosevelt had even asked a State Department official to put together a report on his predecessor Woodrow Wilson's speeches leading up to his 1917 declaration of war on Germany.[8] He was also interested in how President McKinley had asked Congress to declare war on Spain, in 1898, after the sinking of the USS *Maine* in Havana harbour, an event Roosevelt coyly described as 'one of these horrid things they call an episode'.[9]

An incident, an episode: evidently Roosevelt wanted to provoke the Germans in the Atlantic. Over the years the question of whether the president had advance warning of the Japanese attack on Pearl Harbor has produced a cloud of speculative theories, and the answer to that comes later, but even if he had known about this strike beforehand, the decisions he made earlier that year are in many ways more controversial. Rather than turn a blind eye to a coming attack, as he is accused of having done before Pearl Harbor, in this case the US commander-in-chief was deploying American sailors in the hope that they would be attacked, so that he could have a better chance of taking the country to war.

That Roosevelt was even willing to consider this shows how determined he was, as early as March 1941, to find a way into the war. The problem with his plan, however, was Hitler.

The German leader refused to take the bait. Rather than instruct his U-boats to attack American shipping, as Roosevelt hoped he would, Hitler merely recognized the new US security zone. His naval commander, Admiral Raeder, described the latest American move in the Atlantic as 'an act of war'.[10] Hitler disagreed. German forces must not, he said, give Roosevelt 'the excuse' to cast off the mantle of neutrality which had been imposed on him by Congress 'and thus fulfil the dearest wish of the British!'[11] He knew what Roosevelt was trying to do, and was not going to fall for it.

For months now, Stephenson had followed the Foreign Office line. Although he had taken a small risk in seeing Willkie, he had been for the most part a model of perspicacity and caution. This had worked, in the sense that there had been no bad news stories in the press about British spies in the United States. The American people had not been put off the idea of going to war alongside the British, but nor had they been especially won over to it. Their feelings had changed over the last twelve months, but not by much.

When Bill Stephenson first arrived in the United States, in June 1940, just 7 per cent of those questioned in one poll wanted to go to war.[1] By the time Roosevelt announced the Lend-Lease bill, in January 1941, that figure was closer to 12 per cent.[2] Two days after Donovan's return, in March 1941, it had crept up to 17 per cent. But there was no guarantee it would keep moving in this direction: indeed those numbers might just as easily start to drop given the current state of the war.

At that time German forces were winning in North Africa, Yugoslavia and Greece, and soon most of mainland Europe would be controlled by the Nazis, their allies and sympathizers. In March 1941 alone, more than four thousand British civilians were killed in Luftwaffe bombing raids and half a million tons of British shipping sunk by German U-boats. The Germans were winning the Battle of the Atlantic, and again there were rumours of an invasion. The Nazi war machine had acquired an aura of invincibility, which did nothing to improve the chances of the United States coming into the war. Another problem was the British ambassador.

Lord Halifax's first major appearance in the press, at a time when many American factory labourers were working overtime to produce aid for Britain, was to be photographed enjoying a foxhunt in Pennsylvania.

His next public appearance was at a baseball game. 'When asked what he thought of baseball,' ran one report, 'he said it was "more vigorous than cricket which I played at Eton." [. . .] "Do they always argue?" Halifax asked. "We never do that in cricket."'

He was then handed a hot dog.

'What's inside it?' enquired the 3rd Viscount Halifax.[3] He listened thoughtfully to the answer, before placing the uneaten hot dog to one side and then leaving the game early.

'Hot Dog Baffles Lord Halifax', was one of many hot-dog-themed headlines the next day.[4]

Lothian and Halifax seemed to be ambassadors from different versions of Britain, one set in the future and its analogue in the past. The first had been photographed cuddling a kitten, the other killing a fox. Lothian was accessible and modern, Halifax was reserved and stiff, and this mattered. Persuading the Americans to join the British was going to be harder if their spokesman in the US came across as a foxhunting aristocrat who could not bring himself to eat a hot dog.

At around the same time, Roosevelt's health went into decline and he began to receive treatment for flu and high blood pressure. The strain of being in office for more than eight years was starting to show, and in the weeks that followed there was what one presidential biographer has called a 'dangerous pause' in his leadership.[5]

Roosevelt had tried to provoke Hitler into providing him with an incident, but this had failed. The polls he monitored so carefully, always preferring to 'follow public opinion than lead it', as Harry Hopkins remembered it, continued to show little appetite for war.[6] The White House appeared to be stuck, and so were the interventionists and the British. With every day the prospect of America entering the war felt hazier and more distant. Meanwhile British losses were becoming harder to sustain. Lothian was dead. Halifax was a liability. The Blitz had failed to transform American public opinion. The isloationist group America First had never been so strong.

Stephenson was held back both by his orders from London and his desire to follow them. In putting together a sophisticated and forward-thinking organization, it was as if he had built a juggernaut and got it onto the road. But he would not turn the key. By the start of April 1941, the future looked as depressing as the present. Bill Stephenson had reached a crisis. The situation was in fact worse than he realized.

Unknown to Stephenson, Adolf Berle at the State Department was stepping up his investigation into his activities. First he had looked into whether those working for Stephenson were registered with the State Department as foreign agents, which he presumed they should be, given the work they were carrying out on behalf of a foreign government. The penalty for each individual who failed to register was a fine of $5,000, five years in jail, or both.

Berle discovered that most of Stephenson's staff, by then over a hundred men and women, were *not* registered. He passed this on to Sumner Welles, Under-Secretary of State. As far as Berle could tell, Stephenson had secretly built up 'a full size police and intelligence service', which 'regularly employed secret agents and a much larger number of informers'. Berle added: 'I have good reason to believe that a good many of the things done are probably a violation of the espionage acts.'[7]

As Berle saw it, this had been allowed to go on too long. If Germany successfully invaded Britain, which seemed increasingly likely, the intelligence that Stephenson had been sending back to London might fall into German hands. Berle also worried about the effect on his own career if it emerged that he had known about this British enterprise and failed to shut it down.

'My feeling is that the time has come when we should make a square issue with the British Government,' Berle concluded. He wanted to confront Bill Stephenson and explain that legally he and his team were on 'almost impossible ground; they are in fact spies'.[8] Having passed this on to Welles, Berle also sent it up to the Secretary of State, Cordell Hull. The tenacious former child prodigy had made up his mind. Stephenson and his shadowy organization had to be closed down. It only remained for Adolf Berle to decide how to go about this, and when.

Stephenson also faced a choice. He could go on as before or break with the past. He could wait for the situation to improve, trusting that Hitler would make a mistake, and that the American people would eventually come round, or he could go on the offensive. He had the manpower, the expertise, and with the new backing of SOE and several other agencies he had the money. As he saw it, he was in a position to try to save his country, but was prevented from doing so by his instructions from London. He was constrained both by the fear of press exposure, and by the thought of being sent home by 'C'.

This made his decision about what do next an unexpectedly personal one. Everything about his earlier attempts to come to the attention of MI6 and his desire to impress London and to follow his orders suggests a man who coveted working for MI6. The orphan from the red-light district of Winnipeg had been admitted to the most exclusive club in the British Empire, and he did not want to throw away his membership. Now he had to decide whether to cling on to this and follow the line laid down by London, or turn against it and kill off this latest version of himself.

A particular exchange appears to have helped make up his mind. Stephenson was in touch at that time, early April 1941, with several public opinion experts. According to an internal history, he had also 'obtained reports on the situation from Donovan, who was in close touch with the President'.[9]

This last line is revealing. The 'situation' was the American attitude towards war, which Roosevelt and Donovan had been discussing at length. The president had asked 'Wild Bill' to campaign on his behalf to shift public opinion.[10] So Stephenson would have known that the president was looking for ways to change the American attitude to the war. Stephenson had helped Donovan do this in the past, and it followed that he could do so again.

Soon after speaking to Bill Donovan, Stephenson sent his boss in London a long and unusually tetchy cable. 'Axis news reports reach here more quickly than ours,' he told 'C'. German propagandists 'invariably beat our news to headlines' and have a better 'sense of news and timing' and an 'infinitely better understanding [of] US psychology'.[11] Stephenson's underlying message in this telegram was simple: the Germans were winning the propaganda war and the British must do more to fight back.

But this message went 'unheeded'.[12]

Almost every account of Stephenson touches on his decisiveness, or just the speed with which he reached his decisions. He comes across as a man who rarely saw grey, and was good at pulling information together, reaching a conclusion, and acting on it without self-doubt or hesitation. But as well as being swift in his decision-making, Stephenson could be direct and difficult.

'In many ways Stephenson was very uncouth,' one of his officers recalled. 'He knocked the establishment and the rules and pretty much did what he wanted. He wasn't being paid or anything. So if he didn't like what you were doing, he'd tell you to bugger right off.'[13] Which is not what he said to his boss in London. But in the silence that followed his gruff cable to London, in the moments he had to himself each day, as he moved between his penthouse apartment and the Rockefeller Center, walking and thinking, working it through in his mind, Stephenson came to a bold decision: he would 'take action on his own initiative'.[14]

As one internal history recorded it, Stephenson now 'instructed the recently created SOE Division [in his office] to declare a covert war against the mass of American groups which were organized throughout the country to spread isolationism and anti-British feeling'. In his headquarters in the upper reaches of the Rockefeller Center, which now ranged over most of the thirty-fifth floor, 'plans were drawn up and agents were instructed to put them into effect.'[15]

At the same time, a new item was added to the list of SOE objectives in the United States: 'To take any warrantable action likely to influence the entry of the US into the war and to discredit the enemies of the Allies in the US.'[16]

With Adolf Berle angling to shut down this British organization and those in London urging caution, Stephenson decided to launch an all-out attack on the American isolationists. 'He had a sort of fox terrier character,' wrote one colleague, 'and if he undertook something, he would carry it through.'[17] It was as if the cautious spymaster had been replaced at a stroke by the more maverick businessman of his past, a less scrupulous figure who understood what it meant to have nothing, to run away from your debts, and who knew how to be ruthless in pursuit of a goal.

After months of hesitation, Bill Stephenson had decided to dive in.

Left: Bill Stephenson in London in 1938, around the time this businessman and former fighter pilot began to gravitate towards MI6 and the world of intelligence.

Below: Charles Lindbergh, in Chicago in 1940, where the legendary aviator and anti-war campaigner argued for the first time in support of Nazi aggression in Europe.

Franklin D. Roosevelt and Winston Churchill on the HMS *Prince of Wales*, in August 1941, shortly before agreeing on the Atlantic Charter. Churchill came away from this meeting convinced that Roosevelt would provoke an 'incident' at sea to bring the US into the war.

Adolf Hitler on 11 December 1941, in the Reichstag, moments before explaining why he had declared war on the United States.

Above: 'Wild Bill' Donovan, fearless soldier, would-be politician, a hero in search of a role: his friendship with Stephenson would change the history of US intelligence.

Left: Wendell Willkie, the 'dark horse' Republican presidential candidate, who was in conclave with MI6 on the day many had hoped to see him inaugurated as president.

Above: The British ambassador to the US, Lord Lothian. His casual manner was part of his crusade to change the American perception of the British.

Left: Eric Maschwitz, composer of 'A Nightingale Sang in Berkeley Square', typewriter expert, forger: Maschwitz would play a key part in Stephenson's most controversial operation.

Left: Hans Thomsen, Germany's most senior diplomat in the United States, who ran an extensive Nazi influence campaign inside the United States.

Below: Hamilton Fish, staunch isolationist and friend of the German government. Like many others, he abandoned the isolationist cause within hours of the Japanese raid on Pearl Harbor.

Left: Fight for Freedom volunteers in New York City, in the summer of 1941, making the case for war with Nazi Germany.

Below: An America First rally in 1941: at its peak this grass-roots isolationist organization had close to a million members.

GEHEIM

SKIZZE 3

NEUSPANIEN

GUYANA (FRZ.)

CHILE

BRASILIEN

Korridor

ARGENTINIEN

CHILE

CARACAS

TRINIDAD

PARAMARIBO

RIO DE JANEIRO

SANTIAGO

BUENOS AIRES

Falkland Inseln

Galapagos Inseln

LUFTVERKEHRSNETZ
DER
VEREINIGTEN STAATEN
SÜD-AMERIKAS
HAUPTLINIEN

The two Bills: Bill Donovan in 1946 as he pins the Medal for Merit on Bill Stephenson, seen here next to his wife, Mary.

The Hemmings (l-r John, Alice, Harold, Louisa) in late 1941, around the time of their trip to the United States.

PART THREE
MAVERICK

23 APRIL 1941

Days Britain at war – 598
Allied shipping losses in the Atlantic (to date) – 5,817,757 tons
British civilians killed in the Blitz – 43,000 (approx.)[1]

APRIL 1941

Fortune Poll: Would you be in favour of sending an army to Europe?
Yes – 21.5%[2]

On 23 April 1941, a muggy day in New York City, a woman strode down the middle of Eighth Avenue towards a crowd of men. She was carrying a sign calling for the United States to enter the war. Just behind her were ten men with similar banners, and after them came a crowd of fellow interventionists, several thousand strong. In front of them, blocking their way, were 15,000 supporters of America First.

For most of the afternoon this phalanx of interventionists had meandered slowly through the streets of Manhattan, stopping traffic, making themselves heard, and distributing expensively produced handbills which accused Charles Lindbergh of being 'Hitler's secret weapon'.[1] Now they had reached the Manhattan Center, where Lindbergh himself was due to speak. The crowd before them was a volatile blend of isolationist, pro-Nazi, and far right activists. 'German accents were numerous', went one report. Many had been told not to answer questions from the press about which organizations they belonged to or who had sent them, which only added to the roiling, suspicious atmosphere.

The lone female interventionist continued towards the crowd of men.[2] It was ten past eight in the evening. The air was humid and thick, as if it might rain at any moment.

Four minutes earlier, inside the Manhattan Center, Charles

Lindbergh had walked on stage. The roar of applause had been blasted out into the street by a colonnade of loudspeakers.

'We want Lindy!' they had shouted inside the auditorium, over and over, before starting to sing 'The Star Spangled Banner'. Outside, the crowd of America First supporters joined in.

Then conquer we must, when our cause it is just . . .

The female protester was getting closer now.

And this be our motto: 'In God is our trust.'

'Get out of here or we'll kill you,' one of them shouted at her. Others booed and jeered.[3]

And the star-spangled banner in triumph shall wave . . .

But she did not turn back.

O'er the land of the free and the home of the brave.

At this point one man broke away from the America First crowd and ran at the woman. Accelerating towards her, he punched her in the face, knocking her to the ground.[4]

Then it began. Both sides ripped into each other. The street became a violent blur. Lindbergh supporters grabbed placards, smashed them in two and used them as clubs. Police sirens started up. Shouts and grunts, screams, thuds, as men and women punched and kicked each other, tore clothes, wrestled, and shoved each other to the ground. Mounted police cantered into sight.

In the background, oblivious to it all, came Lindbergh's measured voice over the loudspeakers as he explained that Germany would win the war and there was no point helping Britain. Then as quickly as it had flared up, the fight fizzled out. Injured protesters were scooped up by friends and taken off in taxis. Several minutes later it began to rain and everyone took shelter.

The interventionists had done their job. They had not come to the Manhattan Center to change the minds of the isolationists, that was never going to happen, only to hijack the press coverage. Reports in the next day's papers focused on the violence, with most articles also listing the different interventionist groups involved in the march and what their spokespeople had to say about Lindbergh and America First.

Anyone reading these with a keen eye might have noticed that some of the activists used very similar language. It was almost as if they were reading from the same script: which, as it happened, some of them were.

At the heart of Bill Stephenson's assault on the isolationists was a bold new strategy. From April 1941, he instructed a series of British agents to infiltrate some of the American pressure groups pushing for intervention. These agents were to influence these groups from the inside, and to have them all attacking the same targets at the same time. They would also ensure that they were never short of money.

In remarkably little time, Stephenson was starting to see results. His agents were now 'taking part in the activities of a great number of interventionist organizations, and were giving to many of them which had begun to flag and to lose interest in their purpose, new vitality and a new lease of life.'[5]

The best of these agents, the most imaginative and effective, was Joseph Hirschberg. Codenamed X.G.101, Hirschberg was an experienced diamond cleaver, a music lover, an SOE agent and an orthodox Jew. Hirschberg had fled his hometown of Antwerp, in Belgium, just before the German invasion in 1940. At the time he belonged to an organization which smuggled anti-Nazi propaganda into Germany. In London, he offered his services to the British and was sent to New York. Back in Belgium, his extended family began to live under Nazi occupation; many would be sent to concentration camps and later killed.

Deeply religious, Hirschberg would perform the morning prayer every day before breakfast, pulling on his prayer shawl, winding a strap of leather round his forearm to keep the tefilin in place, and reciting a series of prayers, readings and blessings, before embarking on that day's work. During his early months in the United States, as newly declassified documents reveal for the first time, his orders from London included an array of activities, from propaganda to agent recruitment and even planning assassinations of Nazis operating in the Americas.[6] In March 1941 Hirschberg was 'informed' by his SOE paymasters 'that a certain assassination, arranged previously in London, must not take place.'[7] Whether there were others that did go ahead, it is impossible to say.

In early 1941 Hirschberg was told to report for the first time to one of Stephenson's officers, and was given new instructions. The would-be assassin was asked to start infiltrating political pressure groups.

Hirschberg began by targeting the cumbersomely named 'Non-Sectarian Anti-Nazi League to Champion Human Rights', usually known as the Anti-Nazi League, or ANL. Since Hitler had come to power, the ANL had campaigned dutifully for an economic blockade of Nazi Germany, but without great success.

There were several ways Hirschberg could try to infiltrate this New York-based group. Either he could join the ANL and work his way into a senior position, in the hope of exerting influence from within, or he could take a much riskier short cut.

With time against him, Hirschberg approached the chairman of the ANL, a former Boston university professor called James Sheldon. Probably without revealing that he was working for the British, Hirschberg told Sheldon that he could subsidize the ANL. In return, the pressure group had to make certain changes to its policy.

Later described by Hirschberg as 'my very dear friend' who knew 'very well' about his work 'for this cause', Sheldon agreed.[8] Hirschberg had effectively bought control of the ANL. In the weeks that followed, ANL members were told of the group's sudden shift towards activism. 'We should start with a broadside of attacks on the America First organization wherever and whenever it attempts to hold a meeting,' Sheldon told the ANL board, to all-round amazement. 'Wherever possible we should picket such meetings with persons handing out leaflets and attacking that organization and its speakers.'[9] This was unlike anything the ANL had done before. It was more dangerous, involved more manpower and exposure, and it seemed to take the focus away from Nazi Germany. Never before had the ANL showed such interest in America First. But Sheldon stood his ground.

The ANL board was equally surprised by his proposed budget for the coming year. Although they had just a few hundred paying members, Sheldon assured them that $35,000 would be coming in from subscriptions and a whopping $118,000 from 'other sources'.[10]

The ANL was a driving force behind the anti-Lindbergh march that culminated in a brawl outside the Manhattan Center. ANL members and volunteers also handed out on the streets of New York that day as many as 10,000 copies of their leaflet 'What One Hitler Medal Can Do'.[11] This short publication was a scathing attack on Charles Lindbergh and his decision to keep the Verdienstkreuz Deutscher Adler, or Service Cross of the German Eagle, a medal he had been given by Hermann Goering.

The ANL was just one of the pressure groups now being influenced and subsidized by Stephenson's office. His star agent Joseph Hirschberg had also found a way into the League for Human Rights, and the Joint Boycott Council. More would follow, including a new campaign group set up by Hirschberg himself, the Committee for Inter-American Co-operation.[12] Other British agents penetrated the Mazzini Society. Soon the American Committee to Aid British Labor was also being subsidized by the British, as well as Friends of Democracy (yet another one of the groups involved in the anti-Lindbergh march in New York).

Hirschberg's instructions had been simple. Interventionist groups must now 'provide Roosevelt with evidence that the US public is

eager for action'.[13] So for now this was not being done with the connivance of the White House, but was instead part of Stephenson's
attempt to convince the president that the American people wanted
intervention.

Only weeks after Stephenson had quietly declared war on the
isolationists, groups like the ANL were picketing America First
meetings, organizing marches, holding more rallies, or using their
press contacts to make themselves heard. By May 1941, many of these
interventionist groups seemed to be saying the same thing about
Hitler, and how there was a hidden link between the Nazis, America
First and Lindbergh. They were all on the offensive. With British
funding, their voices had become louder. With British infiltration,
these voices were now in harmony.

Some of the groups targeted by the British were tiny, but what
mattered was that they were groups, not individuals. With so many
of these organizations saying roughly the same thing, and at the same
time, it was easy to imagine a wave of popular feeling throughout
America. People across the country began to wonder if the tide was
starting to turn.

Bill Stephenson had never done anything like this before, either in
MI6 or in business. His decision to start infiltrating pressure groups
and to harness their energies to the British cause was audacious and
risky, and in very little time it seemed to be making an impact. But
this was just the start.

On 18 June 1941 reports appeared in the press about a British parachute raid in Nazi-occupied France. It had taken place at Berck-sur-Mer, in the Pas-de-Calais region, and was evidently the most daring British operation of the war so far. 'One party of parachutists, heavily armed with tommy guns and hand grenades, overpowered the airfield guards, rushed the control room and seized its occupants before an alarm could be given,' ran a press report. 'A second party attacked the barracks and captured a number of German pilots who were waiting for orders to take to the air. Meanwhile, the third group scattered over the airport, destroying about thirty planes.' With forty German prisoners in tow, as well as a handful of Frenchmen, who had volunteered on the spot to fight against Hitler, they were met on the beach by British motor torpedo boats that took them home across the English Channel. There were no casualties. 'The whole operation, it was said, was carried out with such precision that the attacking forces were embarked and on their way home before Nazi headquarters knew what had happened.'[1]

This raid had been a blinding success – efficient, deadly and fast. The troops had been courageous and inventive. Their commanders had used the same 'parachute tactics of the type made famous by the Nazis'.[2] Also encouraging was how ordinary Frenchmen had been willing at once to volunteer. Reports on the raid appeared in the *Herald Tribune*, the *Baltimore Sun*, and the *New York Post*; the story also featured in a news bulletin on the short-wave radio station WRUL; the Overseas News Agency filed a piece on it; and in Britain the *Daily Mirror* and its subsidiaries the *Liverpool Echo* and the *Liverpool Evening Express* covered it; the raid even popped up in newspapers further afield in New Zealand and Australia.[3]

But one aspect of this raid did not make it into any of these reports. The entire thing, from start to finish, had been made up.

This British raid on Berck-sur-Mer occurred only in the imaginations of a secretive group in London called the 'Sib Committee', so-called because their job was to produce 'sibs', meaning rumours, from the Latin '*sibillare*', to whisper. Paid for by SOE, the Sib Committee was later described by an American who sat in on its meetings as 'one of the most taboo political warfare mechanisms or activities in Britain'. It would be years before its existence was discovered by historians, and only recently have some details of the stories it produced been released. Run with a strange 'mixture of bureaucratic solemnity and schoolboy zest', this committee produced a stream of rumours that were, the same American observer wrote, 'more imaginative and frequently more ruthless than any Nazi psychological warfare I had studied'.[4]

Formed in November 1940, the Sib Committee was the central hub in Britain's new rumour network. Each week, it met to consider fresh proposals from SOE Section Heads about which rumours to spread around the world. Once the committee had a list of ideas they liked, these were passed on to a network of intermediaries, who would add colour and detail and tailor each one to their audience.

Some rumours were spread by MI5 agents in nightclubs, seamen's hostels, harbours and airports. Others were given to friendly journalists along with instructions to blurt out key details 'with an air of indiscretion' in the vicinity of foreign journalists.[5] Frequently this worked. Rumours were also passed on via secure MI6 cable to SOE stations around the world, including Stephenson's office in New York, which received in mid-June 1941 Sib No. 776, about the imaginary parachute raid on Berck-sur-Mer.

Had this rumour arrived in the Rockefeller Center several months earlier, little would have happened. But by June 1941 the situation had been transformed. Bill Stephenson had now set up an office dedicated to spreading fake, distorted or inaccurate stories, a rumour factory that was so big, so busy, and was putting out so many stories – on average twenty a day[6] – that he had recently registered it with the State Department under a cover name, in the hope that this would kill off any interest from the likes of Adolf Berle.

'British & Overseas Features', the cover name for this new office, was, to all intents and purposes, a harmless British news agency supplying published articles to foreign newspapers. To add verisimilitude, Stephenson had its outer office 'plentifully furnished with the paraphernalia of their trade – ticker tapes and the like'. Behind this façade was the pre-internet equivalent of a troll farm.

The raw materials in this rumour factory were stories. Some came from London in the form of 'sibs', others were produced in-house. Either they were pure fiction, like the raid on Berck-sur-Mer, or they were accurate but had come from a secret source such as a decrypted German radio communication or material stolen from a diplomatic bag passing through British Censorship in Bermuda.

In these cases, the rumour factory's job was to disguise the story's origin. The easiest way to do this was by giving each of these stories what was known in the office as a 'paperclip',[8] shorthand for an invented tale about where the news had come from and how it had ended up in New York. When a collection of photographs showing Nazi atrocities in Poland was published in the US media, the American public was informed that a Luftwaffe pilot had been so fond of these horrific pictures that he kept them in his jacket pocket at all times, which is where they had been when his plane was shot down over Britain. Instead they had almost certainly been smuggled out of Poland by MI6.

Once each story had been written up or given a paperclip there were various ways to feed it into the American news cycle. Some rumours were broken up, with the separate parts fed to different journalists. As the man running this rumour factory, a British journalist called Bill Morrell, explained, 'the natural inquisitiveness of newspapermen will lead them to ferret out further facts.'[9]

On other occasions the 'dope', as Stephenson's officers referred to their rumours, was passed on to a trusted official at the British Press Service (BPS). This was the news service set up by the British ambassador Lord Lothian the year before, ironically to dispel any suspicions that the British were peddling fake news to bring the United States into the war. Now it was helping to do exactly that.

One of the key figures at the BPS was the philosopher Isaiah Berlin, another was the historian John Wheeler-Bennett (who had recently supervised a young John F. Kennedy's master's degree thesis). On receiving the 'dope' from Stephenson's office, Wheeler-Bennett would carry out a rapid rumour triage. Depending on the nature and importance of the story, he would decide where to place it. Some rumours went straight to friendly contacts at interventionist pressure groups, others might go to sympathetic newspaper columnists, influential academics or to political figures within powerful émigré groups.

But for the imaginary raid at Berck-sur-Mer, Stephenson's rumour factory tried something else. Having received the outline of this rumour from London, they chose not to pass it on to the BPS. Instead they wrote it up into a vivid news story, adding colourful details to make it more plausible and memorable. The finished piece was then handed to an unidentified figure at a New York-based news service.

Launched only the year before, the Overseas News Agency (ONA) was already known to many American newspaper and magazine editors as a reliable and dependable source of news.[10] It was just what Stephenson had been looking for. In April 1941 he had approached a controlling figure at the ONA, never named, and they soon came to an understanding. The British would pay the ONA a monthly subsidy. In return, this American outfit would take stories from Stephenson's rumour factory and publish them as if they were true.

From the headquarters of the Overseas News Agency in New York, stories like the 'sib' about the Berck-sur-Mer raid were cabled across the Atlantic to ONA offices in neutral countries such as Switzerland or Sweden. There ONA staff would rewrite these stories and send them to ONA subscribers back in the United States, including editors at the *Herald Tribune*, the *New York Post*, and the *Baltimore Sun*. By now each of these stories had a neutral dateline, which immediately made it sound more credible.

This was how the story of the Berck-sur-Mer raid ended up in print. Having gone from London to New York, New York to Zurich, and now Zurich back to New York, Sib No. 776 had acquired a gleam of authenticity. The dirty news had been laundered, but it was not yet clean.

To make this rumour even more believable, Stephenson's team also passed it to the Press Attaché at the New York consulate of the Czechoslovak government-in-exile, a Dr Jan Loewenbach, 'with whom we have a close understanding'.[11] He rewrote the story again, giving it his own spin, and passed it on to some eighty Czech and Slovak newspapers within the United States. He did the same for most stories the British channelled to the ONA. If pressed on where his information came from, Loewenbach would allude to an underground source in occupied Europe which, for reasons of security, could not be named.

Stephenson and his team also arranged for every rumour that went to the ONA to be translated and sent out simultaneously to other foreign language newspapers within the US. Soon Polish, Serbian,

Croatian and Hungarian papers all over the country were running translations of ONA stories in the hours after their initial release.[12]

To make this dirty news spotlessly clean, the British also used radio. In April 1941, within weeks of coming to an arrangement with the ONA, Stephenson had brokered a deal with a US radio station.

This was another risky move. There might be paperwork involved and a money trail, so it made sense to use a little-known station. Instead he approached the owners of 'the most powerful shortwave station in the US, and the one with the largest European listening audience',[13] the 50,000-watt, Boston-based WRUL. For $400 a month, they agreed to help.

Very soon, a system was in place whereby translations of British rumours were passed on to a senior figure at WRUL, again never named, who would hand them on to the WRUL staff putting together that day's foreign language broadcasts. Within hours, these stories appeared in news broadcasts heard all over the world. If Stephenson's team was lucky, and often they were, these broadcasts were picked up by overseas print journalists listening to the radio, who would then turn them into news stories, and soon these were cabled back to the United States.

The aim was to have each rumour flying back and forth across the Atlantic in a reverberating loop, moving between media and languages, mutating as it went, until it was almost impossible to work out where it had begun, let alone trace it back to an office deep inside the Rockefeller Center.

There was one final weapon in this British fake news operation. As well as radio, news agencies, pressure groups and newspapers, Stephenson's team used a more venerable strategy for spreading rumours, the oldest one there is – they started whispering campaigns.

By the time Stephenson began his assault on American public opinion, one of his officers was also running a network of inform-ants on merchant ships which docked at major US ports. By April

1941, there were more than four hundred of these unpaid informants, most of them Americans, all employed by the main Atlantic
shipping lines. The man running this network was yet another Bill,
the former accountant Bill Ross Smith, whose modus operandi was
simple. He would approach the owner of a major shipping line with
the worrying news that there might be German saboteurs on board
their ships – even if he had no evidence that there were. Usually the
shipping magnate reacted by agreeing to put Ross Smith in touch
with the captains, chief stewards and barmen on board their ships,
and telling them to cooperate with this British official.

During the summer of 1941 the role of these informants changed,
even if they were unaware of it. From that point on, as well as listening
out for interesting rumours they were also being used to spread
them. They became the whisperers in a series of British whispering
campaigns. Ross Smith later revealed his technique.

It was elegantly simple: 'You tell something in "strictest confidence"', he explained. 'That's the best way to start a rumour.'[14]

Another way to start a rumour, as Stephenson was beginning to
understand, involved astrologers.

On a warm night in June 1941, a tall, slender-looking man could
be seen clambering up the fire escape of a luxurious hotel in New
York. High above the street, he paused to knock on a window. After
a while, a plump and bespectacled figure appeared on the other side
of the glass. The window came up. At this point Eric Maschwitz
handed over a large sum of money to the man inside the hotel, before
scuttling back down the fire escape and disappearing into the night.

Maschwitz, whose song 'A Nightingale Sang in Berkeley Square'
was now a global hit, had been summoned to New York to work
for Bill Stephenson, after one of his staff described the good work
Maschwitz had previously done in Section D.

Maschwitz had arrived earlier that month, and right away was introduced to the social complexities of life in Manhattan when his prospective landlord refused to lease him an apartment, explaining that he ran a 'restricted house'.[15] Maschwitz assured him he had no plans to sell liquor on the premises. The landlord replied that 'restricted' meant he would not allow either African-Americans or Jews to live there. Although Maschwitz's father was Jewish, his mother was not; so the apartment was his.

Codenamed G.106, Eric Maschwitz's first job for Stephenson was a peculiar one. He had been told to look after Louis de Wohl, a Hungarian refugee, British secret agent and celebrity astrologer. Maschwitz's main task was making sure he got paid, which involved clambering up the fire escape of de Wohl's expensive hotel once a week.

Louis De Wohl was part of a little-known British campaign to have Hitler's death written in the stars. Department D/Q of SOE had various pet astrologers around the world, including De Wohl and others in Cairo, Istanbul and Lagos. Over the summer of 1941 they were told to start predicting the Nazi leader's sudden demise, which they duly did.

Soon it was reported that a priest called Ulokoigbe in Nigeria had seen astrological evidence of Hitler's coming death. The well-known Egyptian astrologer Sheikh Youssef Afifi was also heard to be saying much the same thing. Reports in several 'Arabic weeklies' about Hitler's death were, SOE reported, 'causing much discussion among Egyptians'.[16] Hitler was 'obsessed' by astrology, De Wohl explained. 'It is impossible that the whole world speaks of the death of one man, without this man becoming aware of it. *It will haunt him.*'[17]

For those who took astrology seriously, including millions of Americans, this might also help to undermine their notions of Nazi invincibility. In this way, De Wohl's predictions were a tiny part of the broader British effort to change public opinion in the United States.

None of this endeared the astrologer-spy to his new handler, Eric

Maschwitz, who later complained that De Wohl was 'a right swindler . . . you never met such a character. He was up to everything and he was paid a lot of money and I know because I used to have to go and pay him once a week.'[18]

By June 1941, Stephenson's operation to bring the United States into the war was larger, more expensive and emphatically more ambitious than it had been at the start of the year. His rumour factory could 'spread a rumour throughout the length and breadth of the US within a few hours'.[19] Using radio, news agency press releases, newspaper columnists, whispering campaigns, the Czechoslovak consulate, foreign language newspapers, and an overweight astrologer looked after by a world-famous lyricist, his office was now putting out a flood of stories. They were designed either to undermine America First and Lindbergh, or to convince the American people that Hitler was bad and he could be beaten.

Not only had Stephenson's operation become larger and more ambitious, it was also more dangerous. Almost as soon as his assault on the American isolationists began, his office started to look into targeted assassinations. On 10 April 1941, as one recently declassified document shows, Stephenson's office cabled SOE headquarters in London to say 'it would be possible for them to arrange for the disposal of Gerhard Hentschke'. Hentschke was a Nazi diplomat stationed at the time in Guatemala.[20] In June 1941, they were at it again. This time they 'recommended' that an American journalist of German origin, Karl von Wiegand, an isolationist and Nazi enthusiast who wrote for the Hearst chain of newspapers, 'should be liquidated'.[21]

These two assassinations were either thwarted or more likely overruled by London. But the fact that they were even suggested is revealing. The character of Stephenson's operation had changed in the space of just a few months; it was now more determined, ruthless and deadly. The man in charge was also becoming more selective about what he shared with London.

One senior figure in Whitehall later said of the British rumour factory in New York 'that the Foreign Office were quite unaware of these operations, and were in fact extremely puzzled at the time by the apparently spontaneous publication of material all over the world'.[22]

Stephenson had by no means gone rogue. But the ties which bound him to some of his colleagues in London had loosened. In his drive to bring the United States into the war, he was taking more risks than ever. But none was as far-fetched as the plan he had recently set in motion involving the White House.

'It was quite clear to me that he could think about seven stages ahead of the average man,' a future professor of mathematics at Columbia University would write of Bill Stephenson, before going on to describe him processing new information: 'it was terrifying to watch. Not a muscle in his face moved, nor did his eyes shift around as people's eyes often do when they're reflective, he looked straight ahead of him, he looked much more like a champion chess player who sees three possibilities for a mate in five and is just wondering which to choose.'[1]

In late 1940, while ruminating on how to bring the United States into the war, Stephenson had seen a possible checkmate. The first two moves would be the hardest. He needed to convince Bill Donovan to run a new American intelligence agency. Then he had to find a way to bring this agency into being.

Stephenson's efforts to win over Donovan had begun with those long drinking sessions in the 21 Club, hugger-mugger among the socialites and businessmen as he made the case for this new agency, occasionally having to shout to be heard over the band. His campaign continued in London, several weeks later, in December 1940, as Donovan was showered with comforts, access and secrets, to the point where the secrets themselves felt less important than the act of their being shared. Each was a gift as much as a test. Keeping one to himself was a nod of loyalty to those who had placed so much faith in him, and none more so than Bill Stephenson.

After being fussed over in London and taken on a tour of the SOE training schools Stations XII and XVII, Donovan appeared to have been won over to the idea of a new American intelligence agency geared towards special operations and 'dirty tricks'. He later confessed that he 'had never been treated in such royal and exalted fashion',[2] and was soon evangelizing in Washington about the need for an American equivalent of SOE. 'Donovan has been working in our interests like a Trojan since his return', Stephenson reported back to 'C'.[3]

Donovan also made the case for this new agency to the president. On 4 April 1941 Roosevelt told his cabinet at length about the need for a new kind of centralised intelligence agency, referring throughout to how the British ran their intelligence operations, information he had been fed by Bill Donovan.

Stephenson's plan was starting to work. What helped was Roosevelt's fascination with intelligence work. It was unusual for an American president to show such an interest in spying. The last one to embrace the possibilities of espionage, counter-espionage, and the need for a centralized intelligence agency, had been George Washington. Since then most US presidents had resisted calls for an all-powerful intelligence organization, partly because spying seemed to be so un-American. Espionage reeked of Europe and the Old World. It was duplicitous and dishonest, and probably best left to the British.

By the start of the war, rather than having a single, controlling agency there were three separate government bodies in the United States which specialized in gathering intelligence: the FBI, the Military Intelligence Department (MID) and the Office for Naval Intelligence (ONI). They operated independently of each other, frequently covered the same ground twice, and seemed to be constitutionally incapable of cooperation.

In an effort to bang their heads together, Roosevelt had told the chiefs of these three rival agencies to have regular meetings. But either they failed to attend these meetings or they sent their deputies. So it was hardly surprising that by April 1941 the president wanted a fresh start. Nor did it come as a shock to anyone in Washington that the three existing intelligence chiefs did not.

In a sudden show of unity, these three men put aside their differences to produce a joint memorandum arguing against this new agency, on the grounds that it offered 'only negligible advantages.'[4] After hearing that Donovan might be running it, Hoover sent the president an unsourced report dismissing 'Wild Bill's' recent trip to Europe as a 'failure' because he was 'not schooled in the art of diplomacy'.[5] For the MID chief, the prospect of a 'super agency controlling all intelligence' was 'very disadvantageous, if not calamitous'.[6]

The president had said he wanted a new, all-powerful intelligence agency. But rather than show him how this could be done, his three intelligence chiefs had told him he was wrong to want it. The teacher had set a demanding essay, and in response most of the class had refused to do it. But one student quietly got to work.

On 26 April 1941 Bill Donovan completed a four-page memorandum explaining how this new intelligence agency could operate. Precise and detailed, his document oozed authority. It covered the relationship between the new organization and, variously, the White House, political parties and existing intelligence agencies. It also explained where funding would come from, who should control this agency, its areas of operation and function, and even the make-up of its advisory committee. Donovan insisted that the new agency must not be limited to gathering intelligence; it should specialize as well in 'the use of propaganda' and 'the direction of subversive operations'.[7] In other words, it should closely resemble Britain's SOE.

This memorandum was so authoritative that in places it read as if it had been put together by someone with experience of running an intelligence agency, which, for the most part, it had been. The student who had quietly gone off to write the essay had also received outside help.

Stephenson later said that 'C' would have been 'horrified' if he had known the extent to which 'I was supplying our friend [Donovan] with secret information to build up his candidacy for the position I wanted to see him achieve here.' When asked about this particular memorandum and two more that followed, Stephenson was clear. 'Of course my staff produced the material for these papers.'[8]

But Roosevelt was not ready to approve this new agency. With every day that he prevaricated, the opposition gathered strength. The chiefs of the FBI, MID and ONI had never been so close. Another figure who began to voice his concerns, rather worryingly given his potential role in the agency, was Bill Donovan himself.

Donovan had cooled on the idea of being a spy chief. He said he 'wouldn't reach for the job', Stephenson explained, and 'felt he shouldn't seek it'.[9] In part, this was to do with pride. Donovan did not like to feel he was angling for a position. He preferred in life to be courted and pursued. His withdrawal was also linked to the dilemma he had been tussling with since the start of the war.

For almost two decades Bill Donovan had been trying so hard to get into politics that he had blinded himself to his failings as a politician. Having recently become much closer to Roosevelt, he imagined that he might be closer than ever to landing a plum political position. More than that, as the prospect of the United States entering the war became clearer, he had begun to feel deep inside himself the call of the military. Donovan remained one of the country's most decorated soldiers. By early June 1941 the pull of both the military and politics had become hard to resist. Rather than push to run this new spy agency, Donovan went to have an army medical examination.

Just when it needed to come together, Stephenson's plan was falling apart. The man he had tried so hard to talk into taking this job had chosen soldiering over spying.

The idea of this new intelligence agency being run by a man so close to the British, like Donovan, had always been a stretch, the type of improbable scheme you might find in a playful spy novel. So it was perhaps fitting that one of the two officials sent from London to help change Donovan's mind, and to bring this agency into being, was the future creator of James Bond.

On 25 May 1941 the luxurious 'Dixie Clipper' seaplane landed on the water at LaGuardia Airport in New York. Once it had pulled up alongside the quay and the gangplanks went up, out stepped the fashion designer Elsa Schiaparelli, carrying a wicker basket reminiscent of the one made famous two years earlier by a seventeen-year-old Judy Garland in *The Wizard of Oz*. 'This is what we now use for luggage in France, you see,' Schiaparelli told the bank of waiting reporters, flashbulbs exploding around her; 'we have no more leather.'[1]

Just behind her came two British intelligence officers in civilian dress. One was Britain's Director of Naval Intelligence, Admiral John Godfrey, the other was his assistant, Lieutenant Commander Ian Fleming. From LaGuardia they were driven in to Manhattan, where their first appointment was with the Bill Stephenson and his friend Bill Donovan.

The atmosphere as these four settled down together would have been lively and loud. Donovan had met Godfrey on his two earlier visits to London and had already offered to put him up in his apartment during his stay; Fleming had met Donovan before in Gibraltar, calling him a 'splendid American, being almost twice the size of Stephenson, though no match for him, I would guess, in unarmed combat';[2] Stephenson, meanwhile, had friends in common with Fleming and probably knew him from before the war.

They all knew and liked each other. But what began as a friendly reunion evolved into something else. The three Britons had two objectives: first, to convince Donovan of the need for a centralized American intelligence agency; then, to persuade him he should run it.

Being a fresh voice and more senior to Fleming, Godfrey took the lead. Donovan's attitude had not changed. He was transfixed by the same dilemma – politics or the military. But somehow Godfrey, one of the future models for Bond's boss 'M', managed to frame the argument in a different way. We do not know how, only that by the end of this session Donovan had again come round to the idea.[3] Next, they had to convince the White House.

Before travelling down to the capital, the two British visitors took a tour of Stephenson's 'highly mechanised eyrie in Rockefeller Center', as Fleming remembered it.[4] Godfrey was in awe. 'How much I admire the wonderful set-up you have achieved in New York,' he told Stephenson. 'As the prototype of what such an organisation should be, I consider it beyond praise.'[5] This was from a man who did not deal in hyperbole. Almost every visitor from London had a similar reaction, with one MI5 officer calling this office 'amazingly good' and Stephenson 'first rate'.[6]

Walking just behind his boss on that tour of the office was Ian Fleming, sweeping up details as he went. One which stuck in his mind was the location of Stephenson's clandestine operation just three floors below the Japanese consulate. In Fleming's first novel, *Casino Royale*, published just over a decade later, James Bond is dispatched to the Rockefeller Center in New York with orders to kill a Japanese cipher clerk.

Fleming was no less intrigued by the man running this operation, later describing Stephenson as a hero of his, 'one of the great secret agents of the last war', a man with 'a magnetic personality and the quality of making anyone ready to follow him to the ends of the earth'.[7] He also remembered watching him mix what seemed to be 'the most powerful martinis in America'.[8] They were so powerful, and so good, that Ian Fleming jotted down Stephenson's recipe: 'Booth's gin, high and dry, easy on the vermouth, shaken not stirred'.[9]

Meanwhile in Washington, the campaign for a new intelligence agency with Donovan in charge had escalated. Shortly before Fleming and Godfrey were shown round the Rockefeller Center, Roosevelt was handed a note from his Navy Secretary, Frank Knox, one of Donovan's closest political allies, saying 'frankly and privately, I am a little disappointed that the Administration is not making better use of Bill Donovan's services. He has made such tremendous sacrifices and contributed in such an outstanding way, that it seems strange to me that some very important job is not assigned to him'.[10] The president was then passed a cutting from the *New York Herald Tribune* in which Major George Fielding Eliot – a stalwart member of the Century Group – called for 'a special intelligence service to act as co-ordinator, responsible directly to the President, acting with his authority'. It should have a budget of $500 million, he went on, to be spent on 'propaganda, counter-espionage and sabotage – yes, sabotage'.[11]

While Roosevelt was considering this article, one of his guests in the White House was Robert Sherwood, another Century Group linchpin who was also in touch with the British. Stephenson later described Sherwood as perhaps 'the most persistent and effective' of his 'avenues of influence' at the White House. Sherwood urged the president to put Donovan in charge of this new intelligence agency.[12]

Several days after he had left, a new guest in the White House was John Winant, the new US ambassador to Britain, the anglophile replacement for the isolationist Joe Kennedy. Later described as a Stephenson 'confidant', he too urged the president to have Donovan installed as the chief of this new agency.[13]

In a different part of the capital, Godfrey, Fleming and 'Wild Bill' himself were now working on a more detailed description of how their agency would look. Again this document was based largely on British expertise.

On 10 June 1941 their 'Memorandum of Establishment of Service of Strategic Information' arrived at the White House. Later that day Admiral Godfrey also arrived at the White House, where he was due to have dinner. His aim was to win over the president to the idea of this new agency. But to his dismay it turned out to be a large dinner and during the meal he did not get the chance to speak to Roosevelt. Afterwards everyone went to watch a film, about snake worship in Laos. Again Godfrey was separated from the president. It was beginning to feel like a wasted venture when Roosevelt ushered him into the Oval Office.

FLYWHEEL, the MI6 codename for Roosevelt, was in a playful mood that night. As soon as the two men were alone the president began to tease the elderly admiral about the decline of the British Empire and the shoddy state of British intelligence. The future model for 'M' was not expecting this, and nor was he used to it. But this was the president of the United States, so he nodded and grunted as best he could, and let FLYWHEEL do most of the talking. But in the momentary gaps, Godfrey jumped in to make his points. He praised Donovan and talked up the need for a centralized intelligence agency, but he was careful not to link the two.

If the president felt he was being pushed by the British into choosing Donovan he might do the opposite. Instead Godfrey suggested half-heartedly that John Winant could be the ideal man to run this agency, because he had such good judgement. Winant had spent the last week talking up Donovan's virtues, as Godfrey knew. Also he had just begun his posting in London, as ambassador, so was unlikely to be called back so soon.

Roosevelt responded as Roosevelt generally did: he gave nothing away. Godfrey left the White House feeling 'doubtful if he'd really made his point'.[14]

Another of Godfrey's meals in the capital was with three government officials each passionately opposed to this new intelligence agency – the Director of the FBI, J. Edgar Hoover, the Director of the Office of Naval Intelligence, Captain Alan Kirk, and the man who continued to pose the greatest threat to Stephenson's organization: Adolf Berle.

This State Department official had not forgotten about Stephenson and his covert operation in New York. It continued to annoy him. But for now Berle held back. It is certainly possible that over lunch in the capital Godfrey assuaged some of Berle's fears concerning Stephenson. Perhaps the admiral reassured him that this undercover office was of little consequence. He certainly did not let on that he and Stephenson were then frantically manoeuvring to bring into existence a new American intelligence agency under their friend and ally Bill Donovan.

Eight days after Godfrey's visit to the White House, shortly before 12.30pm on 18 June 1941, a scene played out in the Oval Office which Bill Stephenson must have imagined many times before. The president of the United States was sitting behind a broad wooden desk cluttered with objects. Bill Donovan was before him, either standing or sitting. After some polite conversation, Roosevelt formally asked him to set up and run a new centralized intelligence agency.

Everything was playing out as Stephenson had hoped, until one of the actors went off script.

'I told the President that I did not want to do it,' Donovan later confessed.

Had he got wind of a political position about to open up? Or heard from a friend in the military that they wanted him back?

The president urged Donovan to reconsider.

Until then, Donovan had been torn between wanting to be a soldier and a politician. But in the moments after turning down this
job something changed. Perhaps he realized finally that running
this new agency was a way of doing both: it would allow him to
be a political soldier. After all, he would be in charge of American
political warfare. Donovan agreed to take the job, but only on three
conditions:[15] other government departments must provide him with
assistance; his funding should be kept secret; and he would report
exclusively to the president.

Roosevelt accepted. He wrote on the cover sheet to Donovan's
memorandum, the one that had been drafted with the help of Stephenson, Fleming and Godfrey, 'please set this up confidentially'.[16]

The Office of the Coordinator of Information, or COI, had been
born. The new Coordinator's first move? He went to see his friend
in MI6.

'Bill saw President today,' Stephenson wrote to 'C' several hours
later. 'After long discussion wherein all points were agreed he accepted
appointment.' He added, 'Bill accuses me of having "intrigued and
driven" him into appointment. You can imagine how relieved I am
after three months of battle and jockeying for position at Washington
that "our man" is in a position of such importance to our efforts.'[17]

The epithet 'our man' is suggestive. It hints at the possibility that
Donovan was now formally working for Stephenson and was on
the books at MI6. Another cable to London confirms that he was
not. Godfrey had suggested Churchill send a 'personal message of
exhortation' to Donovan, in recognition of what had happened. This
idea was shot down immediately. As one British official explained, if
Churchill had written this message and it had leaked then Donovan
would be accused of being a British agent, 'instead of the splendid
free-lance that he is'.[18]

'Splendid free-lance' is the more revealing phrase. Even if it had
been possible for MI6 to recruit Donovan as an agent it was not

in their best interests to do so. He could achieve more for them by remaining outside the formal aegis of MI6. The same is true of most agents of influence.

Although 'Wild Bill' described himself as 'driven' into this job by Stephenson, their relationship had not become lop-sided. It was a partnership. The historian Thomas Troy, who has studied the birth of the COI in forensic detail, concluded it was an 'equal collaboration'.[19] Between them, the two Bills had been instrumental in the birth of America's first centralized intelligence agency, which would later evolve into the OSS and later the CIA. Given the sometimes fractious relationship between the CIA and MI6 in the decades ahead, it is remarkable to consider the role one played in the birth of the other. Today their staff might refer to each other occasionally as 'cousins' or 'friends'. Perhaps 'brothers' is more apt.

Bill Donovan was now responsible for coordinating all American intelligence and for launching 'offensive operations'.[20] He had to build up his organization from scratch. Once that was done Stephenson might be able to activate the next part of his plan, taking him several moves closer to the checkmate he had foreseen in late 1940 that could finally bring the US into the war.

'That night,' Stephenson wrote, 'I took five instead of the usual four hours sleep.'[21]

It had been a strange few weeks for Charles Lindbergh, rounded off by the moment he had a vision of his dead grandfather. The celebrity pilot's world began to unravel when he heard from a friend that Roosevelt had publicly described Lindbergh's analysis of the international situation as 'dumb', as he did on 25 April 1941, before comparing him to the defeatist Civil War politician Clement Vallandigham, leader of the Copperheads,[1] a Unionist who had called for an end to the war because he thought it could not be won. The president had also said that Lindbergh, who had a commission in the US Army Air Corps, would not be called up on account of his political views.

Lindbergh was beside himself. He resigned his commission in protest, an act which had an immediate, liberating effect on him. Only by cutting himself off from the military did he understand the ways in which he had been held back. Having recently become a member of the America First Committee, after months of helping behind the scenes, he could now give as many speeches as he liked, and could be more candid with the American people about his fears for the future. 'If we enter this war, it won't be like the last,' he wrote in his diary, after hearing about Roosevelt's Copperhead jibe, 'and God knows what will happen here before we finish it – race riots, revolution, destruction – America is not immune to any of these.' He finished on a more dangerous note: 'We are due for a bath of fire, possibly it would be the best thing that could happen to us.'[2]

Not long after, Lindbergh was walking through a field near Lake Michigan when he felt as if he had been transported to his childhood, with his grandfather next to him. 'It all came back so clearly that it seemed he was there beside me – that if I turned my head he would be there, walking along with his paper bag for mushrooms in one hand, and a bunch of wildflowers in the other.'[3]

This vision of his grandfather also brought back memories of his father, the congressman. When Lindbergh gave a speech several days later to a 'cheering, frenzied audience of 12,000 people' in Minneapolis, where his father had been a representative, he spoke for the first time in public about Charles Lindbergh Senior. 'His meetings were broken up,' he told the audience, 'his patriotism questioned, and the plates of his book were destroyed by government agents.'[4] The parallels to his own plight were obvious. But his father had been right, Lindbergh added, indignation creeping into his voice: he had predicted that America's involvement in the last war might drag the country into future wars. Lindbergh also told the crowd that his own predictions had been right, and again they applauded, both for Lindbergh and for the memory of his father.

Standing up on stage in his favourite blue suit, Lindbergh experienced a flash of relief. The audience's reaction was all the more poignant because of where he was: Minneapolis, where his father had stood for governor of Minnesota shortly after the First World War and been rejected by the local electorate. 'I think the greatest satisfaction I have had at any of these meetings,' he wrote, 'lay in the applause I received when I spoke of my father tonight. People are beginning to appreciate his vision and his courage.'[5]

When Lindbergh raced back from Europe in 1939 his only aim was to keep the United States out of the war. But since then, as he swam further out from the political shore, and as the situation around him continued to change, he had begun to feel a need to address other issues. The nation he had come home to seemed to be riddled with problems: the president was too strong, the media was strangely hostile to the isolationist cause, and elsewhere he felt that hidden forces were trying to sabotage his campaign and in other ways drag the country into the conflict. As this stewed in his mind a narrative formed that appeared to make sense of it all: everything that was going wrong in the US was down to 'Jewish influence'.

Like most anti-Semites, Lindbergh had convinced himself, first, that a hidden network of wealthy and powerful Jews existed, and that its members were advancing a secret agenda. Once the idea had taken root, he was able to see 'Jewish influence' in almost anything that went wrong.

At a recent America First rally in Philadelphia, in late May 1941, Lindbergh noticed that by the end of the night many people were wiping sweat from their brows.[6] 'It is quite possible that the ventilators were turned off intentionally,' he wrote, calling this 'mostly Jewish inspired'.[7]

Less than a fortnight later, when a friend went to visit Lindbergh at home, he found the pilot with his son 'cleaning and reassembling' an arsenal of firearms, including several new rifles. 'The floor was littered with them,' Lindbergh admitted, 'a real "5th column" reception.'[8] The pilot explained that he had been teaching his son how to shoot.

Charles Lindbergh saw trouble ahead. Not from without but within. He felt the Jewish 'problem' could take America into a new 'civil war',[9] which would climax in a nationwide pogrom against Jewish Americans. It might 'not be pleasant to look forward to', he conceded, but at the same time it would be 'interesting'.[10]

In that one word, 'interesting', you can sense the strange and at times schizophrenic outlook starting to cloud his mind. He believed a civil war was coming, and in writing his diary he wanted future generations to know that he had predicted this and taken precautions, but on the question of whether he *wanted* this civil war to happen, knowing that it might lead to a pogrom, or if he was willing to light the touch-paper to get it started, he was more guarded. Lindbergh seems to have been gripped both by a fear of what was coming and a lurid fascination with how it might play out. He wanted this rupture and at the same time he was afraid of it. Very soon he would have to make up his mind.

30

Meanwhile the actual conspiracy against Charles Lindbergh and America First was gathering momentum. Pressure groups secretly under British control continued to picket America First meetings and distribute leaflets attacking Lindbergh. They also asked awkward questions in the press about the pilot's links to Berlin. In the days before an America First rally at Madison Square Garden, on 23 May 1941, one of these groups, the ANL, had publicly urged Lindbergh to denounce Nazi Germany 'with equal vigor to your denunciation of American participation in the war'.[1] This he would not do.

At the rally itself, more than one hundred interventionist pro-testers showed up, although they had been forbidden to do so by the police. As America First supporters approached the venue they noticed these protesters, most of them women, stationed at street corners with police protection where they handed out what looked like flyers.

On closer inspection, these turned out to be thousands of copies of a derogatory advertisement about 'ex-Col. Charles A. Lindbergh' which had appeared in that day's *New York Times*.[2] The publication of that advertisement, the money to pay for the copies, the speed with which they had been produced, and the presence of so many interventionists: this was all the work of an energetic new pressure group which had begun to galvanize the interventionist movement. It was called Fight For Freedom, and it had not been infiltrated by British agents. That was because there was no need.

Only the month before, the Century Group – that secretive cabal of influential Americans including press baron Henry Luce, well-known commentator Major George Fielding Eliot, and White House speechwriter Robert Sherwood – had reinvented itself as Fight For Freedom. This was a larger, richer and supposedly more transparent version of the Century Group. Their long-term plan was to become the interventionist equivalent of America First. Where the isolationists had Lindbergh, they would use Wendell Willkie.

In their literature they presented themselves as a popular alliance of American interventionists, free from foreign influence or any ties to the administration. The reality was rather different.

By June 1941, Fight For Freedom officials in New York were on the phone to Roosevelt's secretaries at the White House, Steve Early and 'Pa' Watson, 'at least once or twice a day'.[3] Most of Roosevelt's off-the-record press conferences were read out to them over the phone to keep them *au fait* with the president's thinking. The White House even suggested members of his administration to speak at Fight For Freedom rallies, and gave pointers on who to attack and when, and which line to take on vexatious political questions.

From the outset, Fight For Freedom was 'an unofficial propaganda instrument' for the White House.[4] Its leaders were also hand-in-glove with the British. Stephenson's office subsidized Fight For Freedom by paying to have its speeches copied and mailed out. They also used this new interventionist organization as an outlet for some of the stories pouring out of their rumour factory.

As they had done the summer before, during the campaign to get the public behind the transfer of fifty destroyers, the interventionists at Fight For Freedom, the British and the White House were pulling together. Before, they had been united by a desire to defeat Hitler.

Now they were bound together by the realization that to take on Hitler they must defeat Lindbergh and America First. One of the ways to do that was by linking them to Berlin.

'We feel there is German money and German direction behind the America First movement,' one of Stephenson's officers told a new agent at around this time. 'If we can pin a Nazi contact or Nazi money on the isolationists, they will lose many of their followers. It might be the deciding factor in America's entry in the war.'[5]

British agents were trying to find this link. Under Roosevelt's direction, the FBI was also desperate to uncover it. Everyone in the interventionist camp was searching for proof of a connection, but so far they had found nothing. Then Bill Stephenson had a conversation which looked set to change all that.

Tall and good-looking, with wire-framed glasses clamped up against his face, Henry Hoke had spent most of his career in the direct mail advertising business. He knew everything worth knowing about mass mailings, and much that wasn't. He could sense when a marketing mail-out felt wrong or was somehow fishy, even if he was not always able to articulate how.

The year before, Hoke had become intrigued by a series of mail-outs containing isolationist material from the *Congressional Record*. They had been sent in envelopes bearing a series of congressional franks. Hoke estimated that as many as 250,000 German-Americans were receiving these pre-franked letters. Although the congressmen whose signatures appeared on the envelopes represented constituencies from all over the country, most of the mail had been posted from New York. Hoke was convinced this was a Nazi propaganda ploy. But he had no proof.

Henry Hoke had stumbled upon Hans Thomsen's congressional franking scheme, but he did not have the resources to investigate further. He passed on what he had found to the Postmaster General, US

Naval Intelligence (ONI) and the FBI. He wrote articles about what he had found, gave talks, and even issued press releases telling the world that he had 'declared war on German mail activities in this country'.[6]

Nobody seemed to care. The Postmaster General argued correctly that no laws had been broken, and the FBI and ONI felt there was nothing they could do. Hoke was starting to run out of ideas when one of the people he had met suggested he see a Canadian in New York who might be able to help.

Stephenson realized at once that Hoke's investigation could, if he was lucky, uncover proof of a link between the American isolationists and Berlin. He offered to provide all the help he might need. Hoke agreed, and was soon working with members of Stephenson's office.[7]

Their first challenge was to identify who was sending this mail. Hoke had collected a number of letters which he thought might be part of the Nazi franking scheme. All had been addressed automatically using a machine with a distinctive, light blue font. Stephenson had several typewriter specialists in his office, including the multi-talented Eric Maschwitz, and between them they discovered what kind of device was being used.

'We found that the addressing had been done by an old-fashioned Elliott Addressing Machine which had been out of general use for more than twenty years,' Hoke explained.[8] Stephenson's team also discovered that there were just three organizations in New York using this type of machine. One of these, suggestively, was the Steuben Society, a German cultural association with ties to the German embassy.

Either a British agent or Hoke himself went to the Steuben Society headquarters in New York to find out more. In there, they happened to see a notice inviting supporters of the society to a special meeting, at which they would be given copies of a recent speech by the isolationist Senator Wheeler. They would also be given envelopes with his congressional frank, which they were encouraged to use to send copies of his speech on to anyone they could think of.

This was a breakthrough. A US senator had allowed his frank to be used by a German organization with ties to the Nazis. In late May 1941 Hoke wrote an open letter to Wheeler, accusing him of working with the Nazis.[9] Wheeler might have just ignored it. But in this case he had broken the law, as it was illegal for a member of Congress to use their franking privilege for the benefit of a group or association, such as the Steuben Society.

At last, the story attracted more coverage. Wheeler insisted he had done nothing wrong. Stephenson tried to fan the flames by supplying more details of the franking scheme to Fight For Freedom, where senior staff put out press releases designed to bait Wheeler. Details of this investigation even ended up at the White House. Fight for Freedom members urged the president to comment on the story.[10]

But Roosevelt refused, and after the Post Office Department fined the Steuben Society for illegally distributing franked mail the scandal lost momentum. Stephenson and Hoke had made a start, but they needed to dig deeper.

Hans Thomsen, German chargé d'affaires and architect of the Nazi congressional franking scheme, was concerned by what had happened. But he was not especially worried. It did not seem to hurt his propaganda activities. The announcements which came out of the White House several weeks later were different.

On 14 June 1941 Roosevelt ordered all German government assets to be frozen, and two days later he closed every German consulate in the United States, as well as the German Transocean News Service, the German Railway and Tourist Agencies, and the German Library of Information.

This was mainly in response to a recent incident at sea. Several weeks earlier, an American merchant ship, the SS *Robin Moor*, a low-slung, dumpy-looking freighter, had been on its way to Mozambique when it was stopped by a German submarine. The passengers and crew had been ordered onto lifeboats and the ship was torpedoed and sunk. Although this was not the 'incident' that the president had been hoping for, as there had been no loss of life and no US warships involved, Roosevelt would not let it go unpunished.

His closure of the German consulates and the asset freeze was a reaction as well to the recent arrest and deportation of several German undercover agents operating in the US, including two of Thomsen's best propagandists, Manfred Zapp and Guenther Tonn, and the Abwehr agent Kurt Rieth. The first two were uncovered by the FBI, while the identity of the third had been revealed by Stephenson's office.

This was starting to affect Thomsen's work. Americans were more suspicious of him, his staff and his country, and much less willing to work with them than had been the case twelve months previously. Thomsen had fewer agents to call upon and it was harder to make payments. But just as the Nazi influence campaign was starting to stutter, the argument for staying out of the war received an unexpected boost.

Less than a week after the closure of the German consulates, on 22 June 1941, an avalanche of German tanks rumbled into the Soviet Union. They were soon taking territory almost as fast as they could drive. Early reports of Operation Barbarossa suggested a rout. In itself, this unexpected invasion of Russia did nothing to help the isolationist cause in the United States. But the anti-war movement was invigorated by the news that Roosevelt had come out in support of Stalin, as he did several days after the German invasion.

'I should a hundredfold rather be enslaved by Nazi Hitler than by Red Stalin,' Hamilton Fish thundered on the floor of the house,[11] a feeling shared by many Americans.

The isolationist campaign was revitalized.

Until then even the interventionists had described the Soviet Union as an enemy in all but name. Russian financial assets in the

US had long ago been frozen, and the Soviet and Nazi regimes were often depicted as two sides of the same totalitarian coin. Now the interventionists had to persuade the American people of the virtues of the Red Army. It had been hard enough trying to convince them that Britain was worth saving.

By the end of June 1941, the isolationists were on the front foot again. In the days after the invasion of Russia, Churchill was told that Moscow would probably fall within the next three months. Once Stalin was defeated, Hitler would turn to London. Meanwhile British losses in the Battle of the Atlantic were worse than ever. In that year alone they had lost 2.6 million tons of shipping. Even the most bullish Briton would concede that their armed forces stood no chance of defeating Hitler alone. 'We shall lose,' Churchill privately told an American journalist several weeks later, 'unless you come in – and with all you have.'[12]

Events on the Eastern Front gave the campaign to bring America into the war a new urgency. For Stephenson and many others, Britain's future was no longer being measured in years, but months. He had to go further, and risk more.

'The American people,' Stephenson wrote, soon after the German invasion of Russia, 'are like an audience watching an exciting movie. Hitler is the cunning villain; England the brave but not too bright hero. The sympathy of the entire audience is with the hero but that's about all. They do not see that they are called upon to do anything about it.'[1] His job was to change that, to make them feel that this movie was real and it was taking place in their backyard.

In May of that year, J. Edgar Hoover, Director of the FBI, had come to Stephenson for help. The White House wanted the FBI to investigate a rumour that the Nazis might be planning a coup in Bolivia, but Latin America was beyond the FBI purview. So Hoover asked Stephenson to look into it on his behalf.

Roosevelt's interest in this Bolivian coup was partly down to tungsten, a vital material in the production of various machine tools which was abundant in Bolivia. The president's interest was also a reflection of his 'good neighbor' policy towards Latin America. Throughout his time in office Roosevelt had been friendly and protective towards Latin American countries like Bolivia, always looking to improve trading relations and diminish European influence. This policy had its roots in the Monroe Doctrine, developed in 1823 by President Monroe, which held that just as the US would remain aloof from European affairs, Europe must keep out of the Americas. Hitler seemed to have forgotten his side of this unspoken arrangement.

To investigate the rumoured coup, Stephenson sent one of his brightest young officers to Bolivia. This was Montgomery Hyde, who arrived in the Bolivian capital La Paz with just one contact, a British railway manager. Through him, Hyde met a Bolivian, never named, who agreed that he had heard rumours of this impending coup. But that was it. He had no leads. Indeed Hyde was unable to find anything to shed light on who was behind this plot, when and how it was going to happen, or if it even existed.

Aged just thirty-three, Hyde was a combustible blend of ambition, intellect and a bustling imagination. In peacetime he had been a barrister and would later become a prolific author and Conservative politician. As he threw himself around La Paz in search of clues, no doubt feeling the effects of the high altitude, a wild idea formed in his mind.

Hyde arranged to see his Bolivian contact again. He asked how this Nazi coup *might* play out. The two of them agreed that it would no doubt begin with a senior Bolivian diplomat in Germany, perhaps Major Elias Belmonte, the country's military attaché in Berlin and a fervent pro-Nazi, sending plans for the overthrow of the Bolivian government to his fellow plotters in La Paz. He would probably send these plans to the German Legation in Bolivia, most likely in a sealed diplomatic bag.

'Why not anticipate this development by fabricating the kind of letter Belmonte would be expected to write,' Hyde wondered to himself, without pausing to consider the answer, 'and give it the maximum publicity?'[2]

Excited by his idea, Hyde flew back to New York and presented it to his boss.

Those who worked for Stephenson sensed that he enjoyed big decisions, and had a 'refusal to be either hurried or harried'.[3] Nor was he afraid of risk. 'He was quite ruthless when he came up against a situation where it was necessary to take very great measures,' his deputy later said.[4] This was one of them. Rather than being asked to sign off on a fake story about an imaginary British parachute raid, like the one at Berck-sur-Mer, a member of his staff wanted him to sanction a forgery that could easily finish his career as MI6 Head of Station in the US.

But if this forgery worked, in the sense that it was accepted as real and widely publicized, it might help to bring the United States closer to war. Most polls continued to show that the majority of Americans did not think their country should declare war on Nazi Germany. But if the question was adjusted to include German meddling in South America, the result was transformed. When a special Gallup survey asked in May 1941 – 'If Brazil, Argentina, Chile, or any other Central or South American country is actually attacked by any European power, do you think the United States should fight to keep that European power out?' – 81 per cent of those surveyed said yes. The American people felt differently towards Latin America, and had a more sensitive and, at times, proprietorial relationship with their southern neighbours.

The same was true of Roosevelt's administration. Since the start of the war, in almost every meeting of the joint planning committee of US War, Navy and State Departments the first item on the agenda had concerned Latin America. Roosevelt had recently asked the military to draw up a plan for sending an expeditionary force south in the event of a Nazi-backed coup in a country like Bolivia.

Stephenson understood the possible effect of this story about a Nazi plot in Bolivia. The idea of Germans meddling in Latin America was offensive to most Americans, and there was even a chance it could lead to a nationwide call for war, as a similar story had helped to do just over twenty-four years ago.

In early 1917, the British intercepted and decoded a genuine cable from the German Foreign Secretary, Arthur Zimmermann, which had been sent to the German ambassador in Mexico. This telegram revealed the existence of a German plot to form an alliance with Mexico and Japan and attack the United States. The British passed this to the Americans, it was publicized and became known as the Zimmermann telegram.

Today this is seen as the catalyst to America's entry into the First World War. More than any other incident, the Zimmermann telegram destroyed President Wilson's resolve to stay out of the conflict.

The fake letter from Major Belmonte which Hyde had just proposed could have a similar effect. But was anyone in Stephenson's office even capable of producing it? How would they choose the wording of this imaginary letter? Where would the paper come from? What typewriter to use? Who could fake the all-important signature?

Stephenson would soon find out. With German tanks arrowing deeper into Soviet territory, and a feeling taking hold in his office that time was starting to run out, he approved Hyde's plan.

The forgers got to work. 'First, I was able to obtain a genuine letter signed by Belmonte,' Hyde wrote. This came from the British Censorship station in Bermuda, which also supplied an example of the type of official-looking letter a Bolivian diplomat might send, as well as the right paper. Next Hyde asked his Bolivian contact to write a draft of Belmonte's letter, making sure to imbue the text with the right mixture of diplomatic pomposity, cunning and urgency.

It soon became clear that their greatest difficulty would be faking Belmonte's typewriter and his signature. This was where Eric Maschwitz came in.

Hyde had worked with Maschwitz earlier in the war in a subsection of Section D called Section D/L. Both had been involved in 'Operation Letter Bags', a scheme that fed fake anti-Nazi messages into genuine letters destined for Germany. The operation did not last long and achieved little, but by the end of it Maschwitz knew how to open and reseal a letter and had become expert in customizing typewriters. After poring over examples of Belmonte's letters, Maschwitz worked out which brand of typewriter the Bolivian liked to use, before constructing 'a suitable machine'.[5]

Everything was in place apart from the signature. Hyde had a go at faking it and so did Maschwitz, but neither man was particularly good at copying signatures. Luckily they knew someone who was: Hyde's wife.

Dorothy Hyde also worked in Stephenson's office, and with another member of staff, Betty Raymond, she ran the secretive 'Room 99' dedicated to forgeries and counterfeits. This was a vital element in the expanding British rumour factory. Nobody was allowed into Room 99 apart from Raymond, Hyde and Bill Stephenson himself.

Their speciality was faking signatures, but already Belmonte's was proving tricky. 'We practised it,' Raymond remembered, 'because you must practise, and it was a desperately difficult signature to do.'[6] But no matter how many times they tried, it did not look right.

'Until one day we found to our amazement she could do one half, and I could do the other.'[7]

Using their modified typewriter, Hyde and Maschwitz typed out the text of the message on paper purloined from Bermuda. The unsigned forgery was taken into the sanctuary of Room 99, which was quiet and understandably tense. There was only enough of the right paper to produce one fake letter. So Dorothy Hyde and Betty Raymond had to get their signature right first time.

Standing in Room 99 that day it was impossible to hear the merry din of the street below, of Manhattan on a sultry summer's day. Everything about that airless space left you feeling detached from the world outside, from the office and from New York. Instead the two women focused on the sheet of paper before them. The entire operation pivoted on this moment.

'You cannot hesitate on a signature,' Raymond later said. 'Otherwise you are undone. Because nobody pauses on their signature. You just do it. And if there's the slightest hesitation, but the slightest – it is a forgery.'[8]

So they did it.

Everyone inspected the signature. It looked right. But Stephenson wanted to be sure. So he told Hyde to take this forgery to Ottawa and show it to several handwriting experts in the Royal Canadian Mounted Police.

'We think this is a forgery,' Hyde told the unwitting Canadians, handing over what was in fact his, Maschwitz's, Raymond's, and his wife's handiwork.[9]

The experts examined the document carefully, comparing the fake signature to genuine Belmonte specimens. They looked at the weight of the line, the looping curve of the letters, the speed with which it had apparently been written, before concluding that the fake was genuine.

The final precaution involved Hyde and Maschwitz disposing of their customized typewriter. Late one night in July 1941, the two men went for a walk over the Brooklyn Bridge, pausing at one point to remove the typewriter from a bag and hurl it into the East River. With a satisfying splosh, their work was done.

Now the spotlight fell upon Stephenson. He had to find a way to feed this fake letter into the public domain, and to make it believable. One option was to use the *Herald Tribune*. But there was another approach that might be even more effective. If he could devise a suitably good 'paperclip' to explain how this letter had come into his possession, he might be able to have it presented to the world by the Bolivian government itself.

Stephenson contacted Hoover at the FBI with dramatic news. As he explained, MI6 sources had revealed that a German courier called 'Fritz' would soon be arriving at Recife, Brazil, before heading to Bolivia. He had also heard that this courier was carrying documents relating to the imminent Nazi coup. Stephenson explained to Hoover that a British agent was going to intercept the Nazi courier and 'possess himself of the documents'.[10]

The next instalment in this melodrama came several days later. Stephenson contacted Hoover again to say that amazingly his intrepid agent had found the courier and befriended his female secretary, who had revealed that her boss had on him 'a sealed letter addressed to the German Minister in La Paz'.[11] Perhaps he paused for effect at this point. Next, the German courier had flown to Buenos Aires, where another dashing British agent had shadowed him into a crowded lift and relieved 'Fritz' of his secret papers without his realizing. This sealed letter had since been sent securely to New York, and now Stephenson was willing to have it couriered over to Hoover. The FBI Director eagerly agreed.

Today, this 'paperclip' sounds like a plotline from an early James Bond novel, and it is striking that one of the few people to hear this story in its entirety was Ian Fleming, still working in Stephenson's office. But like most of Fleming's tales, this story about the German courier called Fritz sounded a little far-fetched. Stephenson must have realized this. Knowing he had to do more to make this 'paperclip' plausible, he cabled London about the contents of this letter – without letting on that it was a fake – and asked 'C' to have details of the impending coup passed on to the Bolivian government and to the White House.

While this was happening, Hoover began to inspect the forged Belmonte letter. 'Nothing deceives like a document', Stephenson later said.[12] The FBI Director was convinced. He passed the letter on to the Secretary of State, and within hours it was on Roosevelt's desk. Nobody who saw the document appears to have doubted its authenticity. Next the story went public.

On 19 July 1941, the Bolivian government declared a nationwide state of siege. A shocked President Enrique Peñaranda revealed 'the existence of plans and activities against public order and the legal powers, in connivance with foreign political interests of totalitarian character'.[13] The Bolivian police rounded up suspected Nazi sympathizers. Dozens of Bolivian army officers were arrested. Four pro-Nazi newspapers were suspended. The Under-Secretary of State, Sumner Welles, assured the Bolivian government that in the event of 'an international incident' the US would provide full assistance.[14]

The news of this Nazi plot appeared in hundreds of American newspapers. Each report described Belmonte's letter, the alleged coup and the swift reaction from the Bolivian government. Stephenson waited several days before releasing images of the letter itself, which stirred up the controversy further. Seeing a grainy reproduction of the letter blew away any cobwebs of doubt and made this Nazi plot sound unmistakably real.

Stephenson could not have hoped for more from the Bolivian government, the American press, or from Berlin. 'Gangster Methods of the United States President' was the furious headline in the *Berliner Morgenpost*. 'The Belmonte case exposes Roosevelt as a clumsy forger.'[15] Almost every state-backed German newspaper denounced this letter as a forgery, which of course it was. But they also accused Roosevelt of being behind it, which he was not.

By producing this forgery and going to such lengths to make it feel real, Stephenson had created a situation that worked in two different ways. It fuelled the American fear of a Nazi incursion in Latin America, but it also raised concerns in Berlin that Roosevelt might be willing to go further than before, even to the extent of fabricating documents or inventing coups, in his desire to bring the country into the war.

The reality was strikingly different. On 27 May 1941, just seven weeks before the revelation of the Belmonte letter, Roosevelt had told an estimated 85 million people, the largest US radio audience to date, that a state of unlimited national emergency existed. The next

day's press conference in the White House was packed with journalists hoping to hear details of the sweeping presidential measures
to follow. Instead Roosevelt confessed that he had no plans for any
executive orders.

The disappointment in the room was eerie, like the silence after a
bad joke. The bulk of the US Navy would remain at home. Neutrality
was intact. No American warships were to start convoying goods to
Britain. 'One would suppose that such a declaration would mean
a marked change in the national life,' Stephenson complained at
the time, 'that the country would in effect be put on a war footing.
Apparently, however, there is no difference whatsoever in the life of
the country as a result of this solemn declaration.'[16] The problem was
simple. The president was torn between wanting to provoke Hitler
into giving him an excuse for war, while at the same time becoming
a totemic, unifying figure around whom isolationists and interventionists alike could rally.

At that point in his presidency Roosevelt would never have
approved a scheme like the Belmonte letter. But Hitler was unaware
of this, and was too busy with the invasion of the Soviet Union to
respond in public to what he assumed to be a clumsy provocation
from the White House. Yet he was not so busy that he forgot.

In late June 1941, just as Montgomery Hyde flew to Bolivia for the
first time, Charles Lindbergh took a commercial flight home from
Los Angeles after addressing 80,000 supporters at the Hollywood
Bowl. During the flight he received a dazzling proposal. Reuben
'Rube' Fleet, head of the major airline Consolidated Aircraft, offered
him a position in his company running a new aviation research
facility on a salary of $100,000 a year. Here was Lindbergh's way
out of the isolationist quagmire, and what a way out it was. But he
turned it down.

'He asked me what I *did* intend to do,' Lindbergh remembered. 'I
don't know what it is,' he had replied, 'it's more a direction than an
objective; and what it will lead to, I don't know.'[1]

Charles Lindbergh was soon back at his home, Lloyd Manor, an
elegant white-boarded house on the north shore of Long Island, New
York. The front of the house gave on to views out to sea that made
the rest of the world feel ephemeral and distant. Surrounded by his
wife, his children, his staff and his pets, taking his dog for regular
walks to the bluff beyond their house, Lindbergh pondered his next
move, and he was still thinking it through when he heard the news.

On 8 July 1941 Roosevelt announced that US marines had relieved
the British garrison in Reykjavik, the capital of Iceland. US warships

would soon be patrolling the waters around this distant island. The president insisted this was a defensive measure, but Lindbergh disagreed, and so did millions of isolationists. He saw it instead as 'the most serious step we have yet taken. It may mean war.'[2] For months the president had given the nation fiery rhetoric followed by inaction. Now he had tried the opposite: a bold move that seemed to come from nowhere.

Lindbergh was seething, and at the same time he was feeling under siege. The press attacks on him had become more numerous than before, and dirtier. They came from organizations such as the Non-Sectarian Anti-Nazi League and Fight For Freedom, which had recently recruited Lindbergh's cousin, Augustus, in a bid to stir up tensions in the wider Lindbergh family. Even Louis de Wohl, the celebrity astrologer and British agent, had been told to join in, suggesting that Lindbergh's first son might not be dead after all, but was 'being raised in a Nazi school in East Prussia to become a future Führer!'[3]*

Lindbergh was being attacked both by British agents, and by the administration. He had recently been labelled a Nazi by Harold Ickes, Interior Secretary, and had since heard that 'members of Roosevelt's cabinet were going to "gang up" in an attack on me'.[4] Lindbergh had never experienced this kind of pressure before, which seemed to come both from without and within. Nor had he forgotten the pain and humiliation of having his patriotism called into question by the president. More than ever, he wanted revenge. But he was not sure of the form it should take.

Over the next few days Lindbergh took an inventory of his possessions and financial assets, 'in case I should meet with accident or death'.[5] He also arranged for his records, then stored in various vaults

---

* De Wohl's statement may have planted a seed in the mind of a young Philip Roth, leading many years later to his novel *The Plot Against America*.

and warehouses, to be transferred to the womb-like safety of Yale University. 'In times such as we are now going through, when war may start next month, and revolution next year, and when life itself is uncertain from one year to the next, I prefer to have our records in the safest possible location.'[6] The more he talked about it and the longer he spent walking his dog and gazing out to sea, the clearer the picture became in his mind.

Although he conceded that there were numerous groups within the interventionist movement, 'the Jews are among the most active of the war agitators, and among the most influential.'[7] The handful of people he spoke to all agreed. 'We feel that, on the one hand, it is essential to avoid anything approaching a pogrom; and that, on the other hand, it is just as essential to combat the pressure the Jews are bringing on this country to enter the war.'[8]

An identical sentiment was stirring in Berlin. Just days after Lindbergh had reached this conclusion, Hans Thomsen received fresh orders. He was to tell senior American isolationists that 'of all parts of the population in the United States, the Jews, surely, have the greatest interest in America's not entering the war.' This was a novel twist on the Nazi line about American Jews trying to bring the country *into* the war. Now Berlin wanted to plant the supplementary idea that if the country did go to war, and US soldiers were killed in large numbers, non-Jewish Americans would blame their Jewish countrymen for bringing the country into the conflict. 'The end of the story,' the message from Berlin continued, 'will be that one day all the Jews in America will be beaten to death.'[9]

Thomsen did as he was told and passed this on to 'influential leaders of the opposition', including congressmen who had 'show[n] great interest and indicated time and again how very much they agree'. The only problem, Thomsen explained, was a lack of 'leadership and organization for a possible anti-Semitic movement'.[10] Berlin needed to find an American figurehead for their pogrom.

The Nazis were in awe of Charles Lindbergh. One of Thomsen's colleagues eulogized the 'extraordinary importance of this man', writing that 'Lindbergh represents the best of Americans, who are most important for us now and in the future.'[11] He had also been important for them in the past.

Before the war, Lindbergh had visited Nazi Germany on five separate occasions, and been thrilled by what he called the 'organized vitality of Germany' under Hitler.[12] He had been shown aircraft factories and airfields, and his hosts had fed him exaggerated statistics about the size and strength of the Luftwaffe.

The man largely responsible for pulling the wool over his eyes was Goering, commander-in-chief of the Luftwaffe. Lindbergh had fallen for it, and passed on to the US military the numbers he had been given, vouching for their accuracy based on the unprecedented access he had been given. These figures became accepted estimates of German air power and would influence pre-war policy in Washington, Paris and London.

Although the Germans no longer had direct contact with Lindbergh, one of Thomsen's colleagues, von Bötticher, was in touch with a group of men who did. This band of Nazi sympathisers in the US General Staff was led by Colonel Truman Smith, one of Lindbergh's most trusted friends. They would often discuss 'important military matters' with von Bötticher, and communicated through him with Berlin. Now the Germans wanted these American officers to pass on ideas to their friend Lindbergh, the obvious candidate to lead an American pogrom.[13]

Lindbergh was increasingly certain that 'Jewish influence' was responsible for the country starting to turn away from isolationism. Now he had to decide whether he should keep this theory bottled up, or share it with the nation and to hell with the consequences. In some ways this decision was calibrated by the feelings he had about his father, a man who had stubbornly continued his crusade against

America's involvement in the last war, in spite of the opprobrium pouring down on him. For his son to keep his thoughts to himself on such a similar subject was to turn against the memory of his father, and acknowledge to himself that he had been wrong.

In another sense, this question was about the type of man Lindbergh wanted to be. Since becoming a media superstar he had tried to be known as confidently outspoken and iconoclastic. He loathed the idea of being held back by a sentimental need to say what others wanted to hear. He enjoyed causing a stir with his comments.

He was also influenced by his friends. There is little doubt that at least one of the American military officers in touch with General von Bötticher encouraged Lindbergh to go public with his message about 'Jewish influence', and he probably helped to shape it. In August 1941, for reasons to do with his father, his idea of himself and what he had heard from his military friends, Lindbergh decided that for the sake of his country the best response, the bravest response, to the strange situation in which he found himself was to bring this up with the American people. So he began to write a new speech.

The President of the United States was sunburnt. At least this was the official line, explaining why he could be seen on the fantail of his presidential yacht, *Potomac*, with an oversized fedora keeping the sun from his face. The wide brim of the hat also made it hard to pick out his features.

For several days now Roosevelt had reportedly been cruising off Cape Cod. 'All members of party showing effects of sunning,' ran the latest update from the yacht. 'Fishing luck good. No destination announced.'[1]

If you had spotted the *Potomac* as it came in to shore to load up with supplies, as it did on 7 August 1941, and you had reached for your binoculars, you might have seen the president reclining in a deck chair with his trademark black cigarette holder clenched between his teeth. He looked relaxed. It was reassuring in some ways to see the country's most powerful man taking a break like this, just as millions of fellow Americans were doing at that time of year.

Except he was not. The man masquerading as Roosevelt on the *Potomac* was Ed Starling, head of the White House security detail. The president of the United States was at that time on board USS *Augusta*, flagship of the US Navy's Atlantic fleet, as it raced towards a secret rendezvous with Winston Churchill.

In the hope of keeping details of the summit meeting out of the press until after it had happened, Roosevelt had agreed to this small deception. Two days later, off the Newfoundland coast, the crew of the *Augusta* saw a British battleship, HMS *Prince of Wales*, emerge like a phantom out of the mist. A cheer went up from both ships. Within the hour the British prime minister and the US president were shaking hands for the first time since the start of the war.

After several days of talks, Churchill and Roosevelt produced the Atlantic Charter, a clear-eyed statement of principles shared by both governments, and a bold commitment to every nation's right to self-determination, as well as freedom of the seas and a world without trade barriers. Initiated by the Americans, drafted by the British, this text would later inspire the foundational documents of the United Nations (UN) and the North Atlantic Treaty Organization (NATO). The wording was powerful, robust and broad. It had been designed to appeal to those who had not yet come into the war as well as anyone living under Nazi occupation.

When a translation of the Atlantic Charter reached Europe there was 'an outbreak of violence against Nazis', according to an article in the *New York Post*, 'with 150 German officers and 350 men sent to hospitals in France, Belgium and Holland after a wave of assaults'.[2]

At least, this is what the British had hoped to see. The *Post* story was in fact a response to Sib No. 953, a colourful imagining of how the Atlantic Charter might have gone down.

In reality, Churchill and Roosevelt's Atlantic meeting had little immediate impact. The reaction around the world was one of either suspicion or disappointment. Goebbels, the Nazi propaganda chief, dismissed the Atlantic Charter as a 'gigantic propaganda bluff'.[3] Hitler thought it 'can do us no harm at all'.[4]

Churchill had gone to see the US president in the hope of securing an American declaration of war, but had realized early on that Roosevelt had no intention of giving him this. The president would not even sign the Atlantic Charter. On his return to Washington, Roosevelt offered no sabre-rattling statements. Instead he assured the American people they were no closer to war than they had been before he had gone to see Churchill. Having recently frozen all Japanese government assets, he told the press he was willing to meet the Japanese ambassador.

But the British did not leave empty-handed. On his return to Parliament, Churchill had the mischievous, knowing air of a schoolboy who has seen the examination results early and has done better than expected. In confidence, Roosevelt had told him about the new US Navy Western Hemisphere Defense Plan No. 4, WPL-51, which he had recently approved. Under this new directive, US warships operating under war conditions would start escorting convoys from North America to Iceland. Congress had no idea about this, and nor did the American people. There was more.

As Churchill explained to his cabinet, Roosevelt 'was obviously determined that they should come in', and had said 'he would wage war, but not declare it, and that he would become more and more provocative'. The president had even 'made it clear,' Churchill continued, 'that he would look for an "incident" which would justify him in opening hostilities'.⁵ He would order American warships 'to attack any U-boat which showed itself, even if it were 200 or 300 miles away from the convoy. Everything was to be done to force an incident.'⁶

This was an extraordinary report. If Churchill was to be believed, the president of the United States had said he was willing to risk the lives of American sailors in an attempt to bring his country into the war. Of course, this is what Churchill wanted to hear. He may have leaned on the meaning of Roosevelt's words.

But the president was saying essentially the same thing to others. The Under Secretary of the Navy, Jim Forrestal, told friends that the White House agreed to convoying because 'sooner or later some people thought there'd probably be a sinking of American naval vessels'.[7] Bill Stephenson had heard from sources close to the White House, such as Bill Donovan, Vincent Astor and Robert Sherwood, that the president

> does not wish to follow the [President] Wilson precedent of going to the Congress and asking them to declare that a state of war exists between the United States and Germany. For one thing, he wishes to avoid the long debate which would probably ensue. The President would prefer therefore to involve the country suddenly by means of a spectacular and highly successful coup. In this way the people would be swept off their feet by a triumph of American arms, and the isolationists silenced by a burst of patriotic fervor. After such an incident, he might ask the Congress for a formal declaration, but he might even then consider it wiser to continue an undeclared war.[8]

The president of the United States was unable to *declare* war, only Congress could do that, but as commander-in-chief of the US Armed Forces he could *wage* war, so long as this was in the national interest. Isolationists would argue that risking the lives of American sailors was not in the national interest, and could never be. Roosevelt disagreed, and already he was gearing up to wage war against Germany in the Atlantic.

In public, the president's approach was the same as it had been for months. He wanted to lead by appearing to follow, arranging for others to change public opinion on his behalf so that he could graciously respond to it. He longed to see the polls moving towards intervention, and for there to be more stories in the press about Nazi plots against America.

So he would have been pleased by what he saw in the newspapers shortly after meeting Churchill.

34

'Vichy Embassy in U.S. Shown as Heading Clique of Agents Aiding Nazis' was the banner headline on the 31 August 1941 edition of the *New York Herald Tribune*, followed by a sensational piece, syndicated in the *Baltimore Sun* and the *Miami News*, about how diplomats from Vichy France were working with Nazis and American isolationists.[1]

Vichy France was the French state that had controlled the southern rump of the country and its Algerian dependencies since the defeat of France in 1940, with the spa town of Vichy its capital. Although the Vichy regime was nominally independent, it was effectively a puppet Nazi state. Some suspected that Vichy embassies around the world were being used by Berlin for propaganda or espionage purposes. The *Herald Tribune* story appeared to confirm this. It revealed that pro-Nazi agents were operating out of the Vichy embassy and colluding with several prominent American isolationists. Put another way, it underlined the idea that the US anti-war movement was somehow linked to Berlin.

Over the next five days the *Herald Tribune* released more revelations. The story escalated, until the reaction to the story became part of the story itself. 'The New York Herald Tribune was singled out today for an attack,' the newspaper reported, after public complaints from the Vichy ambassador and its government in France.[2] All over the country other newspapers reported on the story, many of them admiring the *Herald Tribune's* investigative work. But the journalist credited with the story, Ansel E. Talbert, was soon starting to feel sheepish. It was not that he disliked praise, but this was not his story.

Talbert's articles on the Vichy French embassy were based on a treasure trove of material handed to him several days earlier by an MI6 officer. The relationship between the British and the *Herald Tribune* was so close that there was no need for the British rumour factory to bother with a 'paperclip'.

Over the past three months Stephenson's staff had put together a seventy-five-page report on Vichy French activities inside the United States. It was based on hours of detailed investigation, documents intercepted by the Bermuda Censorship station, and brave work by undercover operatives.

The most famous of these today is the MI6 agent Betty Pack, codenamed CYNTHIA, a former American debutante later described by *Time* magazine as the 'Mata Hari from Minnesota'.[3] Married to an infirm British diplomat, Pack had begun to work for the British shortly before the start of the war. Earlier that year Stephenson had taken her on at $250 a month. In May 1941, after Stephenson began his assault on the isolationists, she was given a new task.

Betty Pack was told to infiltrate the Vichy embassy in Washington. She decided to concentrate on the press attaché, a married man called Charles Brousse. In short order she had seduced him and they were having an affair. Pack then persuaded him to help her steal secrets, which he did. But the Frenchman would have refused to do so if he had known she was working for MI6, as he could not stand the British. Pack insisted that she was working for the Americans, and valuable intelligence from the Vichy embassy was soon pouring into Stephenson's office. Much of this went into the press exposé.

The relationship between Pack and Brousse did not finish with the publication of the story. By the end of the war, Pack's estranged husband had died and Brousse had left his wife, so they were married and spent the rest of their lives together.

In the hours after the story broke, the mood inside the Vichy embassy was aggrieved and tense. They were under attack, and not just from the *Herald Tribune*. Several days earlier, the results of the latest Gallup poll had included the response to an unusual question. A sample of the US population had been asked if they thought the Vichy government was helping either side in the war. This was odd. No previous Gallup poll had so much as mentioned Vichy France. Perhaps unsurprisingly, a quarter of those surveyed had no opinion.[4]

The wording of the question was also distinctive: 'In the war between Britain and Germany, do you think the Vichy Government is helping one side rather than the other?' Instead of asking if Vichy France had remained neutral in the war, the question implied that this government was already helping one of the two sides and the interviewee had to decide which one. If a typical American knew anything about Vichy France, it was that this new state was effectively controlled by the Germans. So it was predictable that a majority of those who expressed an opinion, 77 per cent, thought Vichy France was helping the Germans. It was almost as if the Gallup Organization, or someone deep inside it, wanted to highlight the connection between Nazi Germany and Vichy France, and in this way prepare the country for the revelations about to be published.

David Ogilvy is today seen an iconic figure in the history of the advertising industry, referred to on his death as the 'Father of Advertising'. Although British, he seemed to possess an intuitive understanding of the American consumer. Interviewers often asked him about this. Usually he referred back to his time at the Gallup Organization, in Princeton, New Jersey, where he had begun to work shortly before the Second World War, and where he learned a lot about the American mind. Sometimes in those interviews he might add that after the US had come into the war he worked for British intelligence. That was true. But he had also been working for them beforehand.

In late 1940 Ogilvy approached a member of Stephenson's team. He wanted to do whatever he could to help the British war effort, 'even if it was shovelling coal into a battleship'.[5] He volunteered to give up his job at Gallup. But Ogilvy was exactly where Stephenson wanted him to be, so he was told to stay put.

By that stage in his career at the Gallup Organization Ogilvy was an associate director. 'I could not have had a better boss than Dr Gallup,' he recalled. 'His confidence in me was such that I do not recall his ever reading any of the reports I wrote in his name. Once he had worked out the methodology of the research, he lost interest and moved on to something new.'[6] From early 1941, Ogilvy was also working for Bill Stephenson, and would describe himself as 'devoted' to his new boss.[7] Later that year the question about Vichy France appeared in the Gallup poll. This was probably the first time Ogilvy inserted a question in the Gallup survey, but not the last.

Interfering in a Gallup poll was dangerous, as for many Americans the authority of these polls was sacred. The US press would have been scandalized by the idea of British spies tinkering with the inner workings of an organization that seemed to articulate the American mind. But it was a different part of Stephenson's assault on the Vichy embassy that now threatened the existence of his office.

The day before the story broke in the *Herald Tribune*, one of Stephenson's officers, John Pepper, had gone to the FBI office in New York and presented them with the British report into Vichy activities. One detail stood out. Buried in this long, exhaustive document was an admission by the British that since April of that year they had been tapping a telephone line used by a Vichy official in the United States. It was not long before word spread beyond the FBI.

One can imagine the colour flooding the face of Adolf Berle, the State Department official who had once been angling to have Stephenson's office shut down, as he read this British report and discovered the line about wire-tapping, as he did several days after the story broke. Berle was incandescent. Congress had outlawed wire-tapping seven years earlier. The FBI had secretly continued this practice, but the idea of British spies involved in the same activity was altogether different.

If Adolf Berle's pursuit of Stephenson had stalled over the summer, reading about this wire-tap brought it spluttering back to life. Berle did not just object to what the British had done, but the way they had gone about it, the blithe manner in which an MI6 officer had sauntered into the FBI office, delivered a report containing incriminating details, and even had the gall to ask if the Bureau might help the British on this investigation. It was as if MI6 had lost sight of the law forbidding wire-tapping, or the other against unregistered foreign agents operating inside the United States.

On the same day that Berle learned of the wiretaps, he was also told that Stephenson's office had refused, for months, to supply the FBI with decoded versions of their messages to London, all of which passed over a secure FBI radio circuit from a station in Chesapeake Bay, Maryland.[1] For the last five months they, or to be more precise,

Stephenson, had hedged. At first, he told the FBI he was waiting to hear back from London. Next he said that handing over the codes might endanger the lives of British agents. More recently he had said this line of communication must remain secret because it was 'utilized by the President in sending messages to high officials in England'.[2]

This last line was dangerous. While it killed off FBI interest in the matter, it had the opposite effect on Berle. On hearing this, he told the FBI 'he intended to take up the matter of these British coded messages with the President'.[3]

In the days that followed, Adolf Berle put together a detailed case against Stephenson and his office. This would go to the White House. Before he had finished, colleagues in the State Department came to him with a series of even more damaging revelations. They told him that a pair of MI6 officers had recently approached the US ambassador in Colombia and suggested he help plant 'some forged documents' implying a Nazi plot against the Colombian government.[4] Berle was also told that British spies had tried to convince the Governor of Dutch Guiana that a German warship had been seen 'in or near Guiana waters'. His State Department colleagues then passed on the most worrying discovery yet: they revealed the truth of the Belmonte letter.[5]

Adolf Berle became aware of these three Latin American incidents in the space of just a few days. In each one, the British had produced fake intelligence designed to damage relations between Germany and the United States. Berle knew how inflammatory stories like this could be. Even a hint of Nazi interference in the Americas could inflame public opinion. Every poll was consistent on this.

'British Intelligence has been very active in making things appear dangerous in this area,' he informed the Secretary of State, referring to Latin America.[6] Meanwhile word began to spread within the State Department. 'British Intelligence is becoming very bold and daring in this hemisphere, stopping at practically nothing,' wrote another senior official at State. 'Some of us here are very disturbed at the extent to which the British appear willing to go in order to attain specific ends. The case of this Belmonte letter is a very good example.'[7]

The size of Stephenson's operation, the illegal wire-tapping, his refusal to hand over their codes to the FBI, and now the Latin American 'incidents'. It was too much for Berle to ignore. He had to take it to the president.

Berle was then working on Roosevelt's next foreign policy speech, so it would be easy for him to bring it up. But he decided to hold back for the next few days. This was mainly because he was busily rewriting the president's speech to accommodate the recent incident at sea.

Early on 4 September 1941 a British Hudson bomber patrolling the waters south of Iceland spotted a German submarine. The bomber's radio operator contacted a nearby *Wickes*-class destroyer, the USS *Greer*, and passed on the submarine's location. Had this happened the day before, that would have been the end of it. The *Greer* would have carried on with its duties, taking care to avoid the German boat. But from the start of that day the captain of the *Greer* had new orders. Rather than avoid all German submarines, he was to pursue them, and if he felt they posed a threat he could open fire. So the *Greer* changed course and began to shadow the U-boat.

Several hours later, the British bomber radioed through to say it was turning back, having used up most of its fuel. Just before leaving, it dropped four depth charges over the last known location of the submarine.

The German captain of *U-652*, a new Type VII-C submarine, felt the four explosions rumble around him with a savage, muffled intensity. For a moment he could not understand what had happened. The only ship in the vicinity was the *Greer*. His orders were to avoid an incident, but this was different. As far as he could tell, he had been attacked without provocation by a US destroyer. He had both a right and a need to defend himself.

Just before midday, local time, the U-boat fired two torpedoes at the *Greer*. These underwater missiles powered towards their target, the water whitening in their wake. But they were spotted by a look-out on the *Greer*. The American captain turned towards them. The torpedoes missed.

Feeling the same anger as the U-boat commander moments earlier, the captain of the *Greer* proceeded to fire nineteen depth charges in the direction of the submarine. They all missed, and several hours later the two boats separated.

The shooting war between Germany and the United States of America had begun. It was strangely apt that this exchange should have been triggered by a British attack – which the Germans mistakenly thought to have come from the Americans. The same could be said of the Belmonte Letter, and of other provocations to come.

As was so often the case in the shadow war now underway in the Atlantic, the American people were fed a different and tendentious account of what had happened. The official line, reported the next day, was that the USS *Greer* had been the victim of an unprovoked German attack.

The Nazis knew this to be untrue and tried to take advantage. 'There is especial interest in this case here at the highest level,' a German official in Berlin told Thomsen. 'The highest level' was Hitler. 'Please, through the channels at your disposal, immediately upon the receipt of this telegram, get in touch with the leading isolationist members of Congress and try in a suitable confidential manner to make it clear to these members of Congress that there is a unique opportunity here to expose Roosevelt's war-mongering policy and deal it a decisive blow to the advantage of the isolationists.'[1]

A detailed plan was sent over. The Germans wanted isolationists to call for a congressional committee to investigate the incident, for the American sailors to be questioned, and for the committee to find out who had given the orders that had led to this incident. Thomsen followed his instructions, and so did the American politicians he spoke to. On 11 September 1941 Senator Nye called for a full investigation by the Senate Committee on Naval Affairs into the *Greer* incident, listing each of the angles proposed by Berlin. This was echoed by other isolationists.

Several hours after Senator Nye had spoken, the president was wheeled into the East Room in the White House and parked before a bank of microphones. Some sixty million Americans across the nation settled down to listen.

'When you see a rattlesnake poised to strike, you do not wait until he has struck before you crush him,' Roosevelt fumed. 'These Nazi submarines and raiders are the rattlesnakes of the Atlantic.'[2] He then gave a list of lesser incidents, before describing German naval aggression as 'but a counterpart' to the Nazi plots and conspiracies in the Americas, Hitler's attempts 'to make ready for him footholds and bridgeheads in the New World'. Then he referred to the Nazis' recent 'endeavor' to 'subvert the Government of Bolivia' – the presiden's first official reference to the Belmonte Letter.

As a result of all this, Roosevelt said, building to a climax, he had authorized a new naval policy, which he called 'active defense'. American warships would no longer wait to be attacked by German raiders and U-boats. Instead they would shoot first. 'From now on, if German or Italian vessels of war enter the waters, the protection of which is necessary for American defense, they do so at their own peril.'[3]

A forgery produced by Stephenson's office had become part of the public justification for this new stance. Fake news was being woven into the story presented to the American people, making it more colourful and compelling.

Goebbels took Roosevelt's speech to be an unofficial declaration of war. The German Foreign Minister, Ribbentrop, responded to this broadcast by seeking assurances from Tokyo that if the United States declared war, they could count on Japan coming in on their side. Many Americans also heard this speech as an informal declaration of war. The Vermont legislature would very soon declare that a state of 'armed conflict' existed between Germany and the United States.

Roosevelt's speech was well crafted and agile. Colourful invective aimed at Hitler was broken up by reassuring reminders of America's glorious past. He had managed to sound reasonable yet firm, like a homeowner who has endured numerous break-ins, and has decided, finally, that if it happens again he will reach for his gun. The subtext throughout this speech was simple: enough is enough.

It was rhetorically pleasing but at the same time disingenuous. Roosevelt had not revealed that he had already instructed US warships to go after German warships or that they were coordinating with the British, which explained why the USS *Greer* was in a position to be attacked by a U-boat, and how the submarine's location was passed on. The origins of this incident lay in the president's aggressive policy in the Atlantic and a far more intimate Anglo-American military collaboration than most Americans were aware of.

But the lack of casualties on board the *Greer*, and the isolationists' stony scepticism about what had happened, made the response to this speech curiously mixed.

The same could not be said of the other speech broadcast across the country that night, which began in the moments after Roosevelt finished speaking.

Charles Lindbergh listened to Roosevelt's speech from behind a curtain at the Coliseum in Des Moines, Iowa, where he was due to address an America First rally. The speech he was about to give would be broadcast live to millions. Rather than take to the stage before the president, Lindbergh had arranged to speak immediately after him. What he planned to say would serve, he hoped, as a powerful corrective to the president's offering.

'Within a minute of the time he finished,' Lindbergh wrote, 'the curtain went up and we filed onto the platform.' Right away he sensed something was not right. 'We were met by a mixture of applause and boos – it was the most unfriendly crowd of any meeting to date, by far.'[1]

Lindbergh advanced to the podium, looked out on the crowd and began to speak, before experiencing every speaker's nightmare: nobody could hear him.

The loudspeakers had failed. In a moment of sublime serendipity a technical fault had given Lindbergh a chance to pull back from the precipice. The text of his speech was sitting before him, and he knew it would be his most controversial one yet. As the engineers hurried around him, he remained rooted to the spot, awkward and alone. The crowd simmered, waiting to reveal itself. At last the loudspeakers were fixed and the microphones went live.

Lindbergh chose to go ahead.

His voice filled millions of living rooms across the United States, as it had done so many times over the past two years, stern but precise, thin yet clear, familiar without being too friendly.

'Foreign interests', he said, had forced the country to the brink of war. There was 'subterfuge and propaganda' at work and that night, he promised, he would 'pierce through a portion of it, to the naked facts which lie beneath'.

Then he came out with it. The real 'war agitators' were 'the British, the Jewish, and the Roosevelt administration'. The British he let off lightly. 'If we were Englishmen, we would do the same.' Next he turned to the Jews.

'No person with a sense of the dignity of mankind can condone the persecution of the Jewish race in Germany,' he began, and yet 'no person of honesty and vision can look on their pro-war policy here today without seeing the dangers involved in such a policy both for us and for them.' Already he had set up an equivalence between the Nazi persecution of German Jews, which was real, and a Jewish conspiracy to bring the US into the war, which was not. He then suggested that if the US went to war, America's Jews 'will be among the first to feel its consequences. Tolerance is a virtue that depends upon peace and strength,' he went on. 'History shows that it cannot survive war and devastations. A few far-sighted Jewish people realize this and stand opposed to intervention. But the majority still do not.' His message was clear. If America went to war, the wave of anti-Semitism that followed would be intense as well as justified. The Jews would have only themselves to blame. It was exactly the message that Berlin had asked his friends to pass on.

Lindbergh finished this part of his speech with two anti-Semitic tropes, telling his audience about the dangerously 'large' Jewish influence in Hollywood, the press, the radio and the US government, before adding that Jewish thinking was 'not American'. He closed this section with a warning: 'We cannot blame them for looking out for what they believe to be their own interests, but we also must look out for ours. We cannot allow the natural passions and prejudices of other peoples to lead our country to destruction.'

A partial recording of this speech exists, which comes in just before this last sentence. Lindbergh's words are followed by a smattering of applause. No cheering or shouting. Just five seconds of staccato claps. But in his diary he described something else. He remembered how, after he had listed the three groups agitating for war, 'the entire audience seemed to stand and cheer' and 'at that moment, whatever opposition existed was completely drowned out by our support.'

While he certainly had some supporters in the audience, the rest of the recording and every newspaper account of the meeting suggest a divided room. There are numerous points in the recording when Lindbergh loses control of the crowd and is forced to stop by eruptions of booing. One reporter noted that, rather than engage with the hecklers or ask them to be quiet, he preferred to stare in silence at the text of his speech.[2] At one point a pack of cards was thrown on to the stage, knocking over the vase before him. Again, he did not look up. Roosevelt's name was cheered every time he mentioned it.[3] But he remained in a bubble. For Charles Lindbergh, the act of telling the country that a Jewish conspiracy was secretly agitating for war was a moment of such exquisite catharsis that the relief seemed to cut through the response around him. Like someone who admits to an affair, and is so liberated by telling the truth that they find it hard to register the reaction, Lindbergh did not at first understand the impact of what he had just said.

'Utterly repugnant,' cried the next day's *Washington Star*. 'The raising of the racial issue by Charles A. Lindbergh,' began a shocked editorial in the *Chicago Herald Examiner*, one of hundreds of angry responses published the next day, 'is the most unfortunate happening that has occurred in the United States since the present tense international situation developed.' With this speech, the *San Francisco Chronicle* put it, Lindbergh had 'sold his birthright'.[4]

The nation blazed with moral outrage. There were calls for his name to be removed from bridges and streets that had been rebranded after his Atlantic crossing. One religious leader called his speech 'zero hour' for anti-Semitism, urging pastors and preachers to turn on Lindbergh.[5] Many obliged, as did a handful of Lindbergh's most prominent supporters. His speech was condemned in an editorial that ran in the chain of Hearst newspapers, otherwise renowned for their isolationist stance and for having the slogan 'America First' on their banners. The senior Republican and leading isolationist Thomas Dewey attacked Lindbergh's Des Moines address as 'an inexcusable abuse of the right of freedom of speech'.[6] When Senator Wheeler mentioned the pilot's name at an America First meeting several days later, six eggs were hurled at him. In the words of Lindbergh's biographer, Scott Berg, 'few men in American history had ever been so reviled'.[7] Once a living god in the eyes of the American public, Lindbergh had become a monster.

In some ways what he had said was less shocking than his decision to say it. Many of those who heard his speech had already detected an undercurrent of anti-Semitism, but had carried on listening anyway. Some were themselves suspicious of Jews and preferred not to admit them to their clubs or permit them to stay in their boarding houses or apartments, as Eric Maschwitz had discovered. In private, millions of Americans believed, like Lindbergh, that large parts of the media and Hollywood probably were controlled by Jews. But to hear a respectable figure say this in a sombre nationwide address was truly shocking. As one of the editorials put it, 'ordinarily such appeals to racial prejudice are heard in America only from hooded speakers at the cow pasture assemblies of the Ku Klux Klan.'[8]

By making these claims in public Lindbergh had done more than endanger American Jews. He had challenged the equilibrium of a society that frequently struggled to blend the emotional ideal of what it should be with the racial reality of what it was. His words were offensive in their own right, but they were also an affront to the possibility of the American dream.

One of the many public figures who tore into Lindbergh's speech was the man who had become the *de facto* spokesman for the interventionist movement, Wendell Willkie. He called it 'the most un-American talk made in my time by any person of national reputation,' adding that a failure to condemn what the pilot had said was like an attempt 'to pull down the temple of liberty'.[9]

Although he may not have seen his second act coming so soon after his defeat in the presidential election, Willkie had thrown himself into the interventionist campaign and had been busy over the summer. He had addressed numerous Fight For Freedom rallies, making the case for the United States to enter the war. Still a hate figure for conservative Republicans, Wendell Willkie had never been so popular among the American people as a whole. Lindbergh, meanwhile, had never been more loathed. His speech in Des Moines and Willkie's virulent condemnation marked the moment when their trajectories crossed.

This turnaround was what Bill Stephenson and those at Fight For Freedom had been working towards for months. Just as they had attacked Lindbergh, they had cultivated Willkie. Stephenson's efforts to win over the Republican leader probably began with that conversation on the day of Roosevelt's inauguration, in January 1941, and there may have been subsequent meetings. Officials at Fight For Freedom had also done what they could to turn Willkie into the poster-boy for interventionism. 'Our brains department is doing its utmost to find some fresh ideas for you,' one Fight For Freedom official wrote to him in June 1941, a note that hints at the way this group was looking after him and offering him encouragement.[10]

With Willkie in the ascendant, Lindbergh was left to mull over what had gone wrong. He struggled at first to understand what the fuss was about. 'I felt that I had worded my Des Moines address carefully and moderately,' he complained. 'It seems that almost anything can be discussed in America except the Jewish problem.'[11] The public reaction to his speech became proof, in his mind, that the press really was under Jewish control. He felt as if he was being attacked for airing an inconvenient truth.

The banal reality was that he had got it wrong. There was no Jewish lobby pushing for war. Nor was there a secretive network of American Jews across the US government, the press, and the radio, insidiously pushing its own agenda. Much of what he imagined to have been carried out by 'Jewish influence' was instead being done by those working for Bill Stephenson and their interventionist supporters. He was right to feel that there was a hidden alliance hoping to bring the country into the war, and that they were targeting him and America First. But he had rounded on the wrong people. His paranoia was justified, his racism was not.

Almost at once, America First came under pressure to distance itself from Lindbergh. The man who had once been their greatest asset was now a liability. The fall-out from his speech was so bad that the chairman of America First, General Wood, raised the idea of suspending the committee's activities entirely. But he was talked out of this. The leadership of America First wanted to keep up the fight. They also hoped to find out who really was agitating to bring the country into the war.

Later that month, Stephenson had a 'delicate conversation' with J. Edgar Hoover about how the isolationists were still 'diligently' looking for proof of collusion between the British and the White House. He found Hoover 'increasingly nervous of [the] possibility of disclosure by Isolationists of our intimate relations with them.'[12]

Stephenson might have begun to keep his distance from Hoover, Donovan and the other leading American interventionists. Instead he wanted to get closer. With the Germans advancing into the heart of the Soviet Union and the United States still out of the war, Stephenson decided to take his influence campaign into new and far more dangerous territory.

PART FOUR

COLLABORATOR

17 SEPTEMBER 1941

Days Britain at war – 745
Allied shipping losses in the Atlantic (to date) – 6,928,695 tons
Russian soldiers killed, injured, or ill since German invasion –
2,817,303 (approx.)[1]

OCTOBER 1941

Gallup Survey: In general do you approve or disapprove of
President Roosevelt's foreign policy?
Approve – 76%[2]

In the days before Lindbergh gave his notorious Des Moines speech, Bill Donovan moved his fledgling intelligence agency into a brutish, granite-faced block on Navy Hill, in Washington DC, that was known locally as 'the Kremlin' on account of its forbidding façade. As Donovan soon discovered, his agency's new home was also filled with the sickening smell of burned, putrid flesh.

Up until the arrival of Donovan and his staff, the 'Kremlin' was used by government scientists investigating syphilis, some of whom were still conducting experiments on animals as Donovan's team moved in. While the staff of America's first centralized intelligence agency unpacked their belongings, men in white coats took a series of syphilitic guinea pigs, goats and sheep out into the courtyard and had them incinerated.

The omens were not good, and the smell was hard to escape, but Donovan's new agency, officially called the Office of the Coordinator of Intelligence, usually known as 'COI', had got off to an exceptional start. Less than three months after Roosevelt had signed it into existence, Donovan had already established different sections responsible for intelligence-gathering, propaganda, research and analysis, and special operations. Reports were now flowing out of the COI, covering a variety of subjects from the recent sinking of the German battleship *Bismarck* through to the Soviet transportation system or the origins of the British commandos. These were read by the president, senior White House officials and a variety of 'consumers' across the US government. Donovan was even starting to act like the head of a dynamic new intelligence agency, and was often seen in the back of a Buick sedan fitted with a state-of-the-art Zenith portable radio which allowed him to speak to the president while on the road.

Most government officials were impressed by the speed with which the COI had established itself. Some were puzzled, given that they had gone out of their way to slow its growth. The State Department had refused to offer guidance on policy, it frequently held up COI communications, and usually failed to help COI officers out in the field.[1] Most of its staff did not want Donovan's agency to succeed, partly because they thought the COI might interfere with their own work. Also they were worried that its aggressive outlook might threaten American neutrality.

Bill Stephenson's fear was that it might not.

From the moment Donovan's agency was born he had done everything in his power to help it succeed. 'Collaboration began at once,' Stephenson recalled. 'Indeed, together we drew up the initial plans for his agency both as regards establishment and methods of operation.'[2] In Donovan's official calendar of telephone calls and meetings during August and September 1941, Stephenson's name appears thirty-six times.[3] 'We practically lived together,' Stephenson later said. 'We were known on all fronts as the two Bills because we were always together.'[4]

Seeing that Donovan's agency was struggling to produce its own intelligence, Stephenson began to supply his friend with a stream of material from MI6 sources and British Censorship in Bermuda. By writing this material up as if it had come from his own agents, Donovan rapidly burnished his agency's reputation. According to the British official who handled this material, Stephenson 'gave him practically everything'.[5] By the time Donovan's agency had moved into the 'Kremlin', most of its intelligence 'product' was simply repackaged British material.

As well as intelligence, Stephenson supplied Donovan with expertise. With backing from his superiors in London, the MI6 man arranged for British scientists to be transferred to the COI; Ian Fleming, for example, wrote detailed reports on how to run an intelligence agency, for which Donovan later rewarded him with a Colt .38 revolver engraved with the words 'For Special Services'. Stephenson had his own deputy, Dick Ellis, an experienced MI6 officer, set up an office in Washington to answer questions from Donovan and his staff; Ellis was later awarded the American Legion of Merit. Besides intelligence and advice, Stephenson and his SOE superiors in London agreed to Donovan's request to establish a British training centre in Canada, 'Camp X', where American agents could be trained by British instructors.[6]

Stephenson also kept Donovan's political warfare section alive. Initially called the Foreign Information Service, this section would later become 'Voice of America'. Realizing the extent to which it was struggling, Stephenson put his entire radio section at its disposal, including 'intermediaries, news gatherers, translators and broadcasters'.[7] He instructed his staff to pass on background material, intelligence and expertise to their American counterparts, and to give them full access to the shortwave station WRUL, then subsidized by the British and frequently used by Stephenson's rumour factory to spread pro-British and anti-Nazi stories around the world. He also arranged for the BBC to offer this American office guidance, rebroadcast their programmes, and coordinate its shortwave schedule to avoid any clashes. The British then vetted Donovan's 'recruits, trained them, [and] transported them to the field where it placed them in touch with their respective British officials who were requested to assist them'.[8]

For all this there was, perhaps inevitably, a quid pro quo. The most carefully guarded secret inside Donovan's political warfare section was that the British were now supplying weekly 'directives' telling them roughly what to say and when.[9] 'In simple words,' one internal history explained, 'Britain was directing the American political warfare organisation.'[10] When Donovan communicated with his office in London, his messages went via MI6 where they were read, commented upon and often added to. In those first few months the agency seen today as the precursor of the CIA was, in practice, an Anglo-American enterprise.

This was without precedent. Until then the relationship between British and American intelligence had been that of a couple which met occasionally for dinner, with MI5 and the FBI exchanging tantalizing scraps of information. Since then this couple had moved in together and opened a joint bank account. 'Bill Stephenson taught us all we ever knew about foreign intelligence,' Donovan later said.[11] Years later another Bill, this time Bill Casey, then CIA director, credited Stephenson with having 'provided the know-how and the training' that allowed the COI to become 'an effective intelligence service'.[12]

Yet by September 1941, from an official perspective, Donovan had never heard of Stephenson. The two Bills may have been spending a great deal of time together but they went to impressive lengths to conceal their relationship from those outside their organizations. Official liaison between their offices was looked after by a man known for his discretion – the president's son, Jimmy Roosevelt. Even Stephenson's colleagues in London were kept partially in the dark. 'Neither MI5's nor "C's" staff at this end,' wrote one government official, 'know anything about the rather complicated background of Donovan's broadcasting and publicity schemes.'[13]

Stephenson's concern was the same as ever. The extent of his collaboration with Donovan was probably illegal under the Foreign

Agents Registration Act, and for most isolationists it was distasteful. The US Attorney General would soon upbraid the British ambassador for just the *possibility* that the British were working with 'Wild Bill' Donovan, telling him such 'activities were completely in error'.[14] The connection between the two Bills had to be dissembled, one of Churchill's advisers warned, 'in view of the furious uproar it would cause if known to the isolationists'.[15] Even Donovan himself, not a man easily spooked, was 'anxious' about it becoming 'publicly known that the British Government are providing him with directives of a provocative nature'.[16] In Washington, the whispers had begun already. 'Rumour that Donovan is British nominee and hireling of British SIS [MI6] is spreading,' Ian Fleming warned.[17]

By then this relationship had gone too far, and was too important to both sides, for either one to call it off. Donovan needed this collaboration to keep his organization alive and learn from the British. Stephenson wanted it for different reasons. His relationship with Donovan gave him influence over the intelligence being circulated within the US government, and it is striking just how well Britain fares in these early reports from Donovan's agency. This helped to restore some faith in the British war machine, at a time when many American officials remained sceptical.

Stephenson's long-term aim was for the COI to become what one British official called 'an extremely valuable offensive weapon'.[18] What he wanted, really, was for Donovan to wage an undercover war against Germany. This was the final move in the checkmate he had once imagined. 'Wild Bill' may have told him that he 'will go practically any distance bar USA actively participating in subversive activities'.[19] But that might change, and Stephenson knew it.

So did the Germans.

'As soon as the Donovan organisation is on track,' Hans Thomsen warned his superiors in Berlin, Germany should expect undercover American agents in Europe carrying out 'acts of sabotage against the occupying army'.[20] What he did not predict, perhaps because it seemed to be so far-fetched, was that the British had already penetrated this new American agency, and were trying to encourage this offensive spirit. It was essential that this collaboration remained secret from the Germans. Another person who must not find out about it was Berle.

At 10.45am on 17 September 1941, the State Department official Adolf Berle was shown into the Oval Office. This was the moment he had been building up to for months, and almost as soon as he crossed the threshold he began to complain to the president about Bill Stephenson.

The British had refused to share their radio codes, Berle told him, they were tapping telephones on American soil, and they were fabricating incidents in Latin America. Berle had brought with him a 'confidential memorandum' that showed in detail how the British had invented Nazi plots in Dutch Guiana, Colombia and Bolivia.

There is no record of whether Roosevelt skimmed through this document with Berle in front of him, or if he read it later instead. But at the very least, by the end of that session the president of the United States had a rough understanding of what the British were up to. He might have flared up in response, asked for more proof or suggested punishments. He had even referred to one of these imaginary incidents in his recent speech on the *Greer*, and had used it to help justify his stance.

Instead the president's reaction was curiously flat. He 'expressed some surprise', Berle recalled, mainly about the British using the FBI radio without sharing their codes, but finished by saying 'he wanted to check into the matter before rendering a decision as to what steps should be taken'. Only towards the end of the meeting did he give his 'somewhat belated blessing' to Berle's requests that something be done 'to make the British intelligence calm down here'.[1]

'Somewhat belated' suggests resistance on the president's part, which must have struck Berle as odd. With hindsight, however, his reaction was understandable given the relationship between Donovan's office, Stephenson's office and the White House – handled, indeed, by Roosevelt's own son. Unknown to Berle, in the days after he went to see the president in the Oval Office, Roosevelt, Donovan and Stephenson were about to embark on their first joint venture.

One of the president's foreign policy priorities by the time Berle stormed into his office in September 1941 was to deliver more aid to the Soviet Union. Kiev was on the verge of surrender to German forces, Leningrad was under siege, Moscow would soon be within the Wehrmacht's reach. More than two million Red Army troops had either been killed, captured, injured or fallen ill. The Soviets urgently needed more help and Roosevelt was willing to provide it. But first he had to overcome the opposition at home.

In a recent poll, fewer than one in ten Americans believed the Soviet regime was much better than the Nazi one.[2] The majority believed they were both as bad as each other. US church leaders were among those who deeply opposed offering any help to Moscow, largely because of what they had read over the past two years about the brutal Soviet state-sponsored attacks on the Catholic church, particularly in Poland.

The reality was even worse than they imagined. By that point, several hundred thousand Poles had been arrested and imprisoned, many of them clerics, as part of the sovietization of occupied Polish territory. Organized religion in Poland had been targeted repeatedly. Over one million Poles had already been deported or sent to gulags deep inside the Soviet Union: others were executed without charge, including some 22,000 Polish military officers, policemen and intellectuals who were murdered by the Soviets earlier that year in and around Katyn Forest.

Roosevelt needed to present a very different picture to the American people. His envoy to Moscow was the businessman and interventionist Averell Harriman, who was due to visit the Russian capital later that month. Shortly before arriving Harriman spoke to several Soviet officials, including one who told him 'the Poles in Russia had complete religious freedom',[3] a dubious line which he passed on nonetheless to the White House.

The president might have just repeated this in a press conference, in the hope of appeasing some of his church leaders. But he knew it was not enough. He wanted to make this line feel authentic and truthful, so he had a word with 'Wild Bill'.

As recently declassified material shows, Donovan was 'instructed' by Roosevelt to give this remark about Poles enjoying complete religious freedom 'the widest dissemination', so that the president 'might have occasion to comment on it'.[4]

Having no idea how to do this, Donovan approached Stephenson.

The MI6 man came up with a ruse. Stephenson cabled London, suggesting the Polish government-in-exile send a message to Polish organizations in the US, including the Polish embassy in Washington, about the surprising lack of religious persecution experienced by Poles in the USSR. 'Roosevelt would then make suitable comment in order to guide Roman Catholic opinion in America, along lines favourable to ourselves.'[5]

It might have pained the Poles in London to lie like this, given the reality of the situation. But Stalin was the lesser of two evils, and so they agreed.

His plan worked. Within days Donovan had a letter from the Polish ambassador to the United States which he showed Roosevelt.

It described in heart-warming terms the new Soviet tolerance towards organized religion, adding that, remarkably, 'a Polish Catholic church is about to be opened in Moscow, as well as a synagogue for Polish Jews'.[6] In London, the Polish government-in-exile announced at a press conference that the USSR had 'granted full religious freedom to 1,500,000 Poles in Soviet territory'.[7] This story was picked up by the United Press agency and appeared in newspapers across the US.

Later that same day, Roosevelt commented on the news. The year before, he had excoriated Stalin for his attacks on the church. Now he was pleased to report a very different picture: 'The Red government guarantees the same protection to religion and freedom of conscience as does the American constitution,' he told the press. 'Russian Religion Rights Same As Ours, Says F.D.R.' was the headline in the *Chicago Tribune*, one of many pieces to report this.[8]

In the Russian capital the next day, the 'First Moscow Protocol' was signed by officials from Britain, the US and the USSR, guaranteeing shipments from London and Washington including a monthly instalment of 400 planes, 500 tanks, 7,000 tons of lead, and 1,500 tons of tin. With the Soviets haemorrhaging territory, men and materiel, this proved to be a lifeline. It might not have happened but for this deft interplay between the White House, MI6 and the precursor of the CIA.

If you were a congressman looking to put together the case for Roosevelt's impeachment, and had miraculously gained access to a transcript of what was said inside the Oval Office, you could do worse than start here. In order to secure the First Moscow Protocol, the president had used distinctly presidential powers and colluded with a foreign nation to mislead the American people. Go back to 1940 and you could probably add to your list of articles for impeachment the two secret arms sales to the British, and possibly the destroyers-for-bases deal several months later.

Of course no congressman had access to this, and the episode remained secret. Indeed it had been such a success from Roosevelt's point of view that right away he wanted to go further.

On the same day the 'First Moscow Protocol' was formally signed, Stephenson passed on the following to London: the president had told Donovan that from now on he – Donovan – 'was to cooperate with the White House on marshalling public opinion behind the President's home and foreign policy'.[9]

That imaginary congressman who knew what was going on inside the White House would have been rubbing his eyes in disbelief. The president had just instructed the chief of America's first centralized intelligence agency, which was technically unable to mount operations inside the US, to campaign within the country to promote the president's own political agenda.

Roosevelt's instructions to Donovan had been specific. He wanted 'Wild Bill' to set up 'secret public opinion polls in order to ascertain beforehand whether any particular project would have the approval of the majority of the American people'.[10] Donovan was unsure how to go about this. So again he went to Stephenson.

As we know, the British already had an agent inside the Gallup Organization, David Ogilvy. Soon Ogilvy and one of his colleagues, Dr Hadley Cantril, were conducting these secret polls on behalf of the White House. The results were passed on to an intermediary, the former White House speechwriter Sam Rosenman, who relayed them to the president.[11]

Donovan then asked his friend at MI6 to pass on to London a rather cryptic message. He wanted to be sure that if he made any controversial statements in the press about the international situation he would not be contradicted by British officials in London.[12] This was an odd request, but it was agreed to at once in London. It was as if Donovan knew that he might soon be making provocative remarks in public – provocative at home, but also in Berlin.

Around the same time the former US ambassador to France, William C. Bullitt, went to see Roosevelt in the White House. The president told him he would not attack Germany, but 'was determined to make Germany declare war first'.[13]

He did not say how.

On the same day that Roosevelt gave the press conference praising Soviet religious tolerance, Bill Donovan went to see a contact of his, Malcolm Lovell, a prominent Quaker and peace campaigner. But he had not come to discuss peace. Donovan had arranged to meet Lovell because this man knew Hans Thomsen at the German embassy. Donovan asked Lovell to make an outlandish proposal to the German chargé d'affaires: the US government was willing to pay him $1,000,000 to denounce the Nazi regime and 'publicly distance himself from Hitler's government'.[14]

Donovan was trying to buy Thomsen's defection. If the German accepted 'Wild Bill's' offer, Hitler would be furious. If he did not accept and reported it to Berlin, Hitler would be furious. If he paused to consider it and the news of this leaked out to Berlin, again, Hitler would be furious. Indeed there were few scenarios in which this did not end up antagonizing Hitler and the Nazi regime. It is also hard to imagine this deeply provocative offer being made without the tacit approval of the White House: and without a word of advice, or at least inspiration, from Bill Stephenson.

Lovell listened carefully to Donovan's offer, and agreed to pass it on to Hans Thomsen.

Several months earlier, Eric Maschwitz had been told to leave Stephenson's office in New York. Although he had worked hard since his
arrival in New York, some colleagues had wondered from the start if
he might be 'more interested in the theatre than in Intelligence and
Special Operations'.[1] Maschwitz spent most of his spare time in Manhattan either working on the draft of his next play, or helping friends
of his on their new Broadway production, where, true to form, he
had fallen in love with the lead, in this case Margot Grahame. At the
time, Maschwitz's music could be heard in two films playing in the
cinemas, including the new Fritz Lang thriller *Man Hunt*, backed by
a haunting, elegiac version of 'A Nightingale Sang in Berkeley Square'.
(This was the first war film to fall foul of the then scrupulously neutral Motion Picture Production Code, or Hays Code, for its negative
portrayal of Germans.)

Maschwitz was clearly enjoying his life in Manhattan, when he
made a chance remark to a colleague in the Rockefeller Center.

'One thing we haven't got is a good forgery section,' he said.[2] Very
soon this was passed up to his boss.

Bill Stephenson had always liked Maschwitz, and admired his 'very
clever, inventive mind'.[3] He called him into his office after hearing
this, and told him he had for a long time wanted to have a dedicated

forgery section, one that could produce fakes 'good enough to defy the most microscopic examination and chemical tests'. Room 99 was useful, but he liked the idea of something bigger and perhaps better. The section he envisaged would only release a document if it was 'an exact imitation down to the smallest detail of what it purported to be'.[4] But Stephenson knew that he could not launch this forgery section on American soil for fear of it being traced back to him. Instead he wanted to set it up in Canada, and until then he had been unsure as to who should run it.

By September 1941 Eric Maschwitz was in Toronto, Canada, running Stephenson's new forgery section. It was called 'Station M' – 'M' was for Maschwitz – and was housed in Casa Loma, a sprawling revivalist mansion on a hilltop overlooking Toronto. Having recently fallen into disrepair, this eccentric building was one of the last places anyone might expect to find a British forgery unit, which was why it had been chosen.

On his daily commute to work, Maschwitz would change into workman's overalls before reaching Casa Loma, so that nobody became suspicious of him or the swarm of men buzzing in and out of this otherwise rundown building. Dressed as a workman, the celebrated lyricist would make his way down a long tunnel beneath the mansion, the sound of his footsteps echoing around him, until he reached the door leading into Station M itself.

Inside was a secretive, crepuscular world. There were chemists from Cambridge, an expert graphologist who could recreate almost anyone's handwriting, and two 'wonderful ruffians', as Maschwitz called them, a pair of 'marvellous' typewriter experts who until recently had run a machine repair shop on a Toronto backstreet. They were 'enormous enthusiasts for the whole thing', he explained, who 'could really reproduce any typewriter imprint, with all the mistakes'.[5] Paper was provided by a large Canadian paper company, which could source almost any weight, grain or colour that might be required.[6] A trove of original documents for reference had also been supplied by British Censorship in Bermuda, as well as sample inks and stationery.

Stephenson's rumour operation had entered a new phase, and so had the story of Eric Maschwitz's war. Not since he had been posted to Yorkshire in 1940, and told to prepare for the German invasion, had Maschwitz felt so removed from the cosmopolitan worlds of theatre, music and film. As he had found earlier, the distance brought out a different side of him, a more serious version of himself and he found it easier to concentrate on the work at hand.

If there had been moments when Maschwitz had forgotten about the war while living in New York, these were less frequent in Canada. News broadcasts were dominated by the latest developments. In mid-October 1941 Maschwitz read about the new administration in Tokyo under the hawkish General Tojo. He also saw the depressing headlines from the Eastern Front: the Soviet government was about to be transferred to an undisclosed location east of Moscow; Stalin was on the edge of defeat.

The day before, 17 October 1941, Maschwitz had heard about a U-boat attack on the British transatlantic convoy SC-48, which might not have been major news but for the presence in the escort of several American destroyers, including one, the USS *Kearny*, which had been hit by a German torpedo.

US warships had been assisting the British in escort duties for just over a month now, but until then there had been no casualties. This was largely due to the British using decrypts from Bletchley Park to keep convoys away from U-boats. But on the night of 16 October 1941, the intelligence had failed. A lone German submarine, U-553, began to attack a British convoy, and was soon joined by a pack of U-boats. Over the next few hours, in the dark of the night, several merchant vessels were sunk and the USS *Kearny* was struck. Although the ship limped back to Reykjavik for repairs, twenty-four American sailors were injured and eleven killed. They were the first casualties in the undeclared war between Germany and the United States.

Berlin dismissed the USS *Kearny* story as 'staged', claiming a British diplomat and White House official had been heard discussing 'the staging of an incident'.[7] 'There is not a single word of truth in this made-up, trumped-up story,' the report continued, dismissing it as 'Jewish trickery' from Roosevelt.[8] Some German sources claimed the Americans had torpedoed their own ship, and this doubt was not confined to Germany. In the days after this incident one US reporter asked the president why the *Kearny* was still afloat if it really had been hit by a torpedo.

The attack on the *Kearny* was concerning, but it did not inspire a nationwide call for war. Ten days later came another incident which looked as if it might do just that.

On the evening of Navy Day, 27 October 1941, the president of the United States was helped up to a temporary podium in the capital's Mayflower Hotel to give what he knew would be his most provocative speech since the start of the war. It was also his angriest. The audience welcomed him with a standing ovation. On either side of the president were explosions of flowers, and overhead a pair of lifebuoys strung from the balcony, a reminder of the day's nautical theme. Behind him was a team of secret service agents in tuxedos, scanning the hall like a battery of searchlights.

They looked out onto distinguished military figures, politicians, judges, diplomats, and their wives, all bathed in a mist of cigarette smoke. Once the applause had died away, everyone returned to their seats and the president began.

Speaking clearly and slowly, enjoying the cadence of each word and often elongating his vowels with an almost theatrical flourish, Roosevelt started with a precis of the international situation. 'The shooting has started,' he intoned. 'And history has recorded who fired the first shot. In the long run, however, all that will matter is who fired the last shot!'

He poured everything into those last few words, finishing with a whinnying flick of his head. It worked. He won the applause he needed to set him up for the next line:

'America has been attacked.' This was crucial. The year before on the campaign trail he had promised never to initiate a military encounter. Acting in self-defence was different.

Next he delivered the news for which this speech would be remembered. 'Hitler has often protested that his plans for conquest do not extend across the Atlantic Ocean. But his submarines and raiders prove otherwise. So does the entire design of his new world order.' He paused for effect.

'For example, I have in my possession a secret map made in Germany by Hitler's government by the planners of the new world order. It is a map of South America and a part of Central America, as Hitler proposes to reorganize it.' He described this map in more detail, before cutting himself off. 'That is his plan. It will never go into effect. This map makes clear the Nazi design not only against South America but against the United States itself.'

Obtaining this map appeared to have been a major intelligence coup. The US government had managed to uncover a document that proved the existence of German plans to take over Latin America, a discovery which could have an effect similar to the Zimmermann telegram during the last war.

That was not all. 'And your Government has in its possession another document made in Germany by Hitler's government,' Roosevelt went on.

It is a detailed plan, which, for obvious reasons, the Nazis did not wish and do not wish to publicize just yet, but which they are ready to impose a little later on a dominated world – if Hitler wins. It is a plan to abolish all existing religions – Protestant, Catholic, Mohammedan, Hindu, Buddhist and Jewish alike. The property of all churches will be seized by the Reich and its puppets. The cross and all other symbols of religion are to be forbidden. The clergy are to be forever silenced under penalty of the concentration camps, where even now so many fearless men are being tortured because they have placed God above Hitler.

The president continued, his voice an irresistible blend of outrage and authority: 'In place of the cross of Christ will be put two symbols – the swastika and the naked sword. A god, the god of blood and iron, will take the place of the God of love and mercy. Let us well ponder that statement which I have made tonight.'

In one speech Roosevelt had given the American people proof of Nazi plans to interfere with two things they held dear – religion and Latin America. He did not produce either the map or the plan for abolishing religion, but the respect most Americans had for his office and the trust they had invested in him as president meant that the majority of those listening believed him anyway.

In Toronto, one of those listening to Roosevelt's speech was Eric Maschwitz. If most people found what the president had to say sobering, for Maschwitz it was strangely thrilling, like hearing one of his songs on the radio for the first time. The Nazi map of South America and the document describing Hitler's plans to abolish religion could shatter relations between the US and Germany. They were controversial, unexpected and potent. They were also exquisite forgeries, Maschwitz's finest yet.

It had all begun several weeks earlier, innocuously, when an Old Etonian stockbroker with one leg two inches shorter than the other made a doodle on his desk blotter. Ivar Bryce was an old friend of Ian Fleming, who had persuaded Stephenson to take him on. Codenamed G.140, good-looking and gung-ho, Bryce was part of Stephenson's Latin American section. He longed to find evidence of a German plot to invade South America, but was also aware that this plot might not exist. Allowing his mind to wander, he had imagined how the map of the continent might look if Hitler took control, until he had sketched out a revised map of South America.

'It was very convincing: the more I studied it the more sense it made.' Crawling further into Hitler's mind, Bryce enlarged or shrank each country, and in the case of Uruguay abolished it altogether, until he was left with one German colony and four vassal states covering the whole continent. 'It made me feel the heady power of king-makers,' he remembered, 'and I drew most carefully a detailed extension of the idea, as it would appeal to Hitler, for submission to the powers that be, to wit Bill Stephenson.'[1]

Bryce stood before his chief, deep inside the Rockefeller Center, scanning his face for a reaction. The idea was similar to the Belmonte forgery which Stephenson had approved several months earlier, albeit bolder, more ambitious and potentially far more effective. Rather than suggest Berlin merely had designs on Bolivia, this implied a plan to conquer South America in its entirety.

Stephenson knew about the sudden and galvanizing effect of the Zimmermann telegram, and was in awe of it. Bryce's map could have a similar impact. It would certainly achieve more than a hundred appeals to conscience. Was there also a moral dilemma for him to resolve? Almost certainly not. Much like the people he was fighting against, Bill Stephenson's political ethics were by then grounded in the singular belief that the end justified the means. He had decided long ago that the threat of Hitler warranted mass deception on a nationwide scale, a feeling shared by most of those working for him on the thirty-fifth floor of the Rockefeller Center, an unlikely blend of émigrés from across Europe, British MI6 and SOE officers, individuals invalided out of the army, Christians and Jews, men and women, including hundreds of Canadian secretaries. They saw their lies as white lies. The constraint they felt was not so much ethical as practical: the fear of being found out.

Stephenson approved Bryce's map idea, and soon passed on the details to Maschwitz and his colleagues in Station M. Applying everything he had learned over the last two years, Maschwitz oversaw the production in just two days of the fake religious document as well as the South American map, 'slightly travel-stained with use' but so convincing that 'the Reich's chief mapmakers for the German High Command would be prepared to swear [it] was made by them.'[2] The paper was right. The inks were consistent with those that might have been used by a Nazi official. The language and jargon was convincing. The handwritten notations looked just like those which might have been written by a German bureaucrat. It was an extraordinary feat of forgery.

The next Bryce heard about this was 'the merest whisper of a hint' in the office that Roosevelt's upcoming radio broadcast 'would be of interest' to him.[3]

The president's Navy Day speech was major news, and the next day's press conference in the White House was packed. Hundreds of journalists wanted more details on the two documents he had referred to.

Roosevelt was the first American president to master the art of the press conference, holding more than any of his predecessors, and to greater effect. His first had been such a delicious contrast to the thin gruel dished up his predecessor, Herbert Hoover, that the journalists 'broke into applause when he finished'.[4] There was no applause this time.

Most journalists had come to see the map for themselves, and while Roosevelt admitted it was in his possession he said that he could not show it to them owing to 'certain manuscript notations' that might 'jeopardize the source and perhaps eliminate a fountainhead of valuable information'. The same went for the Nazi document on religion. Roosevelt added that he 'had not even permitted representatives of any of the American republics to inspect the map', but, thinking about it more, he 'might do so in the future under pledges of strictest secrecy'.[5]

At least one reporter was sceptical. He asked if the map might actually be 'a forgery or a fake of some sort'.

At first, Roosevelt fenced. Of course not. Pushed harder, he explained huffily that the map had come from 'a source which is undoubtedly reliable. There is no question about that.'[6]

The press conference finished, and Roosevelt moved through to a different part of the White House for cocktails and lunch with the Duke and Duchess of Windsor, who were visiting from the Bahamas where the Duke was serving as governor. Roosevelt had seen off the first attack on this South American map and the religious document. The next one would be stronger.

The reaction from Berlin was a foghorn of indignation. 'Drawing on what should be their last reserves of invective, Berlin circles –

both official and semi-official – including press and radio, today discharged a verbal blast of such magnitude against the President of the United States over his Navy Day speech,' reported the *New York Times*, 'that earlier efforts to disparage Mr. Roosevelt, even in the gutter-strength vocabulary of the Stuermer [the notorious Nazi tabloid], pale into insignificance.'[7] 'Slanderous' was how one Nazi official described the documents; 'forgeries intended to outdo all previous forgeries.'[8]

Behind the scenes there was even confusion in the German government as to whether these documents might be genuine. An investigation was launched. After concluding that they were not real, the German press speculated that 'the British made the maps, and the British air forces dropped them from the skies early in October. Where this was done is not stated.'[9] Other German newspapers suggested they came from 'the workshops of Jewish forgers.'[10] The truth was that Berlin did not know where they had come from, only that they were fakes.

The German Foreign Ministry responded formally to Roosevelt's speech with a stern rebuke. 'There does not exist in Germany any map drawn up by the Reich Government regarding partition of Central and South America, nor any document prepared by the Reich Government concerning abolition of religions of the world. In both instances therefore forgeries of the crudest and most brazen kind must be involved,' it began, before describing these allegations as 'so ludicrous and absurd that the Reich Government sees no need for discussing them.'[11]

The president responded to the Nazi government in the most offensive way possible. He failed to take them seriously. 'The President asserted, laughingly, that Nazi denunciations sounded better in German than in English.'[12] The *Pittsburgh Press* reported that Roosevelt called the German allegations of fakes and forgeries 'a scream', adding that Nazi claims about the map 'are to be taken no more seriously than the German charge that he personally torpedoed the destroyer Kearny'.[13]

Roosevelt appeared to be unblemished by even a speck of doubt. Did he know these were British forgeries? Put another way, had he collaborated with one foreign nation to provoke another, a clear abuse of the public trust in his office (and, if it ever got out, another article of impeachment)? Or had he simply been fed bad intelligence?

The answer depends mainly on *how* these documents came into his possession. Stephenson spread one story in his office about having planted them on a German living in Cuba, and later arranging for the FBI to arrest him. The reality was that he gave them to the same man who introduced Roosevelt at the Navy Day dinner, the first person thanked by the president as he began to speak: Bill Donovan.

'Wild Bill' later admitted that the religious document was 'probably supplied by BSC', the official title for Stephenson's office.[14] The text also bears a close resemblance to one produced several months earlier by Douglas Miller, previously an American diplomat in Berlin and soon to be Donovan's assistant. It was in all likelihood an Anglo-American collaboration, while the map was exclusively British in origin. At least one MI6 officer said of the map: 'Stephenson gave it to Colonel Donovan',[15] and there is little doubt Donovan handed both documents to the president when he saw him in the White House on 21 October 1941.

But did Roosevelt have any reason to suspect they could be British forgeries?

Yes, many. The president was fully aware of the relationship between Donovan and Stephenson. His son, Jimmy, was after all the official liaison between the two. Much of the intelligence Donovan passed on to Roosevelt, over two hundred memorandums in the latter half of 1941, had come originally from British sources and, as Donovan's biographer noted, 'Roosevelt suspected he was getting London's reports under a different wrapper, but never complained.'[16]

Even beyond government circles it was said that 'Donovan was Roosevelt's man working with British intelligence.'[17] When the president finally decided to act on Adolf Berle's complaints about Stephenson, it is telling that he did not go to the British embassy. Instead he contacted Bill Donovan.[18]

Roosevelt was not just aware of this relationship. He encouraged it, and was himself part of it. Several weeks after the Navy Day speech, Stephenson made an extraordinary admission, one that has only come to light in recent years. As newly declassified files confirm, he cabled his superiors in London to say that British 'operations of any importance directed against [American] isolationist groups had been approved by President Roosevelt beforehand.'[19] This would have happened via Donovan. One US official revealed, in private, that the president had agreed to setting up Donovan's office partly 'to work out an effective and active cooperation with the British, even to the extent of participation in the war'.[20]

Did Roosevelt have any reason to think the British might supply Donovan with dodgy intelligence concerning Latin America?

Very much so. Only the month before, Berle had given him details of three separate incidents involving British agents either misdirecting American officials, feeding them fake documents or trying to collaborate with them on a forgery. All had served the same goal: to make the American people think the Nazis were looking to establish a foothold in Latin America. The map that Roosevelt had been handed by Donovan, a known conduit to MI6, would have precisely the same effect.

It would imply a troubling lack of imagination if Roosevelt had *not* suspected these documents to be part of a British ruse. All the evidence suggests he knew Eric Maschwitz's documents were indeed fakes. But they served British purposes as well as his, so he used them anyway.

Several weeks earlier, Roosevelt had told Lord Halifax, the British ambassador, that he would keep doing 'whatever he best could' to help Britain, but would not declare war on Germany. 'Declarations of war were, he said, out of fashion,' the ambassador relayed to Churchill. 'It pretty well confirms my view, which I think is yours, that [Roosevelt] is going to move to the undeclared war rather than the other [a declared war], although no doubt things might change overnight if the right things were to happen!'[21]

Churchill knew, Halifax knew, Stephenson knew and Donovan knew that Roosevelt was no longer willing to wait passively for events to unfold before him, in spite of what he told the American people. He wanted to act. He needed an incident. The president understood the threat posed by Hitler, and that to meet it the United States must come into the war. It mattered to him less than ever how this happened. As one of his biographers later suggested, 'what the preservation of the Union had been to Lincoln, the defeat of the Axis now was to Roosevelt.'[22] By this stage in his presidency he was willing to do whatever he could to make 'the right things' happen. His Navy Day speech was the latest example of this.

One of the most recent postings to the British embassy in Washington DC was a twenty-six-year-old assistant air attaché called Roald Dahl. Not yet the renowned children's author, Dahl had been invalided out of the RAF and was now adjusting to life in the US capital, where he became intrigued almost at once by the way his colleagues referred to a shadowy figure called Stephenson.

'I very soon realized that everybody in any position of power either from the British ambassador down or on the American side knew about this extraordinary fellow up there,' he said, meaning New York.[1] On the backstairs of British officialdom, the legend of Bill Stephenson was starting to take shape, and his handling of the South American map proved to be a catalyst. The men and women who had worked for him at the start of his MI6 career, sixteen months earlier, when he seemed to have no idea what he was doing, would have been bemused. Stephenson's reinvention was almost complete. 'C's' experiment had worked.

Stephenson was decisive and had imagination, but above all he was a good administrator. His operation now covered the entirety of the thirty-fifth floor of the Rockefeller Center, and would soon expand into the floor above, but visitors and new recruits alike were struck by the efficiency of this office, and its energetic atmosphere, so hard to maintain in an operation of this size. Nowhere was this more pronounced than within the rumour factory.

'Wounded Germans on the Russian front are being left to die, many commit suicide and others are killed by their comrades to spare them from slow death,' the *Newark Ledger* assured its readers several days before Roosevelt's Navy Day speech, one of many British 'sibs' then being fed to the American press. 'Typhoid Epidemic Reported Raging Behind Nazi Lines', the *New York Post* warned on the same day.[2] Other 'sibs' described the Sicilian Mafia taking on the Fascists; the Germans running out of men; ersatz morphine causing thousands of deaths in the Germany army; Nazi generals spying on behalf of the Soviets or plotting to kill Hitler; desperate Gestapo purges; and, the pick of them all, the story of Italian troops in North Africa who were so terrified by the prospect of fighting the British that they had arranged to be seen by German psychologists.

In just one week in November 1941, twenty-one of these fake news stories appeared in an array of American publications from the *New York Post* and *Boston Globe* to the *Chicago Times* and the *Christian Science Monitor*. Others appeared regularly in the *Herald Tribune*, the *New York Times* and *PM*.[3] British rumours that did not make it into newspapers went out over WRUL radio, or they were turned into whispers and spread among American dockers and stevedores. At the same time, Stephenson's staff continued to run agents like Joseph Hirschberg inside interventionist pressure groups.

These were the central pillars of Stephenson's operation: rumours and groups. Another was his collaboration with Bill Donovan. During the final few months of 1941 he had also developed a fourth and final element of his campaign, arguably more effective than any other.

By 1941, the American Legion was the nation's leading association of military veterans. It had close to one million members and was staunchly isolationist. When polled shortly after the start of the war, almost two-thirds of its delegates said they 'would take no sides' in the conflict.[4] Few had any objection to US manufacturers selling war materiel to Nazi Germany. The Legion was described in the *New York Times* as 'one of the most influential organizations in the United States' whose 'endorsement of proposed measures or policies attracts a large following at once.'[5] If the American Legion came out in support of a particular policy, there was a good chance that many middle-aged white Americans, who could be counted on to vote but who might evade the pollsters' nets, were also likely to support it. Congress followed the pronouncements of the American Legion with interest.

In the days after Lindbergh's speech in Des Moines, in September 1941, thousands of American Legionnaires descended on Milwaukee, Wisconsin, for their annual convention. The night before it began, America First held a rally in Milwaukee that was picketed by members of Fight For Freedom,[6] who also managed to get inside the hall and heckle the speakers. One of those on stage was the ubiquitous Hamilton Fish, who was handed a note in the middle of his address by an elderly female protester labelling him a 'fifth columnist'.[7]

Nothing about this protest was arrestingly unusual, or had the potential to change the way millions of Americans thought about the war. But elsewhere in Milwaukee that night an operation was underway which might.

As Hamilton Fish struggled to make himself heard over the hecklers, British-backed pollsters were conducting a survey. They worked for Market Analysts, a private polling company run by a man called Sanford Griffith, who, since May of that year, had formally joined SOE and begun to work from Stephenson's office in the Rockefeller Center.

The Market Analysts pollsters, paid for by the British, spent the night asking a cross-section of legionnaires whether they wanted their country to go to war. The next day, as thousands of veterans either took part in or watched the legion's parade, described in the press as 'a seemingly endless stream of colourful drum corps, strutting majorettes, gaily attired bands, and marching veterans', witnessed by almost a million spectators,[8] the pollsters carried on with their work. By the end of that day they had interviewed 779 legionnaires from a total of 38 states. They collated their data and passed it on to local representatives of Fight For Freedom, who then put it out in a press release the next day.

The results were astonishing. 'Nearly three-fourths of those attending', the release stated, including many 'officials and delegates', favoured 'breaking diplomatic relations with Germany and Italy'. This would take the US dangerously close to war. The story was picked up by the two major news agencies, Associated Press and United Press, and relayed to newspapers throughout the country, including those in Milwaukee itself, where legionnaires now read that most of their fellow veterans appeared to be moving towards intervention.

The next day, the American Legion approved a controversial resolution, a complete reversal of its earlier position on the war: 'Our present national objective is the defeat of Hitler and what he stands for'.[9]

'Legion Routs Isolationists' was part of a shocked front-page headline in the *New York Times*.[10] A report in the *Chicago Daily News* attributed this turnaround to one thing: 'the wishes of the rank and file', which had been 'borne out by a sampling poll'.[11]

As the last of the legionnaires left Milwaukee, an encrypted message went from Stephenson's office in New York to SOE headquarters in London, confirming that they 'had taken successful steps in connection with a vote taken at the National Convention of the American Legion'.[12]

What were these steps? Did the legionnaires genuinely want to go to war, or had their feelings been misrepresented? The story of another major convention targeted by Stephenson, less than two months later, gives a better sense of how these pollsters worked, and why their technique was so effective.

This was the annual convention of the Congress of Industrial Organizations (CIO), a vast alliance of trade unions that represented over five million American workers. In November 1941 the CIO delegates arrived in Detroit, Michigan, for their annual conclave. Similar to the American Legion, this organization was famously isolationist, and its leader, John L. Lewis, who loathed Roosevelt and had a stranglehold on the CIO, wanted to keep it that way.

Stephenson had other ideas. His efforts to turn the CIO away from isolationism were centred on a poll remarkably similar to the one that had been used in Milwaukee.

As the CIO delegates arrived in Detroit they were approached by pollsters wanting to know if they supported Roosevelt's foreign policy. The pollsters claimed to be working on behalf of Fight For Freedom, but really they were employed by Market Analysts, which was run by the British. According to their 'partial poll', taken as delegates arrived, 92 per cent of their sample 'favoured America's entry into the war against Germany'.[13] The results of the next day's poll were also manically emphatic: 98 per cent of the CIO delegates believed 'it more important that Hitler be defeated than that the United States stay out of the war'.[14]

Both results received national coverage. They were also featured heavily in local papers and newsletters seen by CIO delegates at the convention.[15] This was crucial. Very soon after, on 18 November 1941, to some amazement, the CIO delegates passed a resolution giving their full support to Roosevelt's 'forthright foreign policy'.[16] On the front-page of the New York Times this was described as a 'routing' of 'the isolationist forces'.[17]

How did the British consistently get the results they wanted? They made sure the wording of each question steered the respondent towards particular answers. The order in which the questions were asked mattered, and so did the emphasis pollsters gave to each one, and even the clothes they wore. Interviewees will always respond to the social background of the interviewer. Market Analysts also took the time to test out their questions beforehand on sympathetic CIO delegates, and used their feedback to change the wording. But the key to their success was the speed with which they worked. In both Milwaukee and Detroit, the pollsters had the results of their partial polls published during the first forty-eight hours of the convention, when many delegates were still taking the temperature and working out their position on key issues. Timing was everything.

For any American reading about these two conventions in the closing months of 1941 the message was clear. America's workers had come round to intervention, and so had its military veterans. Few could have guessed at the role played by the British.

The isolationist cause appeared to be on the retreat, and so was the group at the heart of it.

43

The decline and fall of the America First Committee began with Charles Lindbergh's speech in Des Moines, but it accelerated later that month. The final crisis in its short history began on 23 September 1941, when a man called Prescott Dennett received a phone call, after which he put down the receiver, thought for a moment, and panicked.

Prescott Dennett was a senior publicist at the Washington-based agency Columbia News Service. Unknown to most of his clients, he was also the only employee at Columbia News Service. Before the war this one-man band had worked for several isolationist politicians, before being approached by an urbane, witty American of German origin called George Viereck. Author of the acclaimed horror novel *The House of the Vampire*, Viereck was also a Nazi agent reporting to Hans Thomsen. Soon Dennett was working for Viereck, fully aware that he was being paid by Berlin, and a vital cog in the Nazi congressional franking scheme.

Dennett would pass on material from his handler, Viereck, to the likes of George Hill, secretary to Hamilton Fish, and distribute thousands of reprints and pre-franked envelopes to isolationist groups around the country, including various chapters of America First. Their system was detailed and elaborate, which is why it had gone undetected for so long, but it was fallible.

Dennett panicked on the phone because the man on the other end of the line explained that he had been subpoenaed for possible misuse of pre-franked envelopes. The Justice Department's propaganda squad was on its way to seize Dennett's files. Right now. They would be at his office in a matter of hours. This would not have been a problem, but for the twenty bulging sacks of pre-franked envelopes sitting beside him in the room.

Several months earlier, a Grand Jury investigation had begun to look into the alleged misuse of the congressional frank, and earlier that day, 23 September 1941, it had produced its first indictment, of an Ohio attorney accused of working for the Nazis. Dennett was set to be next.

In a panic he contacted George Hill, who arranged for a government vehicle to come round to the office and remove the incriminating sacks. Several hours later, the truck arrived. It was loaded up, and drove off. Not long after, officials from the Justice Department walked through the door.

Dennett had escaped. At least he thought he had. The truck lumbered across the capital, but rather than go to the storeroom used by Hamilton Fish, as it was supposed to, it went to the congressman's office. George Hill was out. His other secretary could not think what to do with these twenty sacks of pre-franked envelopes, and decided to keep eight in the office and send the others to the local chapter of America First.

Bill Stephenson was one of the first to hear about the arrival of these bags, because he had an agent inside this particular chapter of America First.[1] Here was the breakthrough he had been dreaming of. At last, he had a thread clearly linking America First and the isolationists to Berlin. Stephenson called Hoover, and soon the FBI raided the America First premises, where they discovered the twelve bags of pre-franked envelopes.[2]

The weeks that followed saw the indictment of Viereck, the Nazi agent with an interest in vampires, who was later convicted for his failure to give a full account of his activities in the United States. Dennett was indicted on charges of sedition. Officials from America First were called to give evidence to the Grand Jury. A *Washington Post* reporter found members of the local America First chapter burning controversial papers in an alley behind their office late at night. Fish's secretary, George Hill, appeared in court and denied everything, but evidence from the British Censorship station in Bermuda proved he had been lying, and he was convicted on two counts of perjury.

Hamilton Fish, meanwhile, argued he was the victim of 'a smear campaign' and initially refused to appear before the Grand Jury. Eventually he was subpoenaed and forced to testify.[3] Although he was never found guilty of a crime, Fish's reputation was tarnished and two years later he would lose his seat in Congress.

The full details of the Nazi congressional franking scheme in all its byzantine complexity did not emerge for years. But for now, in the eyes of the American people it seemed that the isolationists and America First were somehow in league with the Nazis. The criminal exposure of the congressional franking scheme was a final nail in the coffin of America First. The isolationist cause was on its last legs and staggering. Meanwhile the man who for so long had been its figurehead was turning his attention elsewhere.

In the wake of his Des Moines speech, Charles Lindbergh confessed to feeling 'written out' on the war.[4] He was tired, and had begun to look for an escape. 'This is not a life I enjoy,' he told an audience of just 3,000 supporters at an America First rally on 3 October 1941 in Fort Wayne. 'Speaking is not my vocation, and political life is not my ambition.'[5]

It was not exactly the public apology that so many needed to hear after Des Moines. But it contained at least a note of contrition. On the advice of the America First chairman, Lindbergh did not mention his earlier speech.

In his diary the next day he touched upon his plans to leave politics, make a new home for his family and return to the biological research he had begun to carry out before the war with the Nobel Prize-winning surgeon Alexis Carrel. Little known to his critics or many of his supporters, during the 1930s Lindbergh had invented a pioneering glass perfusion pump which could be used in heart surgery. Now he hoped to continue where he had left off.

By October 1941 Lindbergh was losing interest in the battle to keep the country out of the war, and so were some of the senior figures in America First. What had once been a tiny student protest group, so small it did not have a name, and had gone on to become an enormously popular and influential movement with grassroots support throughout the country, an organization that had faithfully channelled the Founding Fathers' fear of foreign entanglements, had since morphed into a smaller and angrier group with an extremist edge. In the days after Lindbergh's anti-Semitic speech and the escalation of the congressional franking scandal, America First had begun to attract a different type of member. Applications to join were now pouring in from white supremacists, Nazi sympathizers, supporters of the conservative radio priest Father Coughlin, members of the German Bund, the Ku Klux Klan and William Pelley's Fascist Silver Shirts. On hearing Lindbergh's speech in Des Moines, many of them urged the America First leadership to launch a public campaign against American Jews.

Senior figures at America First understood what had happened and were close to giving up, when they heard that the president had launched a contentious new bill.

On 9 October 1941 Roosevelt formally asked Congress to revise the Neutrality Acts, so that in future US merchant ships could be armed and enter combat zones delivering goods to countries taking part in the war. For many isolationists the Neutrality Acts were the symbolic and legislative embodiment of isolationism, and had played a vital part in keeping the country out of the war. Hearing that Roosevelt wanted to have them dramatically rewritten was an affront.

America First threw everything it had at this. Across the country, its remaining supporters handed out lists of congressmen who might vote in favour of the revisions, insisting they 'must be deluged with mail'.[6] In Congress itself, isolationists delivered a drudgery of speeches designed to drag out the debate. For his part, Lindbergh agreed to address one last America First rally.

On 30 October, just a few days after Roosevelt's Navy Day speech, he took to the stage at Madison Square Garden in New York. The turn-out was good, but the atmosphere was somehow off.

Unknown to Lindbergh, in an attempt to disrupt the rally, Stephenson's agents had come up with a cunning plan. They had produced thousands of fake duplicate tickets to the event and handed them out on the streets of Manhattan. They hoped that with two people fighting over each seat there would be chaos in the arena and Lindbergh might be forced to abandon his speech. But they had not anticipated the extent to which his support had withered away. There were so few genuine ticket-holders that those who arrived with fakes were shown to the thousands of empty seats. At some expense, the British had merely increased the size of the audience at an America First rally.

In spite of this, Lindbergh's speech received little coverage, and the press was soon dominated instead by what happened the next day.

An ageing American warship on escort duty, the USS *Reuben James*, had been torpedoed by a German submarine and sunk, with

115 American sailors killed. This was the first time a German attack had led to the sinking of an American warship with significant loss of life. On hearing the news a young folk music star, Woody Guthrie, began a new song. 'The Sinking of the Reuben James' was a protest against the injustice of what had happened, a call for revenge. Unlike the attacks on the *Robin Moor*, the *Greer* or the *Kearny*, the sinking of the *Reuben James* seemed to pierce the public consciousness. It fuelled the desire for intervention.

Seven days after this deadly attack, the Senate voted by a margin of 50 to 37 to repeal articles 2 and 6 of the Neutrality Acts, allowing armed American merchant ships to deliver goods to belligerent nations, and to enter combat zones. The House would soon do the same, with 212 in favour and 194 against.

America First and Lindbergh had lost. 'It cannot now be many days before America is finally in the war,' Churchill said, on hearing the news.[7] Although there had been moments when the revision of the Neutrality Acts seemed politically impossible, the two events that turned the tide of public opinion were the sinking of the *Reuben James* and Roosevelt's revelation on Navy Day of the alleged Nazi map of Latin America.

In the wake of this Charles Lindbergh and America First soldiered on; that was their way. But the mood in the heart of the isolationist movement had soured. Lindbergh would never again address an America First rally. On the day that Roosevelt authorized his attorney general to begin a Grand Jury investigation into the funding of America First, Lindbergh was busy working on an account of his 1927 transatlantic flight.[8] With America's entry into the war looking more likely, he had turned away from what was happening around him, finding solace in the memory of his life as an unknown pilot. At a time when he could open a newspaper and read about a poll in which he had been voted 'America's No. 1 fascist', according to the *New York Daily News* on 19 November 1941, with a third of the respondents calling him 'a fool', it is hardly surprising that he wanted to retreat to a different time.[9] Imprisoned by the present, Charles Lindbergh was left to gaze at the past.

Meanwhile the British campaign to change the American mind continued to expand. Just as it dealt in bold gestures like Eric Maschwitz's South American map, or the early polls at the CIO convention, it was also capable of much smaller actions: tiny, almost forgettable exploits that might change the minds of only a handful of people.

Early in October 1941, a young family – husband, wife, and two children – crossed the Canadian border in a large Buick and drove south into the United States. The mood inside the car was giddy, as for most of the war this family had lived apart. The man behind the wheel telling stories about knights in shining armour was a colonel in the British Army. Next to him was his wife, a journalist and activist, and in the back seat was a nine-year-old girl next to her six-year-old brother, who had almost forgotten what his father looked like after spending more than two years away from him. Bumping along behind them was a trailer containing secret military hardware.

They continued south, past the majesty of the Adirondack Mountains where the leaves had begun to flare up, turning a traffic-light red, before they reached Manhattan where they found a hotel for the night. The next day, Alice and Harold Hemming went to the St Regis Hotel, a few blocks from the Rockefeller Center, to have lunch with Bill Stephenson.

I have always been intrigued by this trip, partly because neither my father nor my aunt – the two children in the back seat of that Buick – have ever been entirely sure why it took place, and exactly what their parents were doing. Growing up, I remember Dad occasionally mentioning the road trip that followed around the United States: the gunsight in the trailer, his father giving talks to American soldiers on a series of US military bases and being told there could be German spies in the audience, or the memory of smiling American women giving him teddy bears and ice cream, and how his mother was repeatedly mistaken for an actress called Greer Garson. But he was six at the time, and there was only so much of this trip he could remember.

Shortly after I began to research this book, Dad lent me his parents' papers, including two large boxes full of daily diaries, cuttings, radio scripts and letters, including many relating to this trip. It was thrilling to piece it all together, and to imagine Dad and his family travelling through the United States while around them the battle played out between the interventionists and isolationists. On the evening Lindbergh addressed the crowd in Madison Square Garden, Harold was speaking to a room full of US Army officers, and as the Senate geared up to its historic vote on the revision of the Neutrality Acts, Alice was giving a talk in a US military base about life in Nazi Germany. Reconstructing this road trip was to enter into a world of day-long drives, diners and flat tyres, forests and mountains, and roads that stretched out to the horizon. It was also a world defined by hospitality and an unthinking friendliness to strangers. Even the most hardened isolationists would treat these British visitors as honoured guests.

But why were Harold and Alice on a tour of US military bases in the months leading up to Pearl Harbor? Was this trip linked in any way to the first person they arranged to see in New York, Bill Stephenson?

*

The origins of this trip lay in the First World War, and the moment Harold, then a twenty-three-year-old British artillery officer on the Western Front, had an unusual idea. He wondered to himself if it was possible to locate enemy artillery positions using trigonometry and a series of observation posts. In theory, at least, if you had three observers at different points on the front, each noting down where on the horizon they saw a flash of an enemy gun, and precisely when, it should be possible to calculate the location of each gun. He tested his idea, and it worked.

Unknown to him, elsewhere on the Western Front the Nobel Prize-winning physicist Lawrence Bragg was formulating a similar idea. Within weeks of each other, Harold and Bragg had invented what became known respectively as 'flash-spotting' and 'sound-ranging'. Both techniques were worked up by the Royal Field Artillery, and gave British gunners an edge in the last two years of the war. For example, in the build-up to the Battle of Vimy Ridge, in 1917, flash-spotting and sound-ranging were used to locate 213 German artillery batteries, the majority of which were destroyed.

Fast forward twenty-four years to the summer of 1941, when America's ranking artillery officer, Major-General Robert M. Danford, DSM, Chief of US Field Artillery, came to visit the Royal Artillery Survey School out on Salisbury Plain, and he was shown round by the school's chief instructor, Harold, by then a Lieutenant-Colonel, who told him about the latest tactical developments in the Royal Artillery. Similar scenes were playing out across the country, with British officers doing all they could to impress their American guests. One of Roosevelt's special envoys to Europe, Averell Harriman, worried that 'all senior British officials spend half their time running a war and the other half entertaining visiting Americans.'[1]

One of the demonstrations Harold put on for General Danford was to introduce him to the latest version of flash-spotting, called 'short base' flash-spotting. This allowed artillery units to locate enemy positions with fewer observers and while on the move. Danford appears to have been taken by flash-spotting, because according to Harold's service record, several weeks later he was 'posted for Special Duty in USA'.

This was the trip I had heard about. The trailer bumping along behind their car contained the flash-spotting apparatus. In the weeks that followed in late 1941 Harold gave a series of lectures and demonstrations to American artillery officers in Forts Monmouth, Bragg and Sill, revealing the intricacies of flash-spotting.

This appears to explain the trip. Danford saw the flash-spotting demonstrations, was impressed, and presumably wanted Harold, who had invented flash-spotting, to lecture his officers on this. Harold would have asked to bring along his family because they missed each other. 'This is so exciting I can hardly bear to think about it,' Alice had written on hearing about this trip.[2] They saw Bill Stephenson in New York because he was Dad's godfather and it would have been rude not to.

This is a plausible explanation, but it does not reveal why Alice ended up giving talks on Nazi Germany during her time in the US. Another problem is that the dates do not fit.

General Danford came to Salisbury Plain in late August 1941. But Harold was talking about his potential trip some time before that, in early July 1941. So Danford could not have proposed the trip. Instead he agreed to it. Also it was Harold who suggested Alice come with him, and the reason he gave only really makes sense in light of who she had become over the past six months.

Before the war, Alice had been a gossip columnist, appearing as 'Girl Friday' in the Marquess of Donegall's 'In Confidence' column in the *Sunday Dispatch*. The highlight of her career until then had been landing the first interview since the Abdication with Wallis Simpson, Duchess of Windsor, a piece syndicated around the world.

Since then, having gone to Vancouver without her husband, she had reinvented herself as a prolific campaigner. As well as writing two columns for the *Vancouver Sun* and presenting a daily radio show, Alice had become a public speaker, and in April 1941 she had gone on a lecture tour of Hollywood calling for more aid to Britain.

She had spoken in Californian aircraft factories and at Los Angeles fundraisers in a series of talks organized by the Victory Loan campaign, the Spitfire Fund and the British War Relief Association. These went down well. One of her hosts wrote to her afterwards, 'I can say, with no hesitation, that I know of no woman who could do the work you are undertaking more effectively'; another described the 'indelible' impression she had left behind.[3] With no previous experience of this, Alice had become a powerful speaker. She was engaging and natural, and had the considerable advantage of being able to speak about life in Nazi Germany from her own experiences.

During Hitler's first two years in power, she and Harold had lived in Berlin, owing to Harold's job with an American stockbroking firm. Alice had seen for herself life under Hitler, including endless examples of the Nazi persecution of Jews. Alice drew on all this in her talks, describing at one point the suicide in Cologne of a Jewish friend of hers. Years later she would recall the strange feeling of looking out onto an audience of wealthy Hollywood socialites and noticing that everyone's mascara was starting to run.

Back in Vancouver, over the summer of 1941, Alice carried on with her campaigning. She organized fundraisers to auction off items she had been given in Hollywood, such as Cary Grant's pyjama top, or the gloves worn by Vivien Leigh in *That Hamilton Woman*. Otherwise she lectured to pretty much anyone who would listen, urging them to give more to the British war effort. 'It would be wicked and foolish to leave any money lying idle now, it would be cutting our own throats,' she reportedly told the Vancouver Junior Board of Trade, on 29 May 1941, and 'I can tell you, from living under the Nazis awhile, that it is hell.'[4]

All this begins to explain a particular line in Harold's letter to Alice of 16 July 1941. After telling her he would be heading to the United States on a military mission, he asked her to come with him, adding, 'if I can fix it for you to tour the States for Dorothy Thompson's or some other organizations would you like that?'[5]

Dorothy Thompson was a legendary American political commentator with her own weekly NBC radio show, and a newspaper column carried by 150 US newspapers. She was also a fierce opponent of fascism, and two weeks before Harold's letter she had set up her own interventionist pressure group called Ring of Freedom. Already it had been infiltrated by Stephenson's office.

Dorothy Thompson was a well-known figure in Britain, and it is of course possible that Harold had simply heard about her new organization and thought this would be the one to approach. But the idea of a British colonel out on Salisbury Plain imagining to himself that he could 'fix it' for his wife, then in Canada, to tour the United States on behalf of an embryonic American organization, to which he had no contact, does not really ring true. Nor was it Harold's style to make a suggestion like this without any prior connection. More likely, someone had planted the idea in his head, and it is easy to guess who that might have been.

Shortly before suggesting to Alice that she come out to the US and speak for an interventionist organization, Harold went for lunch at the Athenaeum, a private members' club in London, with Whitney Shepardson. As well as being a friend of Bill Stephenson's, Shepardson was a key member of the Century Group.[6] When the British ambassador Lord Lothian shared details of the British destroyer situation with the Century Group, the documents had been couriered over to Shepardson. One year on, he had become a driving force in Fight For Freedom, which was organizing countless interventionist rallies and talks across the United States. Now he was having lunch with Harold.

Given that they had never met before, the person who presumably put Harold and Shepardson in touch with each other was Bill Stephenson. After that meal, Harold had the idea of going to the United States, arranging for Alice to join him, and for her to give anti-Hitler talks along the way.

Harold's lectures went down well with his military counterparts, and in a different way so did Alice's. In each of the military bases they visited she lectured to soldiers and their wives about life in Nazi Germany. At the time many senior officers in the US Army were still isolationist in outlook. While Alice and Harold were giving talks, their children were deposited in the army camp schools. My aunt remembers having running battles in the playgrounds with the pro-German children of American soldiers with German ancestry. It was unusual for these soldiers to hear about the horror of Hitler's regime, especially from someone like Alice who had witnessed it for herself. By the end of this trip, late November 1941, Alice was making plans to stay on in the US and to give a series of talks across the Midwest.

Stephenson's influence campaign was capable of grand gestures like the Nazi map of South America, but it was also producing a background hum of much smaller acts: individual conversations, leaflets that were only glanced at for a few seconds, abbreviated articles in local newspapers, radio broadcasts that went out late at night, or a series of lectures by a former gossip columnist that were probably heard by only a few hundred US army personnel and their wives. Harold and Alice's tiny contribution to this vast campaign was testament, in many ways, to Stephenson's understanding of how to change public opinion. He knew that it relied on headline-grabbing stories as well as small, almost incidental exploits designed to support a slow and steady shift towards intervention.

There was one other link between Harold and Alice's trip and Stephenson's campaign. On the night they arrived in New York, 1 October 1941, Harold went for a drink with a friend of his. Federico Stallforth was charming and funny, but something of a rogue. Harold remembered crossing the Atlantic with him before the war, and Stallforth going down to the ship's telegraph office where he dictated a cable to the Prime Minister of France. 'Regret cannot attend lunch on the 19th. Stallforth.' He had never met the Prime Minister of France, nor would he, but Federico Stallforth liked to feel important and he was not above bending the truth.

So when Harold saw him on that night in New York he may not have believed everything he heard about Stallforth's recent trip to Berlin. But on this occasion he was telling the truth, as Bill Donovan had realized earlier that day.

Several hours before seeing Harold, Federico Stallforth sat down with 'Wild Bill' to deliver a message from Nazi Germany. As Stallforth explained, in Berlin he had met an intermediary for a group of German generals including Franz Halder, Alexander von Falkenhausen, Carl-Heinrich von Stülpnagel and the senior diplomat Ulrich von Hassell. They were planning a coup. They hoped to remove Hitler, end the war and return all German territorial gains (apart from those in Austria), but they wanted to be sure of political recognition from Britain and the United States if this coup went ahead. For reasons unknown, they had chosen the American businessman Stallforth as an informal envoy to the White House.

Donovan was enthusiastic. Stallforth reported back to his German contact that their proposal had fallen on 'very fertile ground in America', and that the United States government would recognize their coup.[1] The German plotters were not bluffing. Three of the four who had contacted Stallforth would later take part in what is known today as 'Operation Valkyrie', shorthand for the 1944 attempt on Hitler's life.

In contacting Stallforth these Germans had taken a considerable risk, and to a much lesser extent so had Donovan by offering his support. Berlin knew already about 'Wild Bill's' role as Coordinator of Information and suspected he was responsible for more than coordinating intelligence. In the state-controlled Nazi press, Donovan was described as the American 'super-agitator'.[2] Stallforth's message might easily have been a trap to implicate this super-agitator in a plot against Hitler.

But it was a risk Donovan seemed happy to take. Several days earlier, he had dangled $1 million before a senior German diplomat in an attempt to secure his defection. Since then he had secured from Roosevelt a new budget of $13 million,[3] and was now bombarding Stephenson with ideas for new propaganda schemes, almost all of which were designed to antagonize Nazi Germany.

One of these plans was for British operatives, paid for by Donovan's agency, to paste thousands of American-made posters around the world, printed in a variety of languages and bearing strident anti-Nazi or anti-Japanese messages. Another of Donovan's schemes was for British bombers to drop 'obviously USA propaganda material' over German or German-held territory where, he explained, 'the effect might be good.'[4] The response to this from the Minister of Information in London was apposite: 'Colonel Donovan's suggestion strikes me as being more like a stunt than a serious propagandist effort.'[5]

He was right. Both of these putative operations were stunts, in the sense that they were designed to communicate instantly a simple and provocative message. Roosevelt's comment on this last plan leaves no doubt as to what that message might be. The president agreed to have American propaganda deposited over German-occupied territory on two conditions. First, the material must 'not be dropped in packets which might possibly brain some harmless person'. Second, he wanted it to be absolutely clear to anyone who picked up one of these propaganda leaflets that this publication was the result of Anglo-American collaboration. Roosevelt specifically asked for the following to be added at the bottom: 'Prepared by USA Government, printed London, and dropped by our friends of the RAF'.[6]

In late November 1941, a handful of French civilians saw flurries of these leaflets fall to the ground around them like papery snow. On one side was a picture of Churchill, and on the other was Roosevelt. Next to each portrait was a French translation of near-identical declarations from the two leaders. The message for anyone reading it, whether they were a French citizen living under German occupation, or a government official in Berlin, was unambiguous: Britain and America were now allies in all but name.

This was the point Donovan was trying to drive home in his propaganda efforts during the closing months of 1941. It was provocative and increasingly accurate. Senior British ministers were already referring to 'the Anglo-American war effort'.[7] Bound up within this collaboration was the informal alliance between the White House, the precursor of the CIA, the MI6 station in New York and, more recently, the State Department. In November 1941, as newly declassified files show, officials at State were arranging to smuggle wireless sets out to

US legations in Sofia, Bucharest and Budapest, so that these could be given to undercover British agents.[8]

The US State Department was offering practical support to British spies. British bombers were dropping American leaflets over Nazi-held territory. An American official – Donovan – had tried to secure the defection of Germany's most senior diplomat in the United States, and was offering encouragement to a group of German generals in their plot against Hitler. The president of the United States had used a British forgery to stoke anti-Nazi feeling across the country. Roosevelt was doing almost everything he could to antagonize Hitler – without doing so much that the American public would notice. He was also allowing the tension to build with Japan.

Roosevelt had spent the past two years telling the American people that the greatest threat to the United States came from Nazi Germany, not Japan. But at the same time, in response to Japan's increasingly aggressive foreign policy, he had been quietly ratcheting up the economic pressure on Tokyo.

The president had allowed the trade deal between the two countries to expire. He had also banned the sale of defence materials to Japan, as well as scrap iron, machine tools and certain types of aviation fuel. In July 1941 when Japanese forces moved into parts of Indochina Roosevelt knew that he had to respond. At first he was not sure how.

One option was by refusing to sell oil to Japan, but this was risky. Eighty per cent of Japanese oil imports came from the United States, and Roosevelt knew that this step could lead to war. Although polls suggested that most Americans would welcome this, as they saw the Japanese as a military pushover, Roosevelt did not. He wanted to contain Japan without engaging the country head-on. So in late July 1941 he froze all Japanese assets in the United States. After that he steamed off to meet Churchill and draft the Atlantic Charter.

But while Roosevelt was away, a peculiar episode played out in Washington. To implement the Japanese asset-freeze, a three-man government committee was formed. Its task was to authorize individual American exports to Japan. With the president still at sea, this new committee got to work, whereupon one of its three members went rogue.

His name was Dean Acheson and he was a key member of the Century Group. The year before he had played a part in the Destroyers-for-Bases deal by drafting the *New York Times* letter arguing – erroneously – that it was lawful for the president to transfer fifty ageing American destroyers to the Royal Navy without going to Congress. Acheson was a committed interventionist, and someone who was willing to go to almost any length to help bring the United States into the war. His letter to the *Times* was a start. One year on, as a member of the committee regulating trade with Japan, he had a chance to go further.

Acting against his colleagues' advice, Acheson refused to let Japan pay in dollars for *any* goods. At a stroke, he ended trading relations between the two countries. The US would no longer supply Japan with oil, or indeed anything else. This Century Group member had found himself in a position to make US foreign policy on his own, and he had grabbed it.

Roosevelt did not fully grasp what had happened until after his return from seeing Churchill. He might have simply reversed Acheson's work, but this ban on trade with Japan had played unexpectedly well with the American public. This was helped, in no small part, by press releases and statements from groups like Fight For Freedom, which counted Acheson as a keen member, and the British-backed Anti-Nazi League, all applauding this move. The president did not want to be seen as soft on Japan, and so he did nothing, effectively endorsing Acheson's ban on trade with Japan. Almost unnoticed at the time, the Century Group had put the United States on a collision course with Japan.

*

Several months later, unknown to anyone in either Washington or London, a major decision was reached in Berlin. Although Hitler had often talked about going to war with the United States at some point in the distant future, it had rarely sounded like a priority. The US seemed to be marooned on the periphery of his world-view. But during the course of 1941 that had begun to change. As Roosevelt became more hawkish, Hitler thought harder about how to confront the US, and when.

For most of the year Hitler had said in private that Germany would not declare war on the United States until the Soviet Union was defeated, always preferring to pick off his enemies one by one. His orders to the German navy had been to avoid incidents that could lead to war with the US. He was determined to resist Roosevelt's provocations, until suddenly he changed course.

On 13 November 1941, remarkably, the German leader ordered that 'efforts to avoid incidents are to be abandoned'. Any German vessel being shadowed by a US warship was now free 'to destroy the enemy'.[9] This was partly a response to the revision of the Neutrality Acts, but there was more to it than that, as we shall see.

Several days later, Hitler confided to Ribbentrop, his loyal foreign minister and confidant, that his position on war with the United States had changed. Although the Soviet Union was undefeated, Hitler had a new-found 'willingness', he told Ribbentrop, 'to go to war with the United States'.[10] He did not reveal where this had come from or what had triggered it.

Now it was up to Hitler to find the right moment to declare war.

By the end of November 1941 you could be forgiven for thinking, at times, that America might already be at war. Walking down the street of almost any major American city you would have noticed more military uniforms than at the same time the year before. In airports you were more likely to see bombers parked on the runway, and down the east coast you may have noticed merchant ships decked out in war paint. 'The United States already is in the war,' Wendell Willkie had told a journalist recently, 'and has been for some time.'[1] On 2 November 1941 Roosevelt had the Coast Guard put under the command of the US Navy, an order that usually followed a declaration of war. Five days after that, Admiral Stark told a colleague in private that 'the Navy is already in the war of the Atlantic, but the country doesn't seem to realize it,' adding finally, in case there was any doubt, '*we are at war*.'[2]

But increasingly there were signs that the country did realize it, and that the United States had turned away from isolationism.

Local newspapers throughout the United States continued to come out in favour of intervention. Meanwhile a stream of idealistic young Americans made the journey to Canada where they volunteered to fight. News reports from London had a more positive and pro-British ring to them, partly the result of there being a new Minister of

Information, Brendan Bracken, whose priority was to woo American journalists. There was also more open propaganda from Britain in the form of lectures like the ones Alice had given in US military bases, or publications such as *Britain Today* and *The War in Pictures*. Two years ago the British would not have dared to do so much of this. By November 1941 the mood in the country had changed.

In popular culture you could also sense the shift away from isolationism. There was the runaway success of a new comic strip character 'Captain America', whose speciality was beating up Nazis. Most of that year's bestselling books were either by British authors, or they focused on the war from a partial and pro-British perspective. William Shirer's *Berlin Diary* laid bare the evils of Nazism, Ed Murrow's *This is London*, a collection of his famous radio broadcasts, told first-hand of life during the Blitz. Another popular title was an anthology of Churchill's speeches. Other successful books offered fictionalized accounts of life in Europe, such as Jan Struther's *Mrs. Miniver* about an imaginary Englishwoman adjusting to the war.

Some of these bestsellers could be traced back to Stephenson's office in the Rockefeller Center. *My Sister and I* claimed to be an account of life under Nazi occupation in Holland written by a twelve-year-old boy, but was really the work of an editor at Harcourt, Brace & Co. inspired by a colleague who may have been in touch with Bill Stephenson.[3] Another book Stephenson knew about long before publication was the thriller *Above Suspicion*, by Helen MacInnes, wife of one of his officers, Gilbert Highet.

But the publication of these interventionist books did not in itself drive people away from isolationism. Instead these titles generally confirmed or deepened the reader's existing beliefs.

Film was different, and had much greater potential for changing the way millions of people thought about Britain and the prospect of going to war. In April 1941, most of those who went to see on its release *That Hamilton Woman*, a moving tale of Admiral Nelson's affair with Emma Hamilton, were looking forward to the on-screen chemistry between the glamorous leads, newlyweds Vivien Leigh and Laurence Olivier, and were hoping to enjoy a powerful historical romance. Few expected this love story to be interrupted by stirring accounts of Britain standing up to a vicious European tyrant with plans for global domination – Napoleon in the film, Hitler in the minds of most movie-goers. Nor did many of them imagine that the director and producer of this film was working for MI6.

This was Alexander Korda, who was also using his production company to provide cover for British agents, and was helping his friend Stephenson by reporting on America First activities in California. But the Hungarian-born Korda's greatest contribution to the British influence campaign was *That Hamilton Woman*, a commercial and critical success later said to have been Churchill's favourite film. The year after its release Korda was knighted. (The filmmaker's friendship with Stephenson might also explain how Alice came back from California with Vivien Leigh's gloves to auction off.)

But the film that did the most to change American attitudes to the European conflict had nothing to do with Stephenson's office. While the year 1941 is famous among film buffs for the release of *The Maltese Falcon*, *How Green Was My Valley* and *Citizen Kane*, that year's highest-grossing film was the Warner Brothers production *Sergeant York*, the true story of Alvin York, played by Gary Cooper, a blacksmith's son from Tennessee who was called up during the First World War but refused to fight on religious grounds, before changing his mind, going to France, and becoming one of the country's most decorated soldiers after leading an attack on a German machine-gun position. *Sergeant York* was so unashamedly patriotic, interventionist and anti-German that it might as well have been scripted by Roosevelt himself. Around the time of its release, the president invited to the White House the real-life Sergeant York, as well as the man who played him, telling both he was 'really thrilled' by what he had seen.[4]

The interventionist sails continued to fill. Even Lord Halifax, the aloof British ambassador, was having a positive impact on the campaign to bring the US into the war. But not because of anything he had said.

When Halifax went to see a senior Catholic cleric, Archbishop Mooney, in Detroit, in late 1941, a group of isolationists from the 'Mothers of America' group hurled eggs and rotten tomatoes at him. The ambassador kept his cool and told his aides to 'let them have a good time for their money', before carrying on inside. A report of this incident was sent to the British Press Service in New York. They were impressed with the ambassador's reaction, but wondered to themselves if it could have been better. How would a Bernard Shaw or Oscar Wilde have reacted in that situation?

Within hours the British Press Service had issued a press release giving an alternative version of this incident. As the food rained down on Halifax, they wrote, he had deadpanned: 'My feeling is one of envy that people have eggs and tomatoes to throw about. In England these are very scarce.'

As the historian Nicholas Cull has shown, this one line 'transformed his reputation'. At every subsequent speech he gave in the US, Halifax was greeted like a homecoming hero. 'Even the black laborers on the Washington reservoir stopped work to applaud his morning stroll.'

Halifax was 'bewildered'.[5]

Through the efforts of American interventionists and British officials, those in the middle of the 'Great Debate' were starting to be won over, a section of American society once referred to by the journalist Dorothy Thompson as 'the people',

that class of Americans that historically has always determined the American scene. [. . .] They are native born, northern

European stock, Christian, and protestant. They have a strong
evangelical strain in them, believe without thinking that they
'are' America, and are overwhelmingly middle class, even if many
of them belong to the ranks of skilled workers. They are the
people with incomes between $2500 and $5000 a year, who send
their children to normal schools and freshwater colleges or state
universities, read the *Ladies' Home Journal* and the *Saturday
Evening Post*, voted, most of them for Willkie, but gave enough
votes to Roosevelt to elect him. These people, if they feel the
country is being taken away from them by 'aliens' will furnish a
lot of Fascist support. If they think they are going to be ruled
by a trade union bureaucracy or an economic royalist plutocracy,
they will revolt. They are the best people in this country and the
worst if their minds are not canalized along constructive lines. By
and large they are awfully good, for they believe in the American
tradition and the American dream, which is the best tradition
and dream that any nation has. These people must be reached.[6]

At last, they had been. By November 1941 these people were
reading in the press about military veterans and blue collar workers
coming out in support of intervention. They saw polls suggesting
Americans like them were changing their minds, or they read stories
in the newspapers that seemed to suggest the Nazis were beatable, or
that they were plotting to get a foothold in Latin America.

They read about this in the news, but they were also hearing it
from public figures they trusted. Many of those commentators had
closer ties to the British than they would care to admit, ranging from
the president himself through to his opponent in the last election,
Wendell Willkie, or indeed Dorothy Thompson, described by *Time*
magazine in 1939 as the second most influential woman in the United
States (behind only the First Lady).

Although she had long been a critic of Hitler, and in 1934 was the first American journalist to be expelled from Nazi Germany, it was not until June 1941 that Thompson came out as an interventionist. Very soon after, she began to be fed stories and ideas by an American pollster, Sanford Griffith, who was secretly working for Bill Stephenson. One report from Stephenson's office back to London, which has only recently been declassified, confirms that 'the help of Miss Dorothy Thompson had been satisfactorily enlisted'.[7] Over the following months Griffith supplied her with intelligence to use in her columns, and suggested which line she should take on particular issues. The evidence suggests she did not realize Griffith was working for the British. But like Willkie, she might not have minded if she had known that he was.

Usually the term 'influence campaign' brings to mind a small group of powerful individuals pulling strings from on high and controlling operatives and sympathizers. We look for vertical and 'conscious' relationships: spymaster to spy; controller to agent; employer to employee. Stephenson's campaign was specializing in something else. By the end of November 1941 it relied on more horizontal and sometimes ambiguous ties like the one between Sanford Griffith and Dorothy Thompson. The same went for the links between many of the key actors in this drama, ranging from Roosevelt to Willkie, Donovan and Stephenson, the polling company Market Analysts and Fight for Freedom, and the constellation of pressure groups, sympathetic newspapers, news agencies and radio stations with links to the British. Between them these groups and individuals had combined to heave the country away from isolationism.

But the polls, on the face of it, appeared to tell a different story. The question most regularly asked by Gallup pollsters since the start of the war, one which some commentators saw as a reliable gauge of the nationwide split between isolationists and interventionists, was: 'Should the United States enter the war now?'

When asked this question in November 1941, just 24 per cent of the population said yes, which appears to run counter to the nationwide shift to intervention. But there was a problem with this question.

Usually when a democratic country goes to war two criteria are met, one after the other. The majority of people need to feel threatened by a given enemy. There must also be an inciting incident, some form of transgression that can lead to a declaration of war. One without the other is rarely enough, and if the order is reversed the effect is reduced.

At the start of the Second World War the majority of Americans did not see Nazi Germany as a threat, and there had been no inciting incident. By November 1941, however, that had changed. When asked if they thought the US would 'go into the war in Europe sometime before it is over', 85 per cent said yes.[8] A different poll asked if 'the biggest job facing this country today is to help defeat the Nazi Government': 72 per cent agreed. Another poll, also conducted in November, found that 68 per cent of the respondents thought defeating Germany was *more* important than keeping out of the war.[9] A Gallup poll in October 1941 reported that 76 per cent of those surveyed approved 'in general' of Roosevelt's increasingly aggressive foreign policy.[10] These polls showed that the majority of Americans had come round to the principle of intervention. They saw war with Nazi Germany as necessary and inevitable. Now they were just waiting for the inciting incident.

Of course no poll is a precise gauge of public opinion, and there are reasons to treat these results with some caution. The senior Gallup employee David Ogilvy was after all working for MI6, and on at least one occasion it seems that he may have introduced a new question to the survey. The other major US poll appeared in *Fortune* magazine and was run by Elmo Roper, of Roper Research. Unknown to most of the magazine's readers, Roper was a founding member of the COI and had been working for Bill Donovan since the summer of 1941 (and would later become his deputy).

So by November 1941, Donovan and Stephenson had influential figures working inside the country's top two polling organizations. It is possible that the pressure they applied skewed the results of these polls fractionally towards intervention.

But in many ways this was offset by the bias already hardwired into each poll. At the time, Gallup polls only tried to reflect the views of US *voters*, so as a matter of policy their interviewers paid less attention to the South, to women, to those without college education, and to African-Americans, all of whom were deemed less likely to vote. Other polls taken at the time suggested that the same people routinely ignored by Gallup, especially in the South, were probably more likely to favour intervention. Had the polls been more representative of the American people as a whole, they might have shown a stronger inclination towards war, which is increasingly where the country seemed to be heading by the end of November 1941.

All over this vast nation, in diners and bars, in people's homes and offices, in the bleachers at baseball fields and at the sides of football pitches, at union meetings and at church, from the sleepy hamlets of the Midwest through to the grimy inner suburbs of the industrialized East, amid the millions of lives spooling out in slow motion, the shopkeepers and secretaries, the farmers and their wives, the labourers and waitresses, miners, maids, lawyers and bankers, not forgetting the hustlers and wiseguys, hillbillies, preachers and pastors, cowboys, ranchers and wranglers, the broads and macs, dames and joes, dolls and toms, slowly but steadily, and without ever wanting to be rushed, the people of the United States continued their march away from isolationism.

By the start of December 1941, an unlikely alliance of spies, political campaigners and government officials from both sides of the Atlantic had achieved what Roosevelt and Churchill had asked of them. The country had changed its mind. As one White House analyst concluded: 'the foreign policy issue is now settled.'[11]

The American people were ready for war.

PART FIVE

ALLY

7 DECEMBER 1941

Days Britain at war – 826
Allied shipping losses in the Atlantic (to date) – 7,465,548 tons
British military casualties (to date) – 18,420 men (approx.)[1]

NOVEMBER 1941

Gallup Survey: Do you think the U.S. will go into the war in Europe sometime before it is over, or do you think we will stay out of the war?
Go to war sooner or later with Germany – 85%[2]

The young soldier stared into his oscilloscope in disbelief. He had never seen anything like it. But he was new to radar and this machine had been known to play up.

He had just finished his shift at the Opana Point Radar Station, on the island of Oahu, Hawaii. It was several minutes past 7am on 7 December 1941. The screen on the new SCR-270-B radar suggested a vast fleet of planes, over a hundred miles away, heading towards the island at a speed of roughly 180mph. The soldier passed this on to his commanding officer, who concluded that he had probably just seen the six B-17 bombers due to arrive later that morning, and there was nothing to worry about.

Less than an hour later, the Japanese attack on Pearl Harbor began. In total, 353 planes were involved, including torpedo bombers, horizontal bombers, dive bombers, and the renowned Mitsubishi A6M 'Zero' fighters. Nearby US airbases were targeted first, after which the Japanese bombers concentrated on the warships lined up neatly on Battleship Row. Some of the world's most expensive vessels, with huge, state-of-the-art weapons that could destroy enemy warships from many miles away, had become sitting ducks.

Nothing could prepare the sailors at Pearl Harbor for what followed. Bombs fell, torpedoes exploded, battleships crumpled, capsized, ran aground or sank. Fuel poured out of the damaged ships and caught fire. Soon it was as if the entire harbour was ablaze. Everywhere was the smell of cordite and burning petrol. Bags of black smoke billowed up around the stricken warships, filling the sky, and amid the *thud-thud-thud* of anti-aircraft guns came the metallic whine of machine-gun bullets from Japanese fighters, the splash of injured men falling into the water, the plaintive groan of buckling metal as warships broke open, and, as one sailor remembered, there came 'the screams of our men, their bodies engulfed in flames'.[1]

The first Bill Donovan heard about what had happened was an announcement on the loudspeaker at New York's Polo Grounds. The New York Giants were losing to the Brooklyn Dodgers when a voice rang out around the stadium:

'Attention please! Here is an urgent message. Will Colonel William J. Donovan call Operator 19 in Washington immediately.'

Feeling thousands of eyes on him, Donovan scrambled to find the nearest phone. Soon he was on the line to Jimmy Roosevelt. The president's son explained that his father wanted him in the Oval Office, now. By the time Donovan arrived the extent of the Japanese attack was clear.

In the space of just two hours, 2,335 American servicemen had been killed, 188 American planes destroyed, and 21 US warships seriously damaged, including five battleships. Although 29 Japanese planes had been shot down, most had been flying too high, too low or too fast for the US anti-aircraft batteries.

Not for the last time, the United States had been the victim of a surprise attack on home soil that was brutal, premeditated and had come from the air. Similar to the attack on the World Trade Center in 2001, the assault on Pearl Harbor sixty years earlier had a visceral effect on millions of Americans. Many experienced it as if it had happened in their home town and the victims had been people they knew personally. The nation bristled with a need for revenge.

Roosevelt knew that Congress would agree to a declaration of war on Japan. But should he take this opportunity to ask for declarations of war against Italy and Germany as well?

Some isolationists were sceptical when they first heard about the attack on Pearl Harbor. Charles Lindbergh thought it might be 'just a hit and run raid of a few planes, exaggerated by radio commentators into a major attack'.[2] Others suspected foul play by Roosevelt or Churchill. 'Just what Britain had planned for us,' harrumphed Senator Nye, who was at an America First rally when the news came in, adding, 'Britain has been getting this ready since 1938.'[3] General Wood, chairman of America First, simply blamed Roosevelt. 'Well,' he told Lindbergh, 'he got us in through the back door.'[4]

In spite of this, as the news percolated through the country, many of those who had thought of themselves as staunch isolationists when they woke up that day had changed their minds by the time they went to bed. Although he felt the country had been 'asking for war for months', Lindbergh knew that the attack on Pearl Harbor made his position untenable. The celebrity pilot abandoned his isolationism, writing in his diary the day after the attack: 'I can see nothing to do under these circumstances except to fight.'[5]

Several days before the attack, Hamilton Fish had been testifying tetchily to the Grand Jury about his alleged misuse of the congressional frank. In the wake of Pearl Harbor he sounded like a man reborn, urging the American people to give their full backing to President Roosevelt. 'If there is a call for troops,' he went on, 'I expect to offer my services to a combat division.'[6] But they were only talking about japan.

On 8 December 1941, the day after the assault, President Roosevelt appeared before a joint session of Congress to ask for a declaration of war against Japan. The response was one vote short of unanimous. He said nothing about either Italy or Germany. Although the American people had largely come round to the idea of war against Hitler, Congress had not. The president did not ask for a declaration of war on Italy or Germany that day because he did not think he would succeed.

Although the US declaration of war on Japan produced an immediate and binding sense of unity across the nation, the political rift that had opened up during the so-called 'Great Debate' over the last year did not suddenly disappear. Bridges were built and gaps were filled in, but some cracks remained. Even those former isolationists who were now calling for war harboured a niggling suspicion that the White House might have played some hidden part in Pearl Harbor, and may have known about what was coming beforehand.

This later gave birth to a potent conspiracy theory. In 1944 John T. Flynn, once a leading light in America First, wrote *The Truth About Pearl Harbor*, the first book to argue that either the British or the White House had advance warning of the Japanese attack on Pearl Harbor but had chosen not to pass this on to guarantee America's entry into the war. Even today, this idea lives on.

It is easy to see why. The degree of surprise achieved by the Japanese can seem unnatural and at times suspicious. Roosevelt repeatedly showed he was capable of misleading the American people, and Churchill was desperate to bring the US into the war. When it emerged after the war that American codebreakers had cracked both the Japanese diplomatic cipher, codenamed PURPLE, and the naval cipher JN-25, in the months *before* the attack happened, this conspiracy theory took off. The 1991 book *Betrayal at Pearl Harbor* advanced the argument by suggesting that the British had also cracked this Japanese cipher and discovered evidence of the impending assault but had failed to pass it on.

The problem with any theory centred on naval cipher JN-25 is that by the time of the attack this cipher had been supplanted by a confusion of more complex alternatives, including JN-25B, JN-25B7 and JN-25B8. Another is that the Japanese task force maintained strict radio silence in the days before the assault. More importantly, no historian has found any document showing that British or American cryptanalysts intercepted, decoded and analysed any Japanese message revealing the location, date and nature of this raid.

For all this, Roosevelt could have done much more to prevent the attack from happening.

On 13 November 1941 Bill Donovan passed on to the White House an account of a conversation between one of his informants and Hans Thomsen, who was still mulling over the offer of $1 million to defect. The German diplomat had told Donovan's informant that if Japan attacked the United States, Hitler would follow up with an immediate declaration of war. Roosevelt had just learned that if he allowed the US to be attacked by Japan, or encouraged this to happen, he would achieve his ultimate foreign policy goal: war with Nazi Germany.

Until then, the president had shown little interest in taking on Japan. He wanted to be tough on the Japanese without antagonizing them. But in the days after hearing this from Donovan, his position appears to have changed.

At the time, discussions were taking place between the US Secretary of State, Cordell Hull, and the Japanese Special Envoy, Saburo Kurusu. One of Stephenson's agents, almost certainly Dr Charles N. Spinks, had befriended Kurusu's secretary and was having regular meetings with him in a Washington apartment which the British had bugged. The key points from their conversations were passed on to the president.

Based on these reports, as well as decrypted Japanese cables, Roosevelt understood that there was a split in the Japanese government, with some wanting to improve relations between their countries and others angling for war. He also knew that the Japanese had set themselves a deadline. If by 25 November 1941 their Special Envoy had failed to make substantial progress in Washington then the Japanese would push ahead with plans for war.

At Roosevelt's last war council meeting before that deadline passed the discussion might have been about how to avoid war with Japan. Instead, on 25 November 1941, the president talked about ways to 'maneuver them into the position of firing the first shot without allowing too much danger to ourselves'.[7] The following day, the Secretary of State gave his Japanese counterpart the so-called 'Hull Note', a list of ten uncompromising demands. In Tokyo, the argument about whether to attack the US was over: the militarist faction had won. Later that day the Japanese task force including six aircraft carriers sailed for Pearl Harbor.

'It is said that we went to war because we were attacked at Pearl Harbor,' Dorothy Thompson later wrote. 'That is childish. The attack at Pearl Harbor did not precede but followed the breakdown of peace negotiations opened by the Japanese in Washington. We could have had peace with Japan'.[8]

Thompson was right. Roosevelt could have done much more to avoid war, but he chose not to, probably because he thought war with Japan would lead to war with Germany. Once the 'Hull Note' had been delivered it was no longer a question of 'if' Japan was going to strike, only 'when' and 'where'. The next day, war warnings were sent out to US Army and Navy commanders across the Pacific, anticipating Japanese incursions in territories such as the Philippines, Borneo or Singapore. Earlier that same day, Stephenson had been in Donovan's office when Jimmy Roosevelt told him the Japanese negotiations were off and the military expected 'action within two weeks'.[9]

The following day, Stephenson heard from an agent with links to the Japanese consulate in New York, just a few floors above his office, that the Japanese felt their Washington negotiations had 'completely failed', that 'they expected war' and were now preparing 'to close Consulate offices'.[10]

The intelligence seen by the Americans and the British in the days leading up to Pearl Harbor pointed to an imminent Japanese attack in South East Asia. If either Roosevelt or Churchill had known that an attack was planned at Pearl Harbor, let alone the date, it would have been in their interests to pass this on. Even if the Americans had been forewarned, and as a result the raid had been less successful, the country would have clamoured for war. Their anger had less to do with the severity of the defeat than the scale and nature of the assault.

The only advance warning of Pearl Harbor received by any Briton or American was the one picked up at Opana Point Radar Station less than an hour before the assault began.

Several hours after the Japanese struck at Pearl Harbor, the head of Donovan's political warfare section, Robert Sherwood, contacted his friends at the New York office of Fight For Freedom. He asked them to do a favour 'for the President'.[1] They agreed. Sherwood then dictated a statement over the phone for them to put out in a press release under their own name.

The Fight For Freedom statement went out several hours later, just before midnight on 7 December 1941, a date Roosevelt would soon relegate to infamy. It was picked up by newspapers and radio stations across the country. The Japanese raid on Pearl Harbor was, this statement began, 'a last desperate effort of Hitler to turn American attention from the center of war against our world. That center is Berlin.' Although the assault appeared to be Japanese, it had in fact been 'masterminded by the thugs and gangsters of Berlin'. 'We must remember that Berlin prompted this attack, that Berlin is the world enemy and the world danger.'[2]

In the hurried rhythm of this statement one can sense the speed with which it was put together. It also makes the underlying White House message unmistakeably clear. Very simply, Roosevelt wanted the world to believe that the Nazis were behind Pearl Harbor. He was worried that the attack might take the spotlight away from Berlin, and that Hitler might not do what Thomsen had said he would, which was to declare war immediately on the US. In the hours after the attack there had been silence from Berlin.

Later that day, Bill Donovan heard that Hans Thomsen had *not* been told to prepare for war. In Berlin, an 'authorized spokesman' was asked about Germany's relations with the United States. He described them only as 'no longer of any importance'.[3] Churchill was so worried by the prospect of the US becoming caught up in a war with Japan and remaining at peace with Nazi Germany that he decided that day to cross the Atlantic.

Tuesday 9 December 1941 only seemed to bring more uncertainty. Stephenson had heard that a German newspaper editor had told his New York correspondent to be ready to leave the US 'promptly'.[4] This was passed on to Roosevelt, via Donovan, and was encouraging. But still nothing from Berlin.

Roosevelt decided to act.

Later that day, while the nation was at peace with Germany and Italy, the president declared all German and Italian nationals to be 'enemy aliens', a legal designation meaning they could be arrested and detained, and were forbidden to enter certain parts of the country or carry firearms. Japanese nationals had already been given this status. It was inhumane and racist, but did at least follow from the logic that the US was at war with Japan. Extending this status to nationals of two countries which had peaceful relations with the US was unprecedented. Roosevelt justified this by telling the press 'an invasion or predatory incursion is threatened upon the territory of the United States' by Germany and Italy.

It was not.

That night, as one newspaper reported, 'nearly 400 Germans and Italians were taken into custody by the FBI in sudden swoops'.[5] While those arrests were taking place, Roosevelt delivered a fiery radio address.

The relationship between Tokyo and Berlin was 'a collaboration', he told the country, an 'actual collaboration'. The Germans had urged the Japanese to attack at Pearl Harbor, he claimed. 'We know also that Germany and Japan are conducting their military and naval operations in accordance with a joint plan. [. . .] Remember always that Germany and Italy, regardless of any formal declaration of war, consider themselves at war with the United States'.[6]

Roosevelt was right to say that Tokyo and Berlin were in contact, but the Germans had never urged the Japanese to strike Pearl Harbor. Hitler had been almost as much in the dark about this attack as the US president. He had known an assault was coming, but did not know where or when. For months, Hitler and those around him had urged the Japanese to strike against the USSR in Vladivostok or the British in Singapore. Goebbels described Pearl Harbor as 'a bolt from the blue'.[7] When the news first came in to the German Foreign Ministry it was dismissed as a hoax.

The most provocative part of Roosevelt's speech was his assertion that Germany and Italy were essentially at war with the US already. This was about as close to a declaration of war as the president could go.

Still no word from Berlin, and the two nations remained at peace.

The next day, Bill Donovan contacted the State Department to ask if his 'propaganda broadcasts' were being heard in Germany.[8] Although he did not specify which broadcasts these were, it is easy to guess. Over the past few days Donovan's political warfare unit, still taking directives from London, had been broadcasting into Germany the details of the so-called 'Victory Program'.[9]

This was the leaked US War Department plan showing how American forces could defeat Germany if the two nations went to war. Just three days before the raid on Pearl Harbor, lengthy extracts from this plan had appeared in the *Chicago Tribune* and its affiliated paper, the *Washington Times-Herald*. The irony here was that these had been leaked to the press by the isolationist Senator Wheeler, who had been given them by a disgruntled US Army Air Corps captain, in the hope of killing off the prospect of war with Germany.

But with its detailed maps of Germany, lists of potential targets and stated aim of wiping out the Nazi regime, the Victory Program was like a Zimmermann telegram in reverse. On that occasion, in 1917, the American people had been presented with proof that there was a German plan to invade the United States. The Victory Program, three decades on, was proof of an American plan to invade Germany, which is why the White House made no effort to block its publication. This also explains why Donovan and the British were so keen to have the Victory Program broadcast into Germany.[10]

Still nothing from Berlin.

The attack on Pearl Harbor had taken place on Sunday morning. By Wednesday night, to the growing concern of Roosevelt, Donovan, Stephenson, Churchill, and others, Hitler had not declared war on the United States. Roosevelt had done all that he reasonably could. He had asked Fight For Freedom to demand war on Germany. He had declared all German nationals 'enemy aliens', and had assured the world falsely that the Nazis were behind Pearl Harbor. His political warfare unit had continued to broadcast into Germany details of how the United States was ready to wipe out Hitler's regime. Roosevelt had pinned his hopes on the Nazi leader declaring war. Now he was left to wonder what was really going on in Berlin.

Hitler had been away from Berlin at his eastern headquarters when he was told of the Japanese assault on Pearl Harbor. The following day, Ribbentrop was pressed by the Japanese ambassador for a German declaration of war, but he demurred.

While Japanese officials had tried to amend the Tripartite Pact in the days before the attack, so that Germany and Italy would be forced to come into the war when Japan moved against the United States, they had failed to have this ratified in time. Germany was under no obligation to act, and both sides knew it. Whether Germany would declare war on the United States was a decision that rested exclusively with the German head of state and commander-in-chief of the Wehrmacht: Hitler.

On Tuesday 9 December 1941, two days after the Japanese raid, Hitler returned to Berlin. There were good reasons *not* to declare war on the United States, as he knew. It might divert resources away from the Eastern Front. The German navy had also lost the advantage of surprise: at the time of Pearl Harbor, as the commander-in-chief of the U-boat fleet, Karl Dönitz, regretfully pointed out, 'there was not a single German U-boat in American waters.'[1]

The best reason not to declare war on the US was that Hitler's military chiefs were completely unprepared for it. 'We have never even considered a war against the United States', the German deputy chief of the General Staff told his superior, General Jodl.[2] There was no military plan for how to defeat the United States, nor were there any senior officers arguing it was possible. The country was too large and too far away. Lindbergh had at least been right about this.

Nevertheless, at noon on Thursday 11 December, four days after Pearl Harbor, the US chargé d'affaires in Berlin received a visit from the Nazi Foreign Minister, Joachim Ribbentrop. Preferring not to take a seat, the German politician read out a short declaration of war. He finished with a perfunctory bow, like a conductor at the end of an unremarkable performance, and left the room, knowing that Germany had declared war on the United States.

Germany had declared war on the United States. Hitler had not been required to do this and for most of the previous year had gone to considerable lengths to avoid it. There were many compelling reasons to wait, as he knew. But by the end of November 1941 he had changed his mind.

Why?

There were some strategic advantages to declaring war. It would strengthen Germany's alliance with Japan. Hitler also imagined, wrongly, that war in the Pacific would leave the US unable to fight on two fronts, which allowed him to think there was nothing to lose from a surprise declaration of war. Another reason for going ahead was that by late November 1941 Germany and the United States were effectively at war already, given the situation in the Atlantic. A declaration would merely formalize this state of affairs.

That was the rational case for going to war. But to understand fully what has been described as Hitler's 'last great strategic decision',[3] and one of his costliest mistakes, we must consider Hitler's emotional state.

Three hours after Ribbentrop had delivered the declaration of war, the German leader began a speech in the Reichstag to justify what he had done. This long and often angry address was built around a detailed list of every order, speech, remark or article of legislation from Roosevelt that had pushed the United States closer to war. Hitler left nothing off his list. There was Roosevelt's decision to send fifty destroyers to Britain, and to move US troops to Greenland and Iceland, his efforts to push through Lend-Lease, his instructions to the US Navy to escort convoys and engage German U-boats, and his order to close German consulates and freeze German assets. Hitler also referred to the US mission to Yugoslavia led by Bill Donovan – 'a very inferior character', he told the Reichstag – and how Donovan had given tacit American support to the anti-Nazi coup.

As the historian Ian Kershaw has argued, Hitler's catalogue of grievances in that speech was not 'purely for propaganda effect'. Instead 'it reflected his inner burning desire to get even with President Roosevelt.'[4] This declaration of war was, in many ways, a retaliation. Elsewhere in this speech Hitler slammed Roosevelt as a 'provocateur', someone responsible for 'intolerable provocations', and a man whose government had 'continually been guilty of the most severe provocations toward Germany ever since the outbreak of the European war.'[5]

Hitler clearly felt that he had been provoked, and that until then he had nobly resisted the urge to strike back. Roosevelt's policies, as much as his words and gestures, had produced in Hitler an overwhelming need to feel, for a moment, the hollow joy of revenge.

There is one last reason that explains why Hitler changed his mind about going to war: he now felt that if he did not do this, Roosevelt might beat him to it. This marked a fundamental shift in his thinking. Until then Hitler had seen Roosevelt as a leader shackled to the truth, to democratic propriety, and to the vicissitudes of public opinion. By the end of November 1941, that had changed. Hitler had acquired a different understanding of Franklin D. Roosevelt and what he was capable of. 'This man first incites to war, and then he lies about its causes and makes baseless allegations,' Hitler told the Reichstag, and bemoaned the American's 'shameless misrepresentations of truth'.[6]

Where might this have come from?

In the months leading up to Hitler's speech Roosevelt had bent the truth on several occasions, but there was only one speech which could be described as a 'shameless misrepresentation of truth'. This was the address he gave on Navy Day, 27 October 1941, when he told the world about the alleged Nazi map of South America.

When Hitler made a speech twelve days later, on 8 November 1941, he talked of little else.[7] The South American map appears to have changed the way he saw Roosevelt, turning him into a different type of adversary, one capable of lying to his own people on a grand scale even to the point of using forgeries to deceive them. In Hitler's mind, the US president had become unpredictable and dangerous. Roosevelt might produce another forgery at any moment. Hitler could not tolerate that. Instead he needed to feel a stronger sense of control over his country's destiny. As a senior official at the German Foreign Ministry put it, 'a great power does not allow itself to be declared war on; it declares war itself.'[8] Striking first had become a defining characteristic of the Nazi regime. As soon as Hitler imagined Roosevelt was *capable* of declaring war on him, he had little choice but to act.

The story that Roosevelt told in the months and years that followed was that the United States had been dragged into the Second World War by the Axis powers. it is a version of history that endures to this day: the unprovoked attack at Pearl Harbor led unavoidably to war. But there was more to it than that. Not only did the White House play a meaningful part in bringing the United States into the war, against Germany but so did the British.

Shortly after the United States entered the war, a plane left for Britain carrying a handful of passengers. One of them was Bill Stephenson. As usual, his face gave away little. Those who worked for him remembered his brittle energy as well as his dogged inscrutability. Stephenson had long ago buried any trace of his traumatic childhood. The events of the last eighteen months would remain hidden for years to come. Unknown to anyone but himself, as that plane soared high above the Atlantic, the sound of the engines enveloping each of the passengers, Stephenson had finished an unlikely journey.

Although he had not left his post as MI6 Head of Station in the US, and would soon be back in New York, by the time he made this trip back to London, in late December 1941, a crisis within himself had been resolved. He had reached a new understanding of not only who he was, but what he was capable of.

In June 1940 this quiet, sturdy-looking forty-three-year-old had arrived in Manhattan as a first-time spymaster with a threadbare staff and little sense of the job in hand. Nine months later he had launched an assault on American public opinion that was unlike any-thing which had gone before, certainly in the history of MI6, possibly in that of the United States. Infiltrating pressure groups, spreading rumours, winning over prominent isolationists, using opinion polls and even helping to set up a new American intelligence agency: this operation changed the way Roosevelt was seen in Berlin just as it played a critical part in leading the US away from isolationism.

This meant that very soon after the United States entered the war, Roosevelt was able to announce that US armed forces would concentrate on defeating Germany first, and only after that turn to Japan. This stance was formalized at the end of the Washington War Conference, on 14 January 1942, when it was agreed that 'only the minimum of forces' would be 'diverted from operations against Germany'.[1]

Given that the country had been attacked by Japan, this made little sense. If Pearl Harbor had happened twelve months earlier, when public opinion was firmly opposed to war with Germany, Roosevelt would not have risked this. But by the start of December 1941 most Americans saw war with Hitler as necessary, just and inevitable. As Japanese planes scorched over Pearl Harbor, one young bystander was even heard to shout: 'those dirty Germans!'[2]

Two decisions taken in December 1941 – Hitler's declaration of war on the US, followed by Roosevelt's announcement that the United States would go after Germany first – combined to change the shape of the Second World War. Neither was inevitable. Separated by just a few weeks, these two fateful choices tipped the balance of the conflict. Unknown to all but a handful of people on either side of the Atlantic, Stephenson's office had played a part in each.

Shortly before the end of the war, at Churchill's request, Stephenson was knighted. The following year Sir William Stephenson, as he now was, received the US Medal for Merit by President Truman for his 'timely and invaluable aid to the American war effort', making him only the second non-American to receive this award.[3] The orphan from the red-light district of Winnipeg, who was unafraid of failure and hard to read, a man who liked to take his martinis shaken not stirred, had reinvented himself once more.

In the years after the war Stephenson was not kept on by MI6. To do what he felt had to be done during the darkest days of the Second World War, he had burned some of his bridges with London. He was relieved of the job he so prized. His membership of Britain's most exclusive club was not renewed. Consolation came in knowing he had made the harder choice, and had played a part in saving his country from defeat.

That was all ahead of him. As his plane continued to race across the Atlantic, just days after Hitler had declared war on the US, Bill Stephenson's world felt smaller and simpler. He had reached the point on the horizon he had been driving towards for so long. High above the ocean that separates the old world from the new, with the sky stretching out around him, it was as if he had arrived.

Epilogue

Once the British influence campaign had run its course, a different drama began to play out among those involved. At stake was how this story should be told, or if it should be told at all. In the days after Hitler's declaration of war each of the major players began to move on from what had happened. Evidence was covered up, forgotten about or removed. Many of Stephenson's agents were quietly transferred to Donovan's organization. Others, like Joseph Hirschberg, who had infiltrated so many pressure groups, were reminded of their obligations under the Official Secrets Act and asked to leave the United States.

Although Bill Donovan and his senior colleagues recognized the role played by the British in the birth of their intelligence agency, they preferred to keep this to themselves. The two Bills remained close, and would celebrate the end of the war with 'a raucous private dinner' at the St Regis Hotel, in which they 'shouted toasts and danced about like bears in triumph'.[1] But most of Donovan's wartime recruits were fed a sanitized, Stephenson-free version of how this American agency came into being.

For the rest of the war Stephenson remained in charge of British Security Coordination, in the Rockefeller Center, but from the moment the US entered the conflict this office began to resemble a more

anaemic version of its former self. There were no longer offensive operations aimed at the isolationists, the buccaneering spirit had gone, and
it concentrated instead on the more prosaic gathering of intelligence.

Towards the end of the war, once Stephenson had realized that he
was unlikely to be kept on, his mind turned to the legacy of his office
and how its story might be told. Stephenson also knew there were
some details in his office's records that he did not want to be seen by
'C' or future historians. So he commissioned four members of his staff,
including a young Roald Dahl, to turn his office's records into a sin-
gle-volume classified history. This allowed him to excise from the story
any embarrassing details, while providing future British civil servants
with a guide of sorts to the art of running an influence campaign.

The book-length history that followed was accurate in what it said
but misleading in what it left out. Much of the American involvement
in this operation was airbrushed out, partly because many of the
Americans involved did not want their pre-war work to be preserved
for posterity like this. Stephenson had twenty copies of this history
produced, before having his office's paperwork destroyed.

After that Sir William Stephenson moved to a large house in
Jamaica, renewed his business interests and tried to enjoy the peace.
If asked about his wartime work he clammed up, just as he would
when the conversation touched on his childhood.

His former colleagues and collaborators generally did the same.
Bill Donovan said nothing more than he needed to about his activities
before Pearl Harbor, and instead kept himself busy either working
behind the scenes on the new CIA or trying to run for Senate, which
again, sadly, ended in defeat.

Eric Maschwitz continued to write songs and was later appointed
Director of Light Entertainment at BBC Television where he played a
part in commissioning a new BBC show called *Doctor Who*. When he
came to publish his memoirs, he made sure to obscure many details
of his secret work in North America.

Wendell Willkie was another who preferred not to shed light on his activities leading up to the US's entry into the war, and in particular his relationship with Stephenson and Lothian. But he continued to assist his former adversary, Roosevelt, travelling widely on the president's behalf and meeting Stalin and the Chinese leader Chiang Kai-shek (and finding time for an affair with the latter's wife). Willkie soon became a loud critic of Britain and her empire, much to the annoyance of Churchill, his one-time drinking companion.

Another critic of British imperialism, Adolf Berle, softened his stance on Stephenson's operation, saying after Pearl Harbor that 'in justice to Stephenson it should be remembered that he came here at a time when the United States was not in the war, and probably organized on that basis', later conceding 'it was impossible not to like Bill Stephenson'.[2]

My grandparents, Alice and Harold, spent most of the war apart, and on their reunion in 1944 Alice told her husband that there had been a change in her life: she had become a feminist. In the years after the war she campaigned for Nancy Astor and Ellen Wilkinson's 'Women in Westminster' group, pushing for more women in parliament; she became vice-president of the International Alliance of Women; and for forty years was president of what is today the Commonwealth Girls Education Fund, a charity devoted to achieving better access to education for women across the Commonwealth. She often spoke about her conversion to feminism, which was largely down to the Viennese émigré Anna Askanazy who she got to know in Canada during the war. But I like to think that her experiences in the US during 1941 also played some part in her conversion from journalist to campaigner.

Charles Lindbergh was another who preferred not to speak about his activities during the months leading up to Pearl Harbor. In the wake of the Japanese attack he abandoned isolationism. Although he tried to have his USAAF commission restored, this was blocked by the White House. Nonetheless Lindbergh managed to be taken on in a civilian capacity and, amazingly, flew more than fifty combat missions in the Pacific theatre. After the war, he pursued some of his many interests including engineering, aircraft design and the environment. He also became a prolific adulterer.

Some thirty years after Lindbergh's death in 1974, the man who had once been to many Americans a paragon of modern virtue was revealed to have fathered no fewer than seven children, in Germany and Switzerland, by three different women, and having hidden their existence from his wife and legitimate children. Two of his mistresses were sisters. One was his secretary. All were sworn to secrecy. If any of his illegitimate children asked about their itinerant father they were told he was a little-known American author called 'Careu Kent', which at least allowed Charles Lindbergh to sign his letters to them truthfully with his initial, 'C'.

Lindbergh appears to have acquired an ability to keep secrets just as Stephenson lost his. Once renowned for his discretion, in 1952 Stephenson gave a press interview about his wartime work. We may never know why. Perhaps he was feeling forgotten or frustrated, or just bored. There is also a chance that shortly before this interview he experienced a minor stroke, which may have impaired his memory and decision-making.

In any case, the resulting feature in *Maclean's* magazine in December 1952 was short, inaccurate and full of exaggerations. Sensing, per- haps, that he had made a mistake, Stephenson went initially quiet in the years that followed and refused further interviews.

Meanwhile Bill Donovan began to experience the first symptoms of dementia, and was soon confined to hospital. One of the original Century Group members, Whitney Shepardson, agreed to write Donovan's biography, and in the course of his research went to inter- view Bill Stephenson. Their conversation took place in the late 1950s, and it seems the experience prompted him to think again about his wartime work and how it might be remembered. Fearing that his exploits could be written out of history, Stephenson commissioned a biography of himself, which he envisaged as a companion to the proposed book on Donovan.

The author he chose to write it was Montgomery Hyde, the former British agent who had helped forge the Belmonte Letter. Published in Britain as *The Quiet Canadian* in 1962, and released the following year in the United States as *Room 3603*, with a foreword by Ian Fleming, this book was frequently accurate, and contained many passages lifted verbatim from the internal BSC history that Stephenson had commissioned. But there were also large gaps, moments of fantasy and hagiography, and passages where the author had been told to settle a score on behalf of his former boss.

In the months after publication, Stephenson reacted against the wave of publicity. He refused to have the book reprinted and blocked attempts to turn it into a TV series or film. Again, he seems to have felt that he had gone too far.

This should have been the end of Stephenson's attempts to tell his story, but for two events that combined to change forever the popular perception of Stephenson and his influence campaign. First, Stephenson suffered a major stroke and fell into a coma. One friend who saw him afterwards found to his dismay that 'the stroke seemed to have erased his memory'.[3] Others reported that he had developed the unsettling habit of inserting himself into other people's stories. This would not have been a problem but for the moment several years later when he spoke to a friendly and frequently charming man who wanted to write a book about him.

This was a fellow Canadian named, confusingly, William Stevenson. His book on Stephenson, *A Man Called Intrepid*, came out in 1976 and sold more than two million copies. It was popular, pacey and so inaccurate that allegedly its US publisher later had it reissued as a work of fiction.[4]

The problems began even before anyone opened the book: Stephenson was never codenamed 'Intrepid'. The author continued in this vein, presenting Bill Stephenson as an uber-spook who knew everyone, had spies everywhere, controlled British intelligence in many different parts of the world, was even involved in the assassination of Heydrich, and in his spare time had helped crack the Enigma machine's code. *A Man Called Intrepid* was described by historian Hugh Trevor-Roper as being 'from start to finish, utterly worthless' and stuffed full of 'grotesque claims'.[5] A former SOE section head called it 'a monstrous concoction' and 'a shambles'.[6] Even Stephenson would distance himself from some of its more bizarre assertions.

But for all its faults, this enormously popular book allowed the elderly and by then infirm Canadian one final reinvention. His actual legacy lay in what he had done to help bring the United States into the war, his emphasis on collaboration, his extraordinary abilities as an administrator and a leader, and the impact he had on the character of the CIA. But this book turned him into something else. It created a more mythical figure, an iconoclastic spymaster with unlimited powers: a superhero in all but name.

In Winnipeg, the town where Stephenson grew up and from which he had later fled, he was revered. Today there is an Intrepid Society in Winnipeg, a local street named after him, as well as a library, a scholarship, an award and numerous statues. One of these sits outside the city's legislative building, another statue, a bronze, is currently installed in Langley, Virginia, in the atrium of the CIA Headquarters.

In the years after the publication of this bestselling book and the worldwide fame that followed, Stephenson did not return to Winnipeg. Instead he remained in Bermuda, in a home fitted with the panelled drawing from his Buckinghamshire cottage. Above the fireplace was a copy of the Annigoni portrait of the Queen. This is where he was when he died, in 1989, aged ninety-two. It is perhaps fitting that in the days before his death he managed one final act of press manipulation. Fearing the media circus that might follow the announcement of his death, he arranged for the news to be held back for three days so that his funeral could take place in peace. His instructions were followed, and he received the quiet send-off he desired.[7]

Around the same time, several thousand miles away in London, I began to hear for the first time stories about how my Dad had nearly died when he was very young. The detail that always stuck in my mind was that his life had been saved by a man called Bill.

Afterword

When reading today about the Russian influence campaign which climaxed in the months leading up to the 2016 US presidential election it can be easy to think that this operation was unique, or at least profoundly different to any other attempt by a foreign state to change American public opinion. But strip away the technology involved, the names and the dates, and there are some surprising similarities between the Russian operation which ended in 2016 and the British one which began in 1940.

For one, neither campaign set out to create feelings in millions of Americans that were not already there, only to exacerbate existing tensions, loyalties and suspicions. Both used 'active measures' to achieve specific short-term goals. They produced and exploited rumours, manipulated the media, and stole sensitive correspondence which they then used to their advantage. Each one was popular, in the sense that they tried to shape the way millions of ordinary Americans felt about a political issue. The architects of both understood the importance of message discipline and good timing, and they took care to hide what they were doing. Their agents were often disguised as American activists or journalists. Both ran smear campaigns against prominent figures who got in their way, and each had a preference for the tactic recently described by political scientist Thomas Rid as 'hack-leak-amplify'.[1] (Stephenson's office referred to the same tactic as 'pressure propaganda'.)[2] Having gathered damaging information on a target, they would leak this to a friendly and legitimate outlet – usually the *New York Herald Tribune* for the British, *Wikileaks* for the Russians – before using other tools at their disposal to amplify these leaks. If either operation was unable to find damaging information, they were more than willing to invent it.

In the origins of these two campaigns there are also some abstract similarities. In both cases, a foreign government realized that American public opinion might hold the solution to a national crisis. For the British, this was the existential threat of annihilation at the hands of the Wehrmacht. For the Russians, it was the possibility of further economic sanctions and a more aggressive US foreign policy. Both campaigns were probably approved by their respective leaders, Churchill and Putin, and were successful in the sense that the goal they had been working towards came to pass. To what extent these covert operations were directly responsible for this is an open and contentious question. Cause and effect in the field of influence campaigns will always be hard to measure exactly. But a lack of precision is not the same as a lack of impact.

One of the clearest lessons from these two influence campaigns is just how vulnerable any large Western democracy is to state-sponsored subversion on this scale. The range of opportunities available to both the Russians and the British was remarkable. Our response to this should not be tougher legislation. Instead as consumers we have a responsibility to be more vigilant, to consider where our news has come from, to question the source of polls before accepting their results, to ask about the funding of pressure groups we read about, and to scrutinize the business dealings and contacts of those who represent us politically.

For all the similarities between the British and Russian operations which finished in 1941 and 2016 respectively there are stark and irresolvable differences. While the Russian campaign aimed to deepen the mistrust of American democracy and create a more polarized society, the British one sought to legitimize White House policy and unite the country behind the president. Whereas the British wanted to defeat one of the most tyrannical and murderous regimes in world history, the Russians were motivated partly by a desire to shore up their own authoritarian kleptocracy.

But the most interesting difference between the two campaigns takes us back to Bill Stephenson. While the Russians were relatively conservative in trying to coordinate with individual Americans, such as those around Donald Trump, the British could afford to be bolder given the much stronger ties between the two countries. By the time Hitler declared war on the US in December 1941, the barriers of nationality dividing the White House, Bill Donovan's office, and that of Bill Stephenson, were at times hard to make out. The secret to Stephenson's success was not so much his single-mindedness or an affinity for risk-taking, but his ability to work with his American counterparts. His greatest innovation as MI6 Head of Station in the US came within the first few days of meeting his staff, when he said of the American people: 'They're our friends. They'll help us. And we need them if we're going to win.'[3]

Donovan, Willkie, Roosevelt, Thompson, the leading lights in the Century Group and the hundreds of men and women working in Donovan's office were just some of the Americans who entered into the orbit of Stephenson's office – working *with* them, not *for* them – as part of a joint effort to bring the US into the war against Nazi Germany. Rather than see this behind-the-scenes campaign as an either British or American operation, it was instead a masterclass in collaboration. To protect their country from Hitler, the American interventionists needed to work with and learn from their transatlantic cousins. To ensure their survival and take back control of their destiny, the British forged a meaningful alliance with a powerful rival.

Churchill apparently told King George VI in the wake of Hitler's declaration of war that Britain and America 'were now "married" after many months of "walking out"'.[4] Many historians have picked up on the analogous bond between Churchill and Roosevelt, and their symbolic marriage when pictured standing together on the porch of the White House in late 1941. The friendship between these two was vital, but so was the bond between Bill Stephenson and Bill Donovan. It meant that on the day the United States came into the war there was already an exceptionally close intelligence-sharing relationship between the two nations.

This would change in the years ahead. As Donovan's agency was renamed the Office for Strategic Services (OSS) and later transformed into the Central Intelligence Agency (CIA), a cold wind of suspicion rushed in. Partnership was superseded by rivalry. But the legacy of that initial interplay between the two endures to this day. For the CIA historian Tom Troy, Stephenson's great achievement was the part he played 'in the establishment of the Anglo-American intelligence collaboration', which 'has been an abiding factor in international affairs ever since'.[5] A friendship forged over cocktails in the Stork Club, at the tail end of 1940, made a lasting impression on the close, tense and at times special relationship between the two countries.

Acknowledgements

I wrote this book in a variety of places, from the kitchen at home to a succession of university archives, libraries, airplane seats, a shared office space and a hodge-podge of local cafés. My thanks to everyone in these spaces for putting up with me over the last two years, and in many cases for providing much-needed help. In particular: Katie Young at the University of Arizona, Tara Craig at Columbia University, Vicky Holmes and Helen Ward at the University of Leicester, Sarah McElroy Mitchell at the Lilly Library, Indiana, April Armstrong at Princeton University, Michele Beckerman at the Rockefeller Archive Center, Christine Roussel at the Rockefeller Center Archives, Sarah Patton at Stanford University, Julia Chambers at Syracuse University, Michael Frost at Yale University and most of all to Elizabeth Seitz at University of Regina for her warmth and understanding. I am also grateful to those institutions which gave permission to quote from unpublished archival material.

Many other people have helped along the way, either giving interviews, advice, support, or just pointing me in the right direction. My thanks to William Boyd, Jon Cuneo, Stephen Dorril, Nicholas Ellison, Charlotte Houghteling, Gillian Johnson, Mary Lovell, Bill MacDonald – whose excellent book *The True Intrepid* is full of interesting details on Stephenson's early years – Penel Meredith-Hardy, Giles Milton,

Peter & Jane Pleydell-Bouverie, Edgar Raines, Nicholas Shakespeare, Jared Simard, Rick Stroud, Darren Tromblay, Jay Tunney, Gerhard Weinberg and John Williams. Special thanks to Claire Straw, Gill Bennett, Cutler Cook, Lizzie Lewis, Bea Hemming – for her help throughout – and the superlative Perdita Martell for taking the time to look through the manuscript. Thanks also to the researchers I worked with, including the indefatigable Ashley Sweetman, Ben Barham-Marsh, Steven Kippax, Kevin Leonard, Jeremy Bigwood and Jenny Fichmann.

While much of this book was written in crowded spaces, there were two remarkable exceptions. George and Lizzie Lewis very kindly looked after me in New York, which is where I began to write this book – at their kitchen table with a pet rabbit by my feet. I would also like to thank David Campbell and the trustees of the Hawthornden Literary Institute for generously having me to stay in Casa Ecco, and to Marilena and Margarita for their wonderful cooking and company.

I am indebted to all those who have worked on the book at PublicAffairs and Quercus, from John English and Anthony Hippisley to Ana McLaughlin and Elizabeth Masters, and most of all to the two Bens, a model of transatlantic cooperation to rival the two Bills: Ben Adams in New York, for his encouragement and consistently wise advice; and Ben Brock in London for his excellent judgement and skilful handling of the project. Working with both has been an absolute pleasure. I could not ask for better editors.

Nor could I hope for better film agents in the shape of Gemma Hirst and Katie Snaydon. I'm thrilled to be working on the dramatic adaptation of this book with Rosanne, Jez and Ed at Element Pictures.

None of this, however, would have happened without the support and friendship of my literary agent, Jonathan Conway, who has been involved at every stage of this project. I cannot thank him enough.

Moving steadily closer to home, I am unendingly grateful to my Mum, Sukie Hemming, for her help, her generosity, for her food, and for every time she took Matilda to leave me with a writing window. Without this, the deadline, as Douglas Adams put it, would have whooshed by. Nor could I have done this without the support of the two children in the back of that Buick as it roared into the United States in late 1941: Louisa Service and John Hemming, my aunt and Dad. Their loan of Harold and Alice's papers and their advice and comments were all vital. In a different way, I'm grateful to the two children often to be found in the back of our Prius as it hums around south-west London: Matilda and Sam. Well done Matilda for putting up with Daddy as he finished the book, and Sam, for everything that you are. It may not happen for a while, but I hope you both get to read this one day.

Finally, I want to thank my wife, Helena, whose presence is woven deep into the fabric of this book. She has buoyed me throughout and been a constant source of advice on what's interesting and what's not. She was the first to attack this text with her trusty red pen. She has an incredible flair for storytelling, and is imbued with superhuman patience and love. She is extraordinary. I am indebted to her and could not have written this without her.

Notes

Given that in so many ways the theme of this book is provenance, it is perhaps more important than ever to provide the source of each quotation. Most have come from published material, including memoirs, diaries, public opinion surveys, biographies, histories, newspapers, journals and magazines. There is one caveat on public opinion surveys. During the early 1940s, the Gallup Organization frequently excluded from its survey results any respondents who had no opinion, so that if a third of the interviewees replied 'yes' to a question, another third said 'no' and a final third said 'don't know', Gallup might report that 50 per cent of the population had said 'yes'. Where this has happened I have adjusted the results accordingly.

Other notes relate to unpublished material. Most of these papers I was able to access either in person or virtually at a variety of archives, libraries and institutions in Britain, Canada and the US. Below is a guide to the abbreviations I have used for each. If you would like more detail on any of these please get in touch via my author website and I will do my best to point you in the right direction.

ADM (Records of the Admiralty) – National Archives, London, UK

Adolf A. Berle Papers – Franklin D. Roosevelt Presidential Library, Hyde Park (NY), US

CAB (Cabinet Office files) – National Archives, London, UK

Charles A. Lindbergh Papers – Yale University (CT), US

Dorothy Thompson Papers – Syracuse University Libraries (NY), US

Ernest Cuneo Papers – Franklin D. Roosevelt Presidential Library, Hyde Park (NY), US

Fight For Freedom Papers – Princeton University (NJ), US

FO (Foreign Office records) – National Archives, London, UK

HS (Records of Special Operations Executive) – National Archives, London, UK

KV (Records of the Security Service) – National Archives, London, UK

Lewis W. Douglas Papers – University of Arizona (AZ), US

Nelson A. Rockefeller Private Papers – Rockefeller Archive Center, Sleepy Hollow (NY), US

Non-Sectarian Anti-Nazi League to Champion Human Rights Papers – Columbia University, New York City (NY), US

PREM (Prime Minister's Office files) – National Archives, London, UK

President's Secretary's File – Franklin D. Roosevelt Presidential Library, Hyde Park (NY), US

Rene MacColl Papers – University of Leicester, UK

RG 59 (State Department Papers) – National Archives, Washington (DC), US

RG 226 (George Office Records) – National Archives, Washington (DC), US

Whitney Hart Shepardson Papers – Franklin D. Roosevelt Presidential Library, Hyde Park (NY), US

William Stevenson Papers – University of Regina, Canada

Epigraphs

1 Alexander Hamilton, *Pacificus No. VI*, 17 July 1793 • 2 Charles Eade (ed.), *The War Speeches of the Rt Hon. Winston S. Churchill*, Vol. 2 (London: Cassell, 1952), pp. 151, 202

Preface

1 Nicholas Cull, *Selling War* (New York & Oxford: Oxford University Press, 1995), p. 4 • 2 David Ignatius, 'Britain's War in America', *Washington Post*, 17 September 1989, Outlook, C1–2 • 3 Thomas F. Troy in Bill MacDonald, *The True Intrepid* (Vancouver: Raincoast, 2001), p. 4 • 4 'A Blonde Bond', *Time*, 20 December 1963, p. 23 • 5 Fortune, July 1940, 'Which of these comes closest to expressing what you think the US should do now? Enter the war at once on the side of the Allies: 7.7%; *Public Opinion Quarterly*, Vol. 4 (Princeton: Princeton University, 1940), p. 714 • 6 Gallup, 17 December 1941 (survey period 15–20 November 1941), 'Which of these two things do you think is the more important – that this country keep out of war, or that Germany be defeated?' Defeat Germany – 68%; *Public Opinion Quarterly*, Vol. 6 (Oxford: Oxford University Press, Spring 1942), p. 151 • 7 Psy-Group motto quoted in Adam Entous and Ronan Farrow, 'Deception, Inc.', *New Yorker*, 18 & 25 February 2019, pp. 44–57 • 8 Thomas E. Mahl, *Desperate Deception* (Dulles, VA: Brassey's, 1999), p. 47 • 9 King Tut, 'Fake News', *The Advocate Messenger* (Danville, KY), 5 April 1939, p. 2

PART ONE

1 Losses to the end of May 1940 calculated from Donald P. Steury, 'The Character of the German Naval Offensive', Timothy J. Runyan & Jan M. Copes (eds), *To Die Gallantly* (Boulder, CO, San Francisco & Oxford: Westview Press, 1994), pp. 75–94; Retrieved from https://web.archive.org/web/20090409070707/http://www.spartacus.schoolnet.co.uk:80/2WWbritishA.htm on 22 January 2019; SteveMerc, 'Evaluating The German Army and Luftwaffe's Growth From September of 1939 to June of 1941', 23 October 2017, retrieved from globeatwar.com on 19 March 2019 • 2 Gallup, 29 May 1940 (survey date 18–23 May 1940) 'Do you think the United States should declare war on Germany and send our army and navy abroad to fight?' Yes – 7%; *Public Opinion Quarterly*, Vol. 4 (Oxford: Oxford University Press, 1940), p. 552

Chapter 1

1 Winston Churchill quoted in Warren F. Kimball (ed.), *Churchill and Roosevelt* (Princeton & Woodstock, Oxon: Princeton University Press, 1984), p. 43 • 2 Churchill quoted in Stanley Weintraub, 'Churchill's War', *Washington Post*, 4 December 2005, retrieved from https://www.washingtonpost.com/archive/entertainment/books/2005/12/04/churchills-war/94bcbcf5-fa95-4064-bf53-7bc55c1187b2/ on 4 December 2018 • 3 Churchill, 'We Shall Fight on the Beaches', 4 June 1940, retrieved from https://winstonchurchill.org/ on 18 March 2019 • 4 'Britannic, Athlone's Ship, Here With 760, Including Jan Masaryk', *New York Times*, 22 June 1940, p. 17 • 5 Adolf Berle quoted by Thomas F. Troy in Bill MacDonald, *The True Intrepid* (Vancouver: Raincoast, 2001), p. 1 • 6 Grace Garner in MacDonald, *The True Intrepid*, p. 273 • 7 'Stephenson–Dahl', Roll 2, 83-7, Box 4, File 500.1-4, William Stevenson Papers • 8 David Ogilvy, *Blood, Brains and Beer* (London: Hamish Hamilton, 1978), p. 57 • 9 Charles M. Peters, *Five Days in Philadelphia* (New York: PublicAffairs, 2005), pp. 77–8

Chapter 2

1 Malcolm Muggeridge, *Chronicles of Wasted Time*, Vol. 2 (London: Collins, 1973), p. 136 • 2 Macdonald, *The True Intrepid*, p. 26 • 3 William Stevenson, *A Man Called Intrepid* (London: Macmillan, 1976), p. 4 • 4 Stevenson, *A Man Called Intrepid*, Contributing Material, 83-7, Box 10, File 801.10-11, William Stevenson Papers • 5 Military Cross citation, *Supplement to the London Gazette*, 22 June 1918, p. 7423 • 6 Alice Hemming, Diary, 26 Sept 1937, Private Collection • 7 Gill Bennett, *Churchill's Man of Mystery* (London & New York: Routledge, 2007), p. 193 • 8 Quoted in Bennett, *Churchill's Man of Mystery*, p. 193 • 9 S. Freeman-Mitford, Memorandum, February 1940, FO 371/24237/A.3779 • 10 Gene Tunney, 83-7 Box 4, File 500.1-7, p.1, 'CBC Tuesday Night: The Two Bills', William Stevenson Papers • 11 Edward K. Merritt quoted in Thomas F. Troy, *Wild Bill and Intrepid* (New Haven & London: Yale University Press, 1996), p. 34 • 12 William Stephenson quoted in Keith Jeffery, *MI6* (London: Bloomsbury, 2011), p. 439 • 13 Federal Bureau of Investigation, 'British Intelligence Service in the United States (Running Memorandum)', 1 January 1947, p. 20 • 14 William Donovan quoted in Troy, *Wild Bill and Intrepid*, p. 149 • 15 Stewart Menzies quoted in Bennett, *Churchill's Man of Mystery*, p. 254 • 16 Gallup, 23 May 1940 (survey date 16–21 May 1940), 'If England and France are unable to pay cash for airplanes they buy in this country, do you think we should sell them planes on credit supplied by our Government? No – 46%; *Public Opinion Quarterly*, Vol. 4 (Oxford: Oxford University Press, 1940), p. 552 • 17 John Bruce Lockhart quoted in Christopher Andrew, *For the President's Eyes Only* (London: HarperCollins,

1995), p. 39 • 18 Lord Lothian, 13 June 1940, FO 1093/140 • 19 Jeffery, *MI6*, p. 450 • 20 Gladwyn Jebb, 15 June 1940, FO 1093/140

Chapter 3

1 'New York's Newest Apartment Building Overlooking Central Park', *House and Garden*, October 1937, Vol. 72, pp. 60–1 • 2 Noel Coward, *The Autobiography of Noel Coward* (London: Methuen, 1999), p. 391 • 3 Gill Bennett, *Churchill's Man of Mystery* (London: Routledge, 2007), p. 220 • 4 Bickham Sweet-Escott, *Baker Street Irregular* (London: Methuen, 1965), p. 132 • 5 Colonel John Magruder to Cordell Hull, 3 August 1940, RG 59/4930/841.20211/23 • 6 Stewart Menzies quoted in Bennett, *Churchill's Man of Mystery*, p. 220 • 7 Walter Bell interviewed in Bill MacDonald, *The True Intrepid* (Vancouver: Raincoast, 2001), p. 229 • 8 Bill Ross Smith interviewed in MacDonald, *The True Intrepid*, p. 210 • 9 Roald Dahl, 'Stephenson–Dahl', Roll 2, 83-7, Box 4, File 500.1-4, William Stevenson Papers • 10 Betty Raymond interviewed in MacDonald, *The True Intrepid*, p. 224 • 11 Roald Dahl interviewed in MacDonald, *The True Intrepid*, p. 248 • 12 Walter Bell interviewed in MacDonald, *The True Intrepid*, p. 230 • 13 Dick Ellis, 'Colonel Ellis Roll', Roll C, T83-7, Box 4, File 500.1-4, William Stevenson Papers • 14 Ross Smith interviewed in MacDonald, *The True Intrepid*, p. 208

Chapter 4

1 'Lindbergh is Guarded as he Reaches NY', *Lincoln Star*, 15 April 1939, p. 3 • 2 'Lindbergh Here, Guarded by Police', *New York Times*, 16 April 1939, p. 8 • 3 Lindbergh quoted in A. Scott Berg, *Lindbergh* (London: Macmillan, 1998), p. 387 • 4 'Lindbergh is Guarded as he Reaches NY', *Lincoln Star*, 15 April 1939, p. 3 • 5 Philip Roth, *The Plot Against America* (London: Vintage, 2016), p. 6 • 6 'Lindbergh Here, Guarded by Police', *New York Times,* 16 April 1939, p. 8 • 7 Charles Lindbergh, Diaries, 19 May 1940, Series V, Box 215, Charles A. Lindbergh Papers • 8 Milton Bronner, 'Lindbergh Transformed from Shy Young Air Hero to Political Figure', *Marshfield News-Herald*, 15 April 1939, p. 4 • 9 Charles F. Adams (ed.), *The Works of John Adams*, Vol. 2 (Boston: Little, Brown, 1850), p. 505 • 10 Washington and Jefferson quoted in David Fromkin, 'Entangling Alliances', *Foreign Affairs*, July 1970

Chapter 5

1 Hans Thomsen to Foreign Ministry, 22 May 1940, Document No. 299, *Documents on German Foreign Policy, 1918–1945*, Series D, Vol. 9 (London: HMSO, 1956), pp. 410–12 • 2 Thomsen to Foreign Ministry, 19 June 1940, Document No. 493, *Documents on German Foreign Policy, 1918–1945*, Series D, Vol. 9, pp. 625–6 • 3 Ibid. • 4 Ibid. • 5 Hans Thomsen to Foreign Ministry, 27 June 1940, Document No. 39, *Documents on German Foreign Policy, 1918–1945*, Series D, Vol. 10 (London: HMSO, 1956), pp. 39–40 • 6 Ibid. • 7 Fortune, July 1940, 'Which of these comes closest to expressing what you think the US should do now? Enter the war at once on the side of the Allies: 7.7%, *Public Opinion Quarterly*, Vol. 4 (Princeton: Princeton University, 1940), p. 714 • 8 Thomsen to Foreign Ministry, 4 July 1940, Document No. 108, *Documents on German Foreign Policy, 1918–1945*, Series D, Vol. 10, pp. 119–21 • 9 Lord Lothian to Foreign Office, 26 June 1940, FO 371/24230/A.3464 • 10 Thomsen to Foreign Ministry, 5 July 1940, Document No. 112, *Documents on German Foreign Policy, 1918–1945*, Series D, Vol. 10, pp. 125–6 • 11 Thomsen to Foreign Ministry, 12 June 1940, Document No. 417, *Documents on German Foreign Policy, 1918–1945*, Series D, Vol. 9, pp. 550–1 • 12 Ibid. • 13 'Stop the March to War', *New York Times*, 25 June 1940, p. 19 • 14 Thomsen to Foreign Ministry, 3 July 1940, Document No. 91, *Documents on German Foreign Policy, 1918–1945*, Series D, Vol. 10, pp. 101–2 • 15 David Stout, 'How Nazis Tried to Steer U.S. Politics', *New York Times*, 23 July 1997, p. 17 • 16 Hamilton Fish, 4 April 1940, *Congressional Record*, Vol. 86, Part 4, p. 4027 • 17 'Polish Papers Linking US With War Called Fakes', *Emporia Gazette*, 30 March 1940, p. 5 • 18 Charles Lindbergh, Diaries, 12 June 1940, Series V, Box 215, Charles A. Lindbergh Papers • 19 Lindbergh, Diaries, 15 June 1940 • 20 Alton Frye, *Nazi Germany and the American Hemisphere, 1933–1941* (New Haven & London: Yale University Press, 1967), p. 138 • 21 Ernest Lundeen, 17 June 1940, *Congressional Record*, Vol. 86, Part 8, p. 8357 • 22 Lindbergh, Diaries, 15 June 1940 • 23 Editorial, *Pittsburgh Press*, 17 June 1940, p. 12 • 24 'Our First Duty – To Our Own', *Detroit Free Press*, 18 June 1940, p. 6 • 25 Hamilton Fish, 22 June 1940, *Congressional Record*, Vol. 86, Part 8, quoted in Box 285, Folder 18, Non-Sectarian Anti-Nazi League Papers • 26 Donald Heath to State Department, 29 May 1940, RG 59/4930/ 841.20211/23

Chapter 6

1 Gladwyn Jebb to Stewart Menzies, 7 July 1940, FO 1093/238 • 2 Menzies to Jebb, 12 July 1940, FO 1093/238 • 3 Quoted in Christopher Baxter, 'The Secret Intelligence Service and the origins of the Anglo-American Intelligence Relationship, 1940–1941', FCO Historians, *World War to Cold War: the records of the FO Permanent Under-Secretary's Department, 1939–51* (London: Foreign & Commonwealth Office, 2013), p. 35 • 4 Jay Racusin, 'Hitler's Agent Ensconced in Westchester', *New York Herald Tribune*, 1 August 1940, p. 1 • 5 Helen Reid to Lord Halifax, 13 July 1939, FO 800/324 • 6 British Security Coordination, *The Secret History of British Intelligence in the Americas, 1940–1945* (New York: Fromm, 1999), p. 20 • 7 'Dr. Westrick Living on Scarsdale Estate', *New York Times*, 1 August 1940, p. 3; 'Nazi Agent's Auto Permit Suspended', *Baltimore Sun*, 2 August 1940, p. 1 • 8 Racusin, 'Hitler's Agent Ensconced in Westchester'; 'Mystery Nazi Agent Sees Many Oil Firm Executives', *Philadelphia Inquirer*, 1 August 1940; Editorial, 'The Disappearing Doktor', *New York Herald Tribune*, 2 August 1940, p. 12 • 9 Gerhard Westrick to Ernst von Weizsäcker, 27 June 1940, Document No. 40, *Documents on German Foreign Policy, 1918–1945*, Series D, Vol. 10 (London: HMSO, 1956), p. 40 • 10 'Nazi Agent's Auto Permit Suspended', *Baltimore Sun*, 2 August 1940, p. 13 • 11 British Security Coordination, *The Secret History of British Intelligence in the Americas, 1940–1945*, p. 57 • 12 Hans Thomsen to Foreign Ministry, 5 August 1940, Document No. 287, *Documents on German Foreign Policy, 1918–1945*, Series D, Vol. 10 (London: HMSO, 1956), pp. 411–13 • 13 Lord Lothian, *The American Speeches of Lord Lothian* (London: Oxford University Press, 1941), p. 47 • 14 Winston Churchill, *The Second World War*, Vol. 5 (London: Cassell, 1952), p. 338 • 15 Roald Dahl interviewed in Bill MacDonald, *The True Intrepid* (Vancouver: Raincoast, 2001), p. 239 • 16 Betty Raymond interviewed in MacDonald, *The True Intrepid*, p. 224 • 17 Pat Bayly interviewed in MacDonald, *The True Intrepid*, p. 325

Chapter 7

1 'Co-Operate with the Victor is the Lindbergh Plea', *Kane Republican*, 5 August 1940, p. 1 • 2 Friedrich von Bötticher and Hans Thomsen to Foreign Ministry, 6 August 1940, Document No. 288, *Documents on German Foreign Policy, 1918–1945*, Series D, Vol. 10 (London: HMSO, 1956), pp. 413–15 • 3 Bötticher to Foreign Ministry, 23 May 1940, Document No. 311, *Documents on German Foreign Policy, 1918-1945*, Series D, Vol. 9, pp. 4424–7 • 4 Charles Lindbergh, Diaries,

4 August 1940, Series V, Box 215, Charles A. Lindbergh Papers • 5 'Lindbergh Proposes Accord for America and Germany', *Los Angeles Times*, 5 August 1940, p. 2 • 6 George Tagge, 'Rally Cheers Lindbergh Plea for US Peace', *Chicago Tribune*, 5 August 1940, p. 1 • 7 Lindbergh, Diaries, 8 June 1940 • 8 Gerhard Westrick to Ernst von Weizsäcker, 18 July 1940, Document No. 187, *Documents on German Foreign Policy, 1918–1945*, Series D, Vol. 10, p. 244 • 9 John H. Crider, 'Pershing Would Let Britain Have 50 Old US Destroyers To Guard Our Own Liberty', *New York Times*, 5 August 1940, p. 1 • 10 Bötticher and Thomsen to Foreign Ministry, 20 July 1940, Document No. 195, *Documents on German Foreign Policy, 1918-1945*, Series D, Vol. 10, pp. 254–6

Chapter 8

1 Francis Miller to Sterling Fisher, 15 August 1940, Box 23, Folder 10, Fight For Freedom Papers • 2 Lord Lothian to Frederick Whyte, 27 February 1940, FO 371/24227, A1852/26/45 • 3 Lothian to Foreign Office, 1 February 1940, FO 800/324 • 4 Lothian to Whitney H. Shepardson, Group 91, 'Lord Lothian', Whitney Shepardson Papers • 5 Winston Churchill quoted in Martin Gilbert, *The Churchill War Papers*, Vol. 2 (London: Heinemann, 1994), p. 576 • 6 Lothian to Shepardson, Group 91, 'Lord Lothian', Whitney Shepardson Papers • 7 Mark Chadwin, *The Hawks of World War II* (Chapel Hill, NC: University of North Carolina Press, 1968), p. 75 • 8 Cass R. Sunstein, 'Impeaching the President', *University of Pennsylvania Law Review*, December 1998, Vol. 147, No. 2, pp. 279–315 • 9 Churchill to Franklin D. Roosevelt, 31 July 1940, quoted in Warren F. Kimball (ed.), *Churchill and Roosevelt* (Princeton & Woodstock, Oxon: Princeton University Press, 1984), p. 56 • 10 Herbert Agar, *Britain Alone* (London: Bodley Head, 1972), p. 149

Chapter 9

1 Eric Maschwitz, *No Chip On My Shoulder* (London: Herbert Jenkins, 1957), p. 127 • 2 Ibid. • 3 Ibid., p. 128 • 4 Ibid., p. 127 • 5 Ibid., p. 130 • 6 Ibid., p. 134 • 7 Ibid., p. 135 • 8 Ibid., p. 136

Chapter 10

1 Admiral John Godfrey, 'Interview with Colonel Donovan', 2 August 1940, ADM 223/84 • 2 William Donovan quoted in Douglas C. Waller, *Wild Bill Donovan* (New York: Free Press, 2010), p. 22 • 3 Christopher Andrew, *For the President's*

Eyes Only (London: HarperCollins, 1995), p. 73 • 4 John Wheeler-Bennett, *Special Relationships* (London: Macmillan, 1975), p. 157 • 5 Waller, *Wild Bill Donovan*, p. 57 • 6 William Stephenson to Stewart Menzies, 15 July 1940, quoted in British Security Coordination, *The Secret History of British Intelligence in the Americas, 1940–1945* (New York: Fromm, 1999), p. 9 • 7 Stephenson to Menzies, 16 July 1940, quoted in British Security Coordination, *The Secret History of British Intelligence in the Americas, 1940–1945*, p. 10 • 8 Archibald Sinclair quoted in Thomas F. Troy, *Wild Bill and Intrepid* (New Haven & London: Yale University Press), 1996, p. 79 • 9 Dale Carnegie, *How to Win Friends and Influence People* (New York: Simon and Schuster, 1936), pp. 37–8 • 10 Godfrey, 'Interview with Colonel Donovan', ADM 223/84 • 11 British Security Coordination, *The Secret History of British Intelligence in the Americas, 1940–1945*, p. 9 • 12 Godfrey, 'Interview with Colonel Donovan', ADM 223/84 • 13 Donovan quoted in Thomas E. Mahl, *Desperate Deception* (Dulles, VA: Brassey's), 1999, p. 82 • 14 'Col. Donovan Urges Passage of Draft Bill', *Courier-Journal* (Louisville, KY), 18 August 1940, p. 7 • 15 Donovan quoted in Mahl, *Desperate Deception*, p. 82 • 16 Donovan and Edgar Mowrer, 'Nazi "Fifth Column" Bill For Year Put at $200,000,000', *St Louis Post-Dispatch*, 22 August 1940, p. 10 • 17 British Security Coordination, *The Secret History of British Intelligence in the Americas, 1940–1945*, p. 12 • 18 Ernest Cuneo, 'War Powers of President', undated, Ernest Cuneo Papers • 19 'Flier Who Downed 18 Germans Invents Unique Can Opener', *Winnipeg Tribune*, 29 October 1919, p. 11 • 20 Arthur Krock, 'In the Nation', *New York Times*, 7 August 1940, p. 18 • 21 Joe Kennedy quoted in Martin Gilbert, *Churchill and America* (London: Free Press, 2005), p. 201 • 22 John Balfour, Minute, 19 December 1940, FO 371/24263/A.5194/G • 23 'No Legal Bar Seen to Transfer of Destroyers', *New York Times*, 11 August 1940, p. 58 • 24 Gallup, 18 July 1940 (survey period 5–10 July 1940), 'Do you think we are giving enough help to England, or do you think ways should be found to give England more help than we are at present, but short of going to war?' Give more help 53%; *Public Opinion Quarterly*, Vol. 4 (Oxford: Oxford University Press, 1940), p. 713 • 25 Gallup, 19 August 1940 (survey period 11–16 August 1940), 'General Pershing says the United States should sell to England 50 of our destroyer ships which were built during the last World War and are now being put back in service. Do you approve or disapprove of our Government selling these destroyers to England?' Approve – 57%; *Public Opinion Quarterly*, Vol. 4 (Oxford: Oxford University Press, 1940), p. 713 • 26 Lord Lothian quoted in J. R. M. Butler, *Lord Lothian* (London: Macmillan, 1960), p. 297

Chapter 11

1 Truman Capote, *Breakfast at Tiffany's* (Harmondsworth: Penguin, 2000), p. 76 • 2 Charles M. Peters, *Five Days in Philadelphia* (New York: PublicAffairs,

2005), pp. 168–9 • 3 Thomas E. Mahl, *Desperate Deception* (Dulles, VA: Brassey's, 1999), p. 161 • 4 Willkie quoted in Lord Lothian to Lord Halifax, 29 August 1940, FO 800/324 • 5 Lothian to Winston Churchill, 29 August 1940, PREM 4/25/8

Chapter 12

1 Charles Eade (ed.), *The War Speeches of the Rt Hon. Winston S. Churchill*, Vol. 1 (London: Cassell, 1952), p. 244 • 2 Jock Colville quoted in Martin Gilbert, *Churchill and America* (London: Free Press, 2005), p. 203 • 3 William Stephenson quoted in Keith Jeffery, *MI6* (London: Bloomsbury, 2011), p. 443 • 4 Sir Arthur Salter to Winston Churchill, 17 August 1940, quoted in Thomas F. Troy, *Wild Bill and Intrepid* (New Haven & London: Yale University Press, 1996), p. 60 • 5 Walter Lippmann, 'Today and Tomorrow', *New York Herald Tribune*, 11 February 1941, p. 19 • 6 Gallup, 2 June 1940 (survey period 16–21 May 1940), 'Should the United States require every able-bodied young man 20 years old to serve in the army, navy, or the air forces for one year?' Yes – 47%; *Public Opinion Quarterly*, Vol. 4 (Oxford: Oxford University Press, 1940), p. 551 • 7 Gallup, 29 August 1940 (survey period 11–16 August 1940), 'Do you favor increasing the size of our Army and Navy by drafting men between the ages of 18 and 32 to serve in the armed forces for one year?' Yes – 67%; *Public Opinion Quarterly*, Vol. 4 (Oxford: Oxford University Press, 1940), p. 717 • 8 'Dictator Roosevelt Commits Act of War', *St Louis Post-Dispatch*, 3 September 1940, p. 1 • 9 'Congress Ranks Split on Accord', *New York Times*, 4 September 1940, p. 16 • 10 Winston Churchill, *The Second World War*, Vol. 2 (London: Cassell, 1949), p. 358 • 11 Charles M. Peters, *Five Days in Philadelphia* (New York: PublicAffairs, 2005), p. 172 • 12 Robert H. Jackson, *That Man* (Oxford & New York: Oxford University Press, 2003), p. 74 • 13 Raymond Daniell, 'Capital is Shaken', *New York Times*, 8 September 1940, p. 1

PART TWO

1 Losses to the end of August 1940 calculated from Donald P. Steury, 'The Character of the German Naval Offensive', Timothy J. Runyan & Jan M. Copes (eds), *To Die Gallantly* (Boulder & San Francisco & Oxford: Westview Press, 1994), pp. 75-94 • 2 Gallup, 14 October 1940 (survey period 28 September–5 October 1940), 'If you were asked to vote today on the question of the United States entering the war against Germany and Italy, how would you vote — to go into the war or to stay out of the war?' Go in – 15.6%; *Public Opinion Quarterly*, Vol. 5 (Oxford: Oxford University Press, 1941), p. 159

Chapter 13

1 Charles Lindbergh, Diaries, 3 June 1940, Series V, Box 215, Charles A. Lindbergh Papers • 2 Ibid., 4 September 1940 • 3 Ibid., 7 October 1940 • 4 Mark E. Benbow, 'Birth of a Quotation: Woodrow Wilson and "Like Writing History with Lightning"', *The Journal of the Gilded Age and Progressive Era*, Vol. 9, No. 4, October 2010, pp. 509–33 • 5 Ian Kershaw, *Fateful Choices* (London: Penguin, 2013), p. 388 • 6 NBC News source quoted in https://www.vox.com/2018/1/11/16880750/trump-immigrants-shithole-countries-norway retrieved on 4 July 2018 • 7 R. Douglas Stuart to Lindbergh, 5 August 1940, Series 1, Box 1, Charles A. Lindbergh Papers quoted in Marc Wortman, *1941* (London: Atlantic, 2017), p. 136 • 8 Gallup, 7 July 1940 (survey period 27 June–2 July 1940) 'If the question of the United States going to war against Germany and Italy came up for a national vote within the next two weeks, would you vote to go into the war or to stay out of the war?' Go to war – 13%; *Public Opinion Quarterly*, Vol. 4 (Oxford: Oxford University Press, 1940), p. 714 • 9 'Jap Treaty Stirs Senators', *Chicago Tribune*, 28 September 1940, p. 1 • 10 Milton Ladd quoted in Douglas M. Charles, *J. Edgar Hoover and the Anti-Interventionists* (Columbus: Ohio State University Press, 2007), p. 46 • 11 Franklin D. Roosevelt quoted by Charles, *J. Edgar Hoover and the Anti-Interventionists*, p. 44 • 12 Henry Morgenthau quoted by Charles, *J. Edgar Hoover and the Anti-Interventionists*, p. 44

Chapter 14

1 General George Strong quoted in Bradley F. Smith, *The Ultra-Magic Deals* (Novato, CA: Presidio, 1993), p. 43 • 2 Quoted in Bill MacDonald, *The True Intrepid* (Vancouver: Raincoast, 2001), p. 72 • 3 Jean Peacock in MacDonald, *The True Intrepid*, pp. 169–70 • 4 John Balfour, Minute, 25 August 1940, FO 1093/238 • 5 British Security Coordination, *The Secret History of British Intelligence in the Americas, 1940–1945* (New York: Fromm, 1999), p. 12 • 6 Stewart Menzies to Henry Hopkinson, 3 October 1940, FO 1093/238, C/5073 • 7 John Tracy, *Winnipeg Tribune*, 7 July 1954, quoted in MacDonald, *The True Intrepid*, p. 66 • 8 H. Montgomery Hyde, *The Quiet Canadian* (London: Hamish Hamilton, 1962), p. 32 • 9 Cedric Larson, 'Propagandists Find Nation's Citizenry Allergic to Claims', *Miami News*, 5 May 1940, p. 19 • 10 Robert Calder, *Beware the British Serpent* (Montreal & Kingston, London: McGill-Queen's University Press, 2004), p. 43 • 11 Nicholas Cull, *Selling War* (New York & Oxford: Oxford University Press, 1995), p. 119 • 12 Charles de Gaulle, *War Memoirs: The Call to Honor*,

1940–42 (New York: Simon & Schuster, 1955), p. 104, quoted in Cull, *Selling War*, pp. 97–8 • 13 Winston Churchill quoted in Martin Gilbert, *Churchill and America* (London: Free Press, 2005), p. 204

Chapter 15

1 Charles Lindbergh, Diaries, 9 October 1940, Series V, Box 216, Charles A. Lindbergh Papers • 2 Gallup, 5 August 1940 (survey period 21–26 July 1940), 'If the presidential election were held today, would you vote for the Republican candidate, Wendell Willkie, or the Democratic candidate, Franklin Roosevelt?' Willkie – 43%, Roosevelt – 44%; *Public Opinion Quarterly*, Vol. 4 (Oxford: Oxford University Press, 1940), p. 705 • 3 'Americans Never Had Chance', *Cincinnati Enquirer*, 24 May 1941, p. 5 • 4 Fortune, August, September and October 1940, 'Do you agree with the following statement – never under any conditions should a President hold office for three terms?' Yes – 29.9%, 30.2% and 33.8%; *Public Opinion Quarterly*, Vol. 5 (Oxford: Oxford University Press, 1941), p. 138 • 5 'Text of President Roosevelt's Speeches in Philadelphia and Wilmington', *New York Times*, 24 October 1940, p. 14 • 6 Lindbergh, Diaries, 22 October 1940 • 7 British Security Coordination, *The Secret History of British Intelligence in the Americas, 1940–1945* (New York: Fromm, 1999), p. 72 • 8 Fortune, October 1940, 'Which of the following statements most nearly represents your opinion of Colonel Lindbergh, in the light of his recent public utterances?' Lindbergh is unpatriotic, and he may be deliberately working in the interests of Germany – 2%; *Public Opinion Quarterly*, Vol. 5 (Oxford: Oxford University Press, 1941), p. 155 • 9 Hans Thomsen to Foreign Ministry, 27 March 1940, Document No. 13, *Documents on German Foreign Policy, 1918–1945*, Series D, Vol. 9 (London: HMSO, 1956), p. 30 • 10 Thomsen to Foreign Ministry, 21 May 1940, Document No. 289, *Documents on German Foreign Policy, 1918–1945*, Series D, Vol. 9, pp. 398–400 • 11 Thomsen to Foreign Ministry, 4 November 1940, Document No. 284, *Documents on German Foreign Policy, 1918–1945*, Series D, Vol. 11 (London: HMSO, 1956), pp. 463–4 • 12 Alton Frye, *Nazi Germany and the American Hemisphere, 1933–41* (New Haven & London: Yale, 1967), p. 151 • 13 Thomsen to Foreign Ministry, 4 November 1940, Document No. 284, *Documents on German Foreign Policy, 1918–1945*, Series D, Vol. 11, pp. 463–4 • 14 Lindbergh, Diaries, 5 November 1940 • 15 Ibid. • 16 Ibid. • 17 Fortune, November 1940, 'If it comes to a question of the US declaring war, in whose judgement would you have the greater confidence, that of the President and the Department of State – whoever they are at the time – or that represented by a vote of Congress after debate?' The President – 25.7%; *Public Opinion Quarterly*, Vol. 5, March 1941 (Princeton: Princeton University, 1941), p. 159 • 18 Ted Roosevelt quoted in Marc Wortman, *1941* (London: Atlantic, 2017), p. 125 • 19 Thomsen to Foreign

Ministry, 24 December 1940, Document No. 563, *Documents on German Foreign Policy, 1918–1945*, Series D, Vol. 11, pp. 949–50 • 20 Lord Lothian to Ministry of Information, 5 August 1940, PREM 4/25/8

Chapter 16

1 Lord Lothian quoted in Nicholas Cull, *Selling War* (New York & Oxford: Oxford University Press, 1995), p. 116 • 2 John Wheeler-Bennett, *Special Relationships* (London: Macmillan, 1975), p. 112 • 3 Hans Thomsen to Foreign Ministry, 30 November 1940, Document No. 427, *Documents on German Foreign Policy, 1918–1945*, Series D, Vol. 11 (London: HMSO, 1956), pp. 751–2 • 4 Wheeler-Bennett, *Special Relationships*, p. 111 • 5 Lieutenant-Commander Colin Martell, Diary, December 1940, Private Collection • 6 Rene MacColl, Diary, 13, 27 and 30 December 1940, Rene MacColl Papers • 7 Lord Lothian quoted in H. Montgomery Hyde, *Secret Intelligence Agent* (London: Constable, 1982), p. 94

Chapter 17

1 'Donovan on Mystery Trip', *Minneapolis Star*, 7 December 1940, p. 3 • 2 '"Wild Bill" Leaves on Secret Journey', *El Paso Times*, 7 December 1940, p. 3 • 3 'Col. Donovan Flies Over Atlantic On Secret Mission Tied to France', *New York Times*, 7 December 1940, p. 1 • 4 'Donovan on Mystery Trip', *Minneapolis Star*, 7 December 1940, p. 3 • 5 'Col. Donovan Flies Over Atlantic On Secret Mission Tied to France', *New York Times*, 7 December 1940, p. 1 • 6 '"Wild Bill" Leaves on Secret Journey', *El Paso Times*, 7 December 1940, p. 3 • 7 Thomas F. Troy, *Wild Bill and Intrepid* (New Haven & London: Yale University Press, 1996), p. 61 • 8 British Security Coordination, *The Secret History of British Intelligence in the Americas, 1940–1945* (New York: Fromm, 1999), p. 3 • 9 Ibid., p. 4 • 10 H. Montgomery Hyde, *The Quiet Canadian* (London: Hamish Hamilton, 1962), p. 54 • 11 Troy, *Wild Bill and Intrepid*, p. 61 • 12 Hyde, *The Quiet Canadian*, p. 43 • 13 'British Relations with OSS' quoted in Troy, *Wild Bill and Intrepid*, p. 217 • 14 Douglas C. Waller, *Wild Bill Donovan* (New York: Free Press, 2010), p. 63 • 15 Ibid. • 16 William Stephenson, 'Early Days of OSS (COI)', p. 7, quoted in Troy, *Wild Bill and Intrepid*, p. 220 • 17 'Colonel Ellis Roll', Roll C, T83-7, Box 4, File 500.1-4, William Stevenson Papers • 18 William Langer and Sarell Gleason, *The Undeclared War* (London: Royal Institute of International Affairs, 1953), p. 397, quoted in Troy, *Wild Bill and Intrepid*, p. 78 • 19 Keith Jeffery, *MI6* (London: Bloomsbury, 2011), p. 446 • 20 Lord Lothian to Foreign Office, 5 December 1940, FO 371/24263/A.4925/4925/45 • 21 Jeffery, *MI6*, p. 446 • 22 Stephenson quoted in Jeffery, *MI6*, p. 447 • 23 Ibid., p. 446 • 24 Ibid.,

p. 447 • 25 Ibid. • 26 Donovan quoted in John Balfour, Minute, 19 December 1940, FO 371/24263/A.5194/G • 27 H. Montgomery Hyde, *Secret Intelligence Agent* (London: Constable, 1982), p. 92 • 28 Hyde, *The Quiet Canadian*, p. 48

Chapter 18

1 Eric Maschwitz, *No Chip On My Shoulder* (London: Herbert Jenkins, 1957), p. 138 • 2 Billboard Chart retrieved from http://www.old-charts.com/charts40/pdf1940USA/Wk51_Dec%2021.pdf on 27 July 2018 • 3 Maschwitz, *No Chip On My Shoulder*, p. 139 • 4 Ibid. • 5 Ibid., p. 141 • 6 John Grierson quoted in Nicholas Cull, *Selling War* (New York & Oxford: Oxford University Press, 1995), p. 114 • 7 'A Raid-Free Christmas', *The Times*, 27 December 1940, p. 2

Chapter 19

1 'Firemen Return from War Scene', *New York Times*, 15 January 1941, p. 12 • 2 Federal Bureau of Investigation, 'British Intelligence Service in the United States (Running Memorandum)', 1 January 1947, pp. 21–2 • 3 'Home Defence (Security) Executive Special Operations Executive', 15 July 1940, CAB 301/49 • 4 'Directorate of Security Coordination in America', Part III: Special Operations (SOE), HS 7/72 • 5 SOE Survey of Global Activities, February 1941, HS 7/213 • 6 Ibid., March 1941, HS 7/214 • 7 Ibid. • 8 Ibid., February 1941, HS 7/213 • 9 British Security Coordination, *The Secret History of British Intelligence in the Americas, 1940–1945* (New York: Fromm, 1999), p. 53 • 10 Federal Bureau of Investigation, 'British Intelligence Service in the United States (Running Memorandum)', 1 January 1947, pp. 21–2 • 11 British Security Coordination, *The Secret History of British Intelligence in the Americas, 1940-1945*, p. 17 • 12 Stewart Menzies quoted in Keith Jeffery, *MI6* (London: Bloomsbury, 2011), p. 448

Chapter 20

1 Adolf Berle, Diaries, 3 June 1940, Container 211, Adolf A. Berle Papers • 2 Ibid., 9 April 1940; Berle, Memorandum, 19 June 1941, Container 212, Adolf A. Berle Papers; Berle, Diaries, 20 April 1940, Container 211, Adolf A. Berle Papers; ibid., 2 October 1940 • 3 Minute, 13 December 1940, FO 371/24263/347 • 4 Berle, Diaries, 10 October 1940 • 5 Ibid., 15 October 1940 • 6 R. L. Bannerman quoted in Thomas F. Troy, *Wild Bill and Intrepid* (New Haven & London: Yale University Press, 1996), p. 221

Chapter 21

1 Robert Sherwood, *Roosevelt and Hopkins* (New York: Harper, 1950), p. 224 • 2 Raymond P. Brandt, 'Roosevelt Plan For Lease-or-Lien Arms Aid to Britain', *St Louis Post-Dispatch*, 18 December 1940, p. 2 • 3 'President's Call for Full Response on Defense', *New York Times*, 30 December 1940, p. 6 • 4 Harold B. Hinton, 'Lindbergh Urges Negotiated Peace', *New York Times*, 24 January 1941, p. 6 • 5 Charles Lindbergh, Diaries, 23 January 1941, Series V, Box 216, Charles A. Lindbergh Papers • 6 'US and Britain can't Win the war, Aid a "Mistake", Lindbergh says', *Baltimore Evening Sun*, 23 January 1941, pp. 1–2 • 7 Robert Calder, *Beware the British Serpent* (Montreal & Kingston, London: McGill-Queen's University Press, 2004), p. 13 • 8 Hans Thomsen to Foreign Ministry, 7 February 1941, Document No. 34, *Documents on German Foreign Policy, 1918–1945*, Series D, Vol. 12 (London: HMSO, 1956), pp. 60–2 • 9 Thomsen to Foreign Ministry, 24 December 1940, Document No. 563, *Documents on German Foreign Policy, 1918–1945*, Series D, Vol. 11 (London: HMSO, 1956), pp. 949–50 • 10 Thomsen to Foreign Ministry, 7 February 1941, Document No. 34, *Documents on German Foreign Policy, 1918–1945*, Series D, Vol. 12, pp. 60–2 • 11 Thomsen to Foreign Ministry, 28 January 1941, Document No. 721, *Documents on German Foreign Policy, 1918–1945*, Series D, Vol. 11, pp. 1213–1214 • 12 'Editor White of "Aid to Britain" Committee Declares Yanks Not Coming, Says Joining War Would Be Stupid', *Austin Statesman*, 23 December 1940, p. 7 • 13 Lindbergh, Diaries, 23 December 1940 • 14 Ibid., 7 January 1941 • 15 Winston Churchill quoted in Martin Gilbert, *Churchill and America* (London: Free Press, 2005), p. 211

Chapter 22

1 Rene MacColl, Diary, 22 December 1940, Rene MacColl Papers • 2 David Ogilvy, *Blood, Brains and Beer* (London: Hamish Hamilton, 1978), p. 61 • 3 William Stephenson quoted in Stewart Menzies to Henry Hopkinson, 21 January 1941, FO 1093/238, C/5730 • 4 Pat Bayly interviewed in Bill MacDonald, *The True Intrepid* (Vancouver: Raincoast, 2001), p. 314 • 5 H. Montgomery Hyde, *The Quiet Canadian* (London: Hamish Hamilton, 1962), p. 48 • 6 H. Montgomery Hyde, *Secret Intelligence Agent* (London: Constable, 1982), p. 92 • 7 Winston Churchill to Dudley Pound, 17 February 1941, quoted in Thomas F. Troy, *Wild Bill and Intrepid* (New Haven & London: Yale University Press, 1996), p. 220 • 8 Douglas M. Charles, *J. Edgar Hoover and the Anti-Interventionists* (Columbus: Ohio

State University Press, 2007), p. 64 • 9 'Warns US of Axis', *New York Times*, 12 February 1941, p. 1 • 10 Steve Neal, *Dark Horse* (Lawrence, KS: University Press of Kansas, 1989), p. 184 • 11 'Warns US of Axis', *New York Times*, 12 February 1941, p. 1 • 12 'Aid Britain or War in 60 Days – Willkie', Richard L. Turner, *Indianapolis Star*, 12 February 1941, p. 12; 'Willkie Plea May Speed Aid to Britain', *Circleville Herald*, 12 February 1941, p. 1; 'Give Britain 10 Destroyers a Month – Willkie', *The Waco News-Tribune*, 12 February 1941, p. 1 • 13 'Outline of Dinner Meeting', 11 November 1940, Lewis W. Douglas Papers • 14 Frederic Coudert to Lewis Douglas, 31 December 1940, Lewis W. Douglas Papers • 15 Neal, *Dark Horse*, p. 188 • 16 Ibid., p. 191 • 17 British Security Coordination, *The Secret History of British Intelligence in the Americas, 1940–1945* (New York: Fromm, 1999), p. 17 • 18 'Mr. Willkie Checks Out', *Chicago Tribune*, 18 January 1941, p. 8 • 19 Stephenson quoted in Menzies to Hopkinson, 21 January 1941, FO 1093/238, C/5730 • 20 Ibid. • 21 Ibid. • 22 Ibid. • 23 Report, 6 June 1941, PREM 4/26/6 • 24 Robert Sherwood, *Roosevelt and Hopkins* (New York: Harper, 1950), p. 635 • 25 Carlton Savage quoted in Neal, *Dark Horse*, p. 206 • 26 Samuel Grafton, 'I'd Rather be Right', *New York Post*, March 1941

Chapter 23

1 Stewart Menzies to Alexander Cadogan, 1 April 1941, FO 1093/238, C/6122 • 2 'Donovan Tour "Impudent"', *New York Herald Tribune*, 29 January 1941, p. 3 • 3 H. Montgomery Hyde, *The Quiet Canadian* (London: Hamish Hamilton, 1962), p. 46 • 4 Menzies to Cadogan, 1 April 1941, FO 1093/238, C/6122 • 5 Lord Halifax to Foreign Office, 2 May 1941, FO 371/26147 • 6 Harold Ickes, *The Secret Diary of Harold L. Ickes*, Vol. 3 (New York: Da Capo, 1974), p. 466 • 7 Churchill quoted in Martin Gilbert, *Churchill and America* (London: Free Press, 2005), p. 219 • 8 Adolf Berle, Memorandum, 18 February 1941, Container 212, Adolf A. Berle Papers • 9 Berle, Diaries, 18 February 1941, Container 212, Adolf A. Berle Papers • 10 'Reich Warns US', *New York Times*, 26 May 1941, p. 1 • 11 Adolf Hitler quoted in Marc Wortman, *1941* (London: Atlantic, 2017), p. 51

Chapter 24

1 Gallup, 29 May 1940 (survey period 18–23 May 1940), 'Do you think the United States should declare war on Germany and send our army and navy abroad to fight?' Yes – 7%; *Public Opinion Quarterly*, Vol. 4 (Oxford: Oxford University Press, 1940), p. 552. Fortune, July 1940, 'Which of these comes closest to expressing what you think the US should do now? Enter the war at once on the side of the Allies – 7.7%, *Public Opinion Quarterly*, Vol. 4, (Oxford: Oxford University Press, 1940), p.

714 • 2 Gallup, 30 December 1940 (survey period 1–6 December 1940), 'If you were asked to vote on the question of the United States entering the war against Germany and Italy, how would you vote — to go into the war or to stay out of the war?' Go in – 12%; *Public Opinion Quarterly*, Vol. 5 (Oxford: Oxford University Press, 1941), pp. 325–6 • 3 Steve Snider, 'Hot Dog Baffles Lord Halifax', *Austin American*, 11 May 1941, p. 19 • 4 Ibid. • 5 Kenneth S. Davis, *FDR, The War President, 1940–43* (New York: Random House, 2000), p. 152 • 6 Harry Hopkins quoted in David Roll, *The Hopkins Touch* (Oxford & New York: Oxford University Press, 2013), p. 105 • 7 Adolf Berle quoted in Thomas F. Troy, *Wild Bill and Intrepid* (New Haven & London: Yale University Press, 1996), p. 74 • 8 Ibid., p. 221 • 9 British Security Coordination, *The Secret History of British Intelligence in the Americas, 1940–1945* (New York: Fromm, 1999), p. 69 • 10 Stewart Menzies to Henry Hopkinson, 27 March 1941, FO 1093/166, C/6094 • 11 William Stephenson quoted in British Security Coordination, *The Secret History of British Intelligence in the Americas, 1940–1945*, p. 69 • 12 Ibid. • 13 Walter Bell interviewed in Bill MacDonald, *The True Intrepid* (Vancouver: Raincoast, 2001), p. 231 • 14 British Security Coordination, *The Secret History of British Intelligence in the Americas, 1940–1945*, p. 69 • 15 Ibid. • 16 'Directorate of Security Coordination in America', Part III: Special Operations (SOE), HS 7/72 • 17 Canadian Broadcasting Corporation, interview with Roald Dahl for 'A Man Called Intrepid', take 1-2, William Stevenson Papers

PART THREE

1 Losses to the end of April 1941 calculated from Donald P. Steury, 'The Character of the German Naval Offensive', Timothy J. Runyan & Jan M. Copes (eds), *To Die Gallantly* (Boulder, CO, San Francisco & Oxford: Westview Press, 1994), pp. 75-94 • 2 Fortune, April 1941, 'Would you be in favour of sending an army to Europe?' Yes – 21.5%; *Public Opinion Quarterly*, Vol. 5 (Oxford: Oxford University Press, 1941), p. 487

Chapter 25

1 Press Release, 24 April 1941, Box 273, Folder 11, Non-Sectarian Anti-Nazi League Papers • 2 'Fights Flare at Lindbergh Talk', *Indianapolis News*, 24 April 1941, p. 11 • 3 Ibid. • 4 'British Seek Another AEF, Lindbergh Tells 10,000 Here', *New York Times*, 24 April 1941, pp. 1 and 12 • 5 British Security Coordination, *The Secret History of British Intelligence in the Americas, 1940–1945* (New York: Fromm, 1999), p. 69 • 6 SOE Survey of Global Activities, March 1941, HS 7/214 • 7 Ibid. • 8 Joseph Hirschberg to James Sheldon, 21 February 1943,

Box 31, Folder 19, Non-Sectarian Anti-Nazi League Papers • 9 James Sheldon, 'Memorandum on Future Purposes of the NSANL', 19 May 1941, Box 418, Non-Sectarian Anti-Nazi League Papers • 10 'Budget', 28 February 1941, Box 418, Non-Sectarian Anti-Nazi League Papers • 11 Press Release, 24 April 1941, Box 273, Folder 11, Non-Sectarian Anti-Nazi League Papers • 12 SOE Survey of Global Activities, April 1941, HS 7/215 • 13 Bill Morrell, 10 July 1941, FO 898/103

Chapter 26

1 'British 'Chute Raid on Nazi Base Reported', *Baltimore Sun*, 18 June 1941, p. 2 • 2 'British 'Chutists Smash Airport in France, Flee With Prisoners', *New York Herald Tribune*, 18 June 1941, p. 5 • 3 'British 'Chute Raid on Nazi Base Reported', *Baltimore Sun*, 18 June 1941, p. 2; 'British 'Chutists Smash Airport in France, Flee With Prisoners', *New York Herald Tribune*, 18 June 1941, p. 5; 'Chutists Seize Nazi Airport', *New York Post*, 18 June 1941, p. 1; 'Paratroops Hit Nazis', *Daily Mirror*, 19 June 1941, p. 8; 'British Skymen's Raid', *Liverpool Echo*, 19 June 1941, p. 3; 'Paratroops', *Liverpool Evening Express*, 19 June 1941, p. 1; 'Land in France', *New Zealand Herald*, 20 June 1941; 'Parachute Raid', *Barrier Miner*, 19 June 1941, p. 2 • 4 Edmond Taylor, *Awakening from History* (London: Chatto & Windus, 1969), p. 240 • 5 SOE Survey of Global Activities, October–December 1940, HS 7/211 • 6 Bill Morrell, 10 July 1941, FO 898/103 • 7 British Security Coordination, *The Secret History of British Intelligence in the Americas, 1940–1945* (New York: Fromm, 1999), p. 59 • 8 Nicholas Cull, *Selling War* (New York & Oxford: Oxford University Press, 1995), p. 129 • 9 Morrell, 10 July 1941, FO 898/103 • 10 Ibid. • 11 Ibid. • 12 'Directorate of Security Coordination in America', Part III: Special Operations (SOE), HS 7/72 • 13 Ibid. • 14 Bill Ross Smith interviewed in Bill MacDonald, *The True Intrepid* (Vancouver: Raincoast, 2001), p. 189 • 15 H. Montgomery Hyde, *Secret Intelligence Agent* (London: Constable, 1982), p. 140 • 16 SOE Survey of Global Activities, June 1941, HS 7/217 • 17 Louis de Wohl, 'The Orchestra of Hitler's Death', WO 208/4475 • 18 Maschwitz, 83-7 Box 4, File 500.1-7, p.1, 'CBC Tuesday Night: The Two Bills', William Stevenson Papers • 19 'Directorate of Security Coordination in America', Part III: Special Operations (SOE), HS 7/72 • 20 SOE Survey of Global Activities, April 1941, HS 7/215 • 21 Ibid. • 22 'Directorate of Security Coordination in America', Part III: Special Operations (SOE), HS 7/72

Chapter 27

1 83-7 Box 4, File 500.1-7, p.1, 'CBC Tuesday Night: The Two Bills', William Stevenson Papers • 2 William Donovan quoted in H. Montgomery Hyde, *Secret Intelligence Agent* (London: Constable, 1982), p. 98 • 3 Stewart Menzies to Winston Churchill, 6 April 1941, FO 1093/166 • 4 'Report on Coordination of the three Intelligence Services,' 29 May 1941, quoted in Troy, *Wild Bill and Intrepid*, p. 120 • 5 J. Edgar Hoover quoted in Douglas C. Waller, *Wild Bill Donovan* (New York: Free Press, 2010), p. 68 • 6 Sherman Miles quoted in Thomas F. Troy, *Wild Bill and Intrepid* (New Haven & London: Yale University Press, 1996), p. 90 • 7 Donovan to Frank Knox quoted in Troy, *Wild Bill and Intrepid*, p. 116 • 8 William Stephenson quoted in Troy, *Wild Bill and Intrepid*, p. 121 • 9 Troy, *Wild Bill and Intrepid*, p. 121

Chapter 28

1 'Immigrant Schiaparelli Here, Clothes in Basket', *New York Daily News*, 26 May 1941, p. 4 • 2 Ian Fleming, Foreword, H. Montgomery Hyde, *Room 3603* (New York: Farrar, Straus, 1963), pp. ix–xii • 3 Keith Jeffery, *MI6* (London: Bloomsbury, 2011), p. 448 • 4 Fleming, Foreword, Hyde, *Room 3603*, pp. ix–xii • 5 Jeffery, *MI6*, p. 450 • 6 John Maude to Guy Liddell, 23 May 1941, KV 4/446/0h • 7 Fleming, Foreword, Hyde, *Room 3603*, pp. ix–xii • 8 Ibid. • 9 Fleming quoted in William Stevenson, *Spymistress* (New York: Arcade, 2011), p. 155 • 10 Frank Knox quoted in Thomas F. Troy, *Wild Bill and Intrepid* (New Haven & London: Yale University Press, 1996), pp. 122–3 • 11 'Major Eliot Urges U.S. to Fight Hitler with His Own Weapons', *New York Herald Tribune*, 8 May 1941, p. 10 • 12 Stephenson quoted in Troy, *Wild Bill and Intrepid*, p. 121 • 13 Jay Jakub, *Spies and Saboteurs* (London: Macmillan, 1999), p. 25 • 14 Donald McLachlan quoted in Troy, *Wild Bill and Intrepid*, p. 127 • 15 William Donovan quoted in Ibid., p. 130 • 16 US Bureau of the Budget, Records, Folder 211, quoted in Ibid., p. 128 • 17 Stewart Menzies to Henry Hopkinson, 19 June 1941, FO 1093/238 • 18 John Godfrey and Victor Cavendish-Bentinck quoted in Jeffery, *MI6*, p. 449 • 19 Troy, *Wild Bill and Intrepid*, p. 133 • 20 Menzies to Hopkinson, 19 June 1941, FO 1093/238 • 21 Stephenson, 'The Story of OSS', taped interview, quoted in H. Montgomery Hyde, *Secret Intelligence Agent* (London: Constable, 1982), p. 253

Chapter 29

1 'President Defines Lindbergh's Niche', *New York Times*, 26 April 1941, p. 5 • 2 Charles Lindbergh, Diaries, 25 April 1941, Series V, Box 216, Charles A. Lindbergh Papers • 3 Ibid., 5 May 1941 • 4 'Lindbergh Says Father's Patriotism Was Questioned, Too', *Santa Cruz Sentinel*, 11 May 1941, p. 1 • 5 Lindbergh, Diaries, 10 May 1941 • 6 George M. Mawhinney, 'British Flee Crete, Nazis say; 16,000 Hail Lindbergh Here; Says Roosevelt Seeks World Rule by US', *Philadelphia Inquirer*, 30 May 1941, p. 1 • 7 Lindbergh, Diaries, 29 May 1941 • 8 Ibid., 4 June 1941 • 9 Ibid., 4 February 1941 • 10 Ibid., 27 June 1941

Chapter 30

1 'Lindy Says U.S. Led to War', *The Tennessean*, 24 May 1941, p. 1 • 2 'How about telling the whole truth, Mr. Lindbergh – not just part of it?' *New York Times*, 23 May 1941, p. 15 • 3 Mark Chadwin, *The Hawks of World War II* (Chapel Hill, NC: University of North Carolina Press, 1968), p. 201 • 4 Ibid., p. 203 • 5 Dick Ellis quoted in Donald Downes, *The Scarlet Thread* (London: Derek Verschoyle, 1953), p. 60 • 6 'Fights Nazi Propaganda', *New York Times*, 13 June 1940, p. 5 • 7 British Security Coordination, *The Secret History of British Intelligence in the Americas, 1940–1945* (New York: Fromm, 1999), p. 77 • 8 Henry Hoke, *Black Mail* (New York: Reader's Book Service, 1944), p. 29 • 9 H. Montgomery Hyde, *The Quiet Canadian* (London: Hamish Hamilton, 1962), p. 88 • 10 Ulric Bell to Franklin D. Roosevelt, 4 June 1941, Box 28, Folder 1, Fight For Freedom Papers • 11 Hamilton Fish, 26 June 1941, *Congressional Record*, Vol. 87, Part 5, quoted in Box 285, Folder 18, Non-Sectarian Anti-Nazi League Papers • 12 Winston Churchill quoted in Peter Kurth, *American Cassandra* (Boston: Little, Brown, 1990), p. 337

Chapter 31

1 William Stephenson, 'If Time Permits', 23 July 1941, FO 371/26172/A.6153 • 2 H. Montgomery Hyde, *Secret Intelligence Agent* (London: Constable, 1982), p. 153 • 3 Ernest Cuneo, EM, 83-7 Box 4, File 500.1-7, p.1, 'CBC Tuesday Night: The Two Bills', William Stevenson Papers • 4 'Colonel Ellis Roll', Roll 4, 83-7, Box 4, File 500.1-4, William Stevenson Papers • 5 Hyde, *Secret Intelligence Agent*, p. 153 • 6 Betty Raymond interviewed in Bill MacDonald, *The True Intrepid* (Vancouver: Raincoast, 2001), p. 216 • 7 Ibid. • 8 Ibid., p. 217 • 9 Ibid., p.

216 • 10 Hyde, *Secret Intelligence Agent*, p. 154 • 11 Ibid. • 12 Stephenson quoted in William Stevenson, *The Bormann Brotherhood* (London: Corgi, 1975), p. 21 • 13 'Axis Plot Punctured By Bolivia', *Miami News*, 19 July 1941, p. 13 • 14 Sumner Welles quoted in Hyde, *Secret Intelligence Agent*, p. 159 • 15 'German Anger is Mounting', *Tipton Daily Tribune*, 29 July 1941, p. 3 • 16 Stephenson, 'If Time Permits', FO 371/26172/A.6153

Chapter 32

1 Charles Lindbergh, Diaries, 22 June 1941, Series V, Box 216, Charles A. Lindbergh Papers • 2 Ibid., 8 July 1941 • 3 Lee Richards, *The Black Art* (United Kingdom: www.psywar.org, 2010), p. 95 • 4 Lindbergh, Diaries, 27 July 1941 • 5 Ibid., 13 July 1941 • 6 Ibid., 19 July 1941 • 7 Ibid., 11 July 1941 • 8 Ibid. • 9 Joachim Ribbentrop to Hans Thomsen, 18 July 1941, Document No. 139, *Documents on German Foreign Policy, 1918–1945*, Series D, Vol. 13 (London: HMSO, 1956), p. 201 • 10 Thomsen to Foreign Ministry, 24 July 1941, Document No. 150, *Documents on German Foreign Policy, 1918–1945*, Series D, Vol. 13, pp. 213–14 • 11 Bötticher and Thomsen to Foreign Ministry, 27 April 1941, Document No. 411, *Documents on German Foreign Policy, 1918–1945*, Series D, Vol. 12 (London: HMSO, 1956), pp. 651–2 • 12 Charles Lindbergh, *Autobiography of Values* (New York: Harcourt Brace Jovanovich, 1978), p. 147, quoted in Marc Wortman, *1941* (London: Atlantic, 2017), p. 130 • 13 Bötticher and Thomsen to Foreign Ministry, 27 April 1941, Document No. 411, *Documents on German Foreign Policy, 1918–1945*, Series D, Vol. 12, pp. 65–2

Chapter 33

1 'Roosevelt's Yacht Sets "No Destination" As Rumors of Purpose of Trip Increase', *New York Times*, 8 August 1941, p. 6 • 2 *New York Post*, 22 August 1941, S/953, quoted in Folder 'PWE/SIBS', General File: 1941–1945, Folder 'Come-backs: 1940–1943', FO 898/71 • 3 Joseph Goebbels quoted in Ian Kershaw, *Fateful Choices* (London: Penguin, 2013), p. 407 • 4 Adolf Hitler quoted in Kershaw, *Fateful Choices*, p. 408 • 5 Winston Churchill quoted in Martin Gilbert, *Churchill and America* (London: Free Press, 2005), p. 234 • 6 'War Plans Laid to Roosevelt', *New York Times*, 2 January 1972, p. 7 • 7 Nelson A. Rockefeller, Oral Histories, Series 1, FA 344, Nelson A. Rockefeller Private Papers • 8 William Stephenson, 'If Time Permits', 23 July 1941, FO 371/26172/A.6153

Chapter 34

1 Ansel E. Talbert, 'Vichy Embassy in U.S. Shown as Heading Clique of Agents Aiding Nazis', *New York Herald Tribune*, 31 August 1941, p. 1 • 2 'Vichy is Angry at Articles in Herald Tribune', *New York Herald Tribune*, 6 September 1941, p. 1 • 3 'A Blonde Bond', *Time*, 20 December 1963, p. 23 • 4 Gallup, 16 August 1941 (survey date 31 July–4 August 1941) 'In the war between Britain and Germany, do you think the Vichy Government is helping one side rather than the other?' Vichy is helping Germany – 58%; *Public Opinion Quarterly*, Vol. 5 (Oxford: Oxford University Press, 1941), p. 676 • 5 Bill Ross Smith interviewed in Bill MacDonald, *The True Intrepid* (Vancouver: Raincoast, 2001), p. 191; see also Malcolm Atkin, 'Section D for Destruction Forerunner of SOE Appendix 2: Officers, Agents and Contacts of Section D of the Secret Intelligence Service' downloaded from https://www.academia.edu/35641341/ Section_D_for_Destruction_Forerunner_of_SOE_Appendix_2_Officers_Agents_ and_Contacts_of_Section_D_of_the_Secret_Intelligence_Service on 5 September 2018 • 6 David Ogilvy, *Blood, Brains and Beer* (London: Hamish Hamilton, 1978), p. 51 • 7 Ogilvy quoted in MacDonald, *The True Intrepid*, p. 251

Chapter 35

1 Federal Bureau of Investigation, 'British Intelligence Service in the United States (Running Memorandum)', 1 January 1947, pp. 55 and 57 • 2 Adolf Berle, Memorandum, 3 September 1941, Container 213, Adolf A. Berle Papers • 3 Federal Bureau of Investigation, 'British Intelligence Service in the United States (Running Memorandum)', 1 January 1947, p. 56 • 4 Berle, Memorandum, 4 September 1941, Container 213, Adolf A. Berle Papers • 5 Berle to Cordell Hull, 5 September 1941, Container 213, Adolf A. Berle Papers • 6 Ibid. • 7 Laurence Duggan to Spruille Braden, 12 September 1941, RG 59/4930/ 841.20211/23

Chapter 36

1 Joachim Ribbentrop to Thomsen, 6 September 1941, Document No. 282, *Documents on German Foreign Policy, 1918–1945*, Series D, Vol. 13 (London: HMSO, 1956), pp. 454–6 • 2 Retrieved from http://www.usmm.org/fdr/rattlesnake.html on 9 March 2018 • 3 Retrieved from http://www.presidency.ucsb.edu/ws/index. php?pid=16012 on 19 October 2018

Chapter 37

1 Charles Lindbergh, Diaries, 11 September 1941, Series V, Box 216, Charles A. Lindbergh Papers • 2 Cliff Millen, 'Cheers and Jeers Greet Lindbergh as he Takes Stage', *Des Moines Tribune*, 12 September 1941, pp. 1 and 7 • 3 'Lindbergh Sees a Plot For War', *New York Times*, 12 September 1941, p. 2 • 4 'As the Press of America Views the Lindbergh Speech', *Daily Times* (Davenport, IA), 16 September 1941, p. 3 • 5 'Assail Lindbergh For Iowa Speech', *New York Times*, 13 September 1941, p. 3 • 6 'Dewey Denounces Lindbergh's Talk', *New York Times*, 15 September 1941, p. 2 • 7 A. Scott Berg, *Lindbergh* (London: Macmillan, 1998), p. 428 • 8 'As the Press of America Views the Lindbergh Speech', *Daily Times* (Davenport, Iowa), 16 September 1941, p. 3 • 9 'Willkie Terms Lindbergh's Des Moines Talk Un-American', *Baltimore Sun*, 14 September 1941, p. 1 • 10 Ulric Bell to Wendell Willkie, 18 June 1941, Box 37, Folder 1, Fight For Freedom Papers • 11 Lindbergh, Diaries, 15 September 1941 • 12 William Stephenson to Frank Nelson, 25 September 1941, FO 898/102

PART FOUR

1 Losses to the end of August 1941 calculated from Donald P. Steury, 'The Character of the German Naval Offensive', Timothy J. Runyan & Jan M. Copes (eds), *To Die Gallantly* (Boulder, CO, San Francisco & Oxford: Westview Press, 1994), pp. 75–94; G. F. Krivosheev, *Soviet Casualties and Combat Losses in the Twentieth Century* (London: Greenhill Books, 1997), p. 94 • 2 Gallup, 17 October 1941, 'In general do you approve or disapprove of President Roosevelt's foreign policy?' Approve – 76%; *Public Opinion Quarterly*, Vol. 6 (Oxford: Oxford University Press, 1942), p. 163

Chapter 38

1 'Summary of Events Early 1941 and July 1942: US Office of War Information', 1 September 1942, HS 7/75 • 2 William Stephenson, 'The Story of OSS', taped interview, quoted in H. Montgomery Hyde, *Secret Intelligence Agent* (London: Constable, 1982), p. 253 • 3 'Appointments and Telephone Calls, August 9, 1941– September 29, 1945', Donovan Papers, quoted in Thomas F. Troy, *Donovan and the CIA* (Frederick, MD: Aletheia, 1981), p. 83 • 4 Interview with Stephenson, 83-7 Box 4, File 500.1-4 green transcript sheets in folder Part 1 of 2, William

Stevenson Papers • 5 'Colonel Ellis Roll', Roll E, 83-7, Box 4, File 500.1-4, William Stevenson Papers • 6 Tommy Davies to Frank Nelson, 9 September 1941, HS 8/116 • 7 'Directorate of Security Coordination in America', Part III: Special Operations (SOE), HS 7/72 • 8 'Summary of Events Early 1941 and July 1942: US Office of War Information', 1 September 1942, HS 7/75 • 9 Minute, 14 September 1941, FO 898/103 • 10 'Summary of Events Early 1941 and July 1942: US Office of War Information', 1 September 1942, HS 7/75 • 11 Donovan quoted in Albin Krebs, 'William Stephenson, British Spy Known as Intrepid, Is Dead at 93', *New York Times*, 3 February 1989, p. 17 • 12 Retrieved from https://www.cia.gov/library/readingroom/document/cia-rdp85m00364r000600980018-3 on 3 January 2018 • 13 Hugh Dalton to Brendan Bracken, 24 October 1941, FO/954/24A/20 • 14 Federal Bureau of Investigation, 'British Intelligence Service in the United States (Running Memorandum)', 1 January 1947, p. 26 • 15 Desmond Morton to Edward Jacob, 18 September 1941, Churchill Papers, Box 145, Folder 463, Item 2, quoted in Thomas E. Mahl, *Desperate Deception* (Dulles, VA: Brassey's, 1999), p. 19 • 16 SOE Survey of Global Activities, October 1941, HS 7/221 • 17 Ian Fleming quoted in Gill Bennett, *Churchill's Man of Mystery* (London & New York: Routledge, 2007), p. 257 • 18 'Godfrey Report', 7 July 1941, ADM 223/84 • 19 Davies to Nelson, 9 September 1941, HS 8/116 • 20 Thomsen to Foreign Ministry, 27 August 1941, quoted in Douglas C. Waller, *Wild Bill Donovan* (New York: Free Press, 2010), p. 74

Chapter 39

1 Federal Bureau of Investigation, 'British Intelligence Service in the United States (Running Memorandum)', 1 January 1947, p. 56 • 2 Fortune, October 1941, 'Which one of the following statements most nearly describes your present feelings about the Russian and German governments?' The Russian Government is far better than the German Government – 8.5%; *Public Opinion Quarterly*, Vol. 6, (Oxford: Oxford University Press, Spring 1942), p. 152 • 3 SOE Survey of Global Activities, September 1941, HS 7/220 • 4 Ibid. • 5 Ibid. • 6 William Donovan to Franklin D. Roosevelt, 27 September 1941, Coordinator of Information, President's Secretary's File • 7 'Religious Rights Restored To Poles', *Wilmington Daily Press Journal*, 30 September 1941, p. 1 • 8 Walter Trohan, 'Russian Religion Rights Same As Ours, Says F.D.R.', *Chicago Tribune*, 1 October 1941, p. 12 • 9 SOE Survey of Global Activities, October 1941, HS 7/221 • 10 Ibid. • 11 British Security Coordination, *The Secret History of British Intelligence in the Americas, 1940–1945* (New York: Fromm, 1999), pp. 222–3 • 12 SOE Survey of Global Activities, October 1941, HS 7/221 • 13 Derek Hoyer-Millar to Harold Butler, 19 September 1941, FO 371/26173 A.8892 • 14 'Bureau Memo, 14 March 1946 re: Malcolm Lovell 100-25944-47', quoted in Christof Mauch, transl. Jeremiah

M. Riemer, *The Shadow War Against Hitler* (New York: Columbia University Press, 2003), p. 234

Chapter 40

1 H. Montgomery Hyde, *Secret Intelligence Agent* (London: Constable, 1982), p. 141 • 2 Interview with Eric Maschwitz, 'The Great Canadian Spy', Roll 2, 83-7 Box 4, File 500.1-7, 'CBC Tuesday Night: The Two Bills', William Stevenson Papers • 3 Interview with William Stephenson, 83-7 Box 4, File 500.1-4 green transcript sheets in folder Part 2 of 2, William Stevenson Papers • 4 H. Montgomery Hyde, *The Quiet Canadian* (London: Hamish Hamilton, 1962), p. 137 • 5 Interview with Maschwitz, 'The Great Canadian Spy', Stevenson Papers • 6 Ibid. • 7 'Russians Hold Foe West of Moscow; Nazis Report Eight Armies Crushed, Claim Sinking of 12 Ships in Convoy', *New York Times*, 19 October 1941, p. 1 • 8 '12 Ships in Convoy Claimed By Reich', *New York Times*, 19 October 1941, pp. 1 and 6

Chapter 41

1 Ivar Bryce, *You Only Live Once* (London: Weidenfeld & Nicolson, 1984), p. 65 • 2 Ibid., p. 66 • 3 Ibid. • 4 William O'Neill, *A Democracy at War* (New York: Free Press, 1993) pp. 40–1 • 5 'Roosevelt Insists on Map's Validity', *The Pittsburgh Press*, 29 October 1941, p. 9 • 6 Marc Wortman, *1941* (London: Atlantic, 2017), p. 312 • 7 George Axelsson, 'Nazis Excoriate Navy Day Speech', *New York Times*, 29 October 1941, p. 5 • 8 'British Jubilant Over Speech, Berlin Calls it Slanderous', *Leaf-Chronicle*, 28 October 1941, p. 1 • 9 Ibid. • 10 George Axelsson, 'Nazis Excoriate Navy Day Speech', *New York Times*, 29 October 1941, p. 5 • 11 Joachim Ribbentrop to Foreign Ministry, 31 October 1941, Document No. 439, *Documents on German Foreign Policy, 1918–1945*, Series D, Vol. 13 (London: HMSO, 1956), pp. 724–5 • 12 Frank L. Kluckhorn, 'Nazi Ire Over "Secret Map" Is a "Scream" to Roosevelt', *New York Times*, 29 October 1941, pp. 1 and 4 • 13 'Roosevelt Insists on Map's Validity', *Pittsburgh Press*, 29 October 1941, p. 9 • 14 Christopher Andrew, *For the President's Eyes Only* (London: HarperCollins, 1995), p. 103 • 15 H. Montgomery Hyde, *The Quiet Canadian* (London: Hamish Hamilton, 1962), pp. 149–50 • 16 Douglas C. Waller, *Wild Bill Donovan* (New York: Free Press, 2010), p. 77 • 17 Milton Wolff quoted in Studs Terkel, *The Good War* (London: Hamish Hamilton, 1985), p. 480 • 18 Franklin D. Roosevelt, 'Memorandum for Bill Donovan', 13 October 1941, Subject File "C", Box 141, President's Secretary's File • 19 SOE Survey of Global activities, December 1941, HS 7/223 • 20 Frank Nelson to Stewart Menzies, 20 November 1941, HS

9/1584/6 • 21 Lord Halifax to Winston Churchill, 11 October 1941, PREM 4/27/9 • 22 Denis W. Brogan, *The Era of Franklin D. Roosevelt* (New Haven: Yale University Press, 1961), p. 326

Chapter 42

1 'Stephenson - Dahl', Roll 1, 83-7, Box 4, File 500.1-4, Interview with Sweet-Escott, Roll R, 83-7 Box 4, File 500.1-4, William Stevenson Papers • 2 'Report Nazi Wounded Left To Die', *Newark Ledger*, 22 October 1941, R/415; 'Typhoid Epidemic Reported Raging Behind Nazi Lines', *New York Post*, 22 October 1941, R/535; both quoted in Folder 'PWE/SIBS', General File: 1941–1945, Folder 'Come-backs: 1940–1943', FO 898/71 • 3 'Fortnightly Report of Activities of the Propaganda Section', 20 November 1941, HS 8/232 • 4 'Opposition is in Lead', *Lincoln Journal Star*, 2 October 1939, p. 3 • 5 Arthur Krock, 'Anti-War Group Losing Strength in Congress', *New York Times*, 23 September 1941, p. 103 • 6 H. Montgomery Hyde, *The Quiet Canadian* (London: Hamish Hamilton, 1962), p. 73 • 7 'Clark, Fish Charge FDR Forcing War', *Argus Leader* (Sioux Falls, SD), 14 September 1941, p. 2 • 8 Thomas Morrow, 'Pro-War Plank Shaped Up For Legionnaires', *Chicago Tribune*, 17 September 1941, p. 1 • 9 Byron Darnton, 'Escort of Convoys By Navy One of Methods Being Used in Defense Areas, Knox Says', *New York Times*, 18 September 1941, p. 1 • 10 Ibid. • 11 Clem Lane quoted in Thomas E. Mahl, *Desperate Deception* (Dulles, VA: Brassey's, 1999) • 12 SOE Survey of Global Activities, September 1941, HS 7/220 • 13 'CIO Poll 92% For War', *New York Daily News*, 17 November 1941, p. 8 • 14 George Tagge, 'CIO Delegates Put Approval on Mine Strike', *Chicago Tribune*, 18 November 1941, p. 2 • 15 British Security Coordination, *The Secret History of British Intelligence in the Americas, 1940–1945*, p. 83 • 16 'Roosevelt Message to C.I.O. and Foreign Policy Resolution', *New York Times*, 19 November 1941, p. 16 • 17 A. H. Raskin, 'C.I.O. Backs Foreign Policy In Rout of the Lewis Forces', *New York Times*, 19 November 1941, p. 1

Chapter 43

1 British Security Coordination, *The Secret History of British Intelligence in the Americas, 1940–1945* (New York: Fromm, 1999), p. 79 • 2 H. Montgomery Hyde, *The Quiet Canadian* (London: Hamish Hamilton, 1962), p. 89 • 3 Henry Hoke, *Black Mail* (New York: Reader's Book Service, 1944), p. 52 • 4 A. Scott Berg, *Lindbergh* (London: Macmillan, 1998), p. 430 • 5 Ibid. • 6 America First publication, Box 70, Folder 24, Non-Sectarian Anti-Nazi League Papers • 7 Winston Churchill quoted in Martin Gilbert, *Churchill and America* (London: Free Press, 2005), pp. 239–40 • 8 Douglas M. Charles, *J. Edgar Hoover and the Anti-Interventionists*

(Columbus: Ohio State University Press, 2007), p. 96 • 9 'Stopping Hitler Means More Than Peace to CIO', *New York Daily News*, 20 November 1941, p. 38

Chapter 44

1 Adolf Berle, Diaries, 28 February 1941, Container 212, Adolf A. Berle Papers • 2 Alice Hemming, 16 July 1941, Private Collection • 3 Ian MacDonald to Alice Hemming, 26 November 1941; J. Lamprey to Alice Hemming, 28 November 1941; Private Collection • 4 'Junior Board Supports Loan', *Vancouver Sun*, 30 May 1941, p. 20 • 5 Harold Hemming, Diary, 16 July 1941, Private Collection • 6 Thomas F. Troy, *Wild Bill and Intrepid* (New Haven & London: Yale University Press, 1996), p. 6

Chapter 45

1 Christof Mauch, transl. Jeremiah M. Riemer, *The Shadow War Against Hitler* (New York: Columbia University Press, 2003), p. 233 • 2 Joseph E. Persico, *Roosevelt's Secret War* (New York: Random House, 2001), p. 114 • 3 Douglas C. Waller, *Wild Bill Donovan* (New York: Free Press, 2010), p. 76 • 4 SOE Survey of Global Activities, November 1941, HS 7/222 • 5 Brendan Bracken to Anthony Eden, 13 November 1941, FO 954/24A/35 • 6 SOE Survey of Global Activities, November 1941, HS 7/222 • 7 Hugh Dalton to Bracken, 24 October 1941, FO/954/24A/20 • 8 SOE Survey of Global Activities, November 1941, HS 7/222 • 9 Admiral Raeder, 13 November 1941, *Documents on German Foreign Policy, 1918–1945*, Series D, Vol. 13, p. 779 • 10 Gerhard L. Weinberg, 'Hitler's image of the United States', *American Historical Review*, Vol. 69, No. 4, pp. 1006–21

Chapter 46

1 Wendell Willkie quoted in 'U.S. Nazis Near Air, Sea Battles, Willkie Declares', *Philadelphia Inquirer*, 21 October 1941, p. 11 • 2 Admiral Harold Stark quoted in Patrick Abbazia, *Mr. Roosevelt's Navy* (Annapolis, MD: Naval Institute Press, 1976), p. 306 • 3 Paul Fussell, 'Writing in Wartime: The Uses of Innocence', *Thank God for the Atom Bomb and Other Essays* (New York: Summit, 1989), pp. 53–81, quoted in Nicholas Cull, *Selling War* (New York & Oxford: Oxford University Press, 1995), p. 177 • 4 David D. Lee, *Sergeant York* (Lexington, KY: University Press of Kentucky, 1985), p. 110 • 5 Cull, *Selling War*, p. 163 • 6 Dorothy Thompson to Meyer Weisgal, 28 September 1941, Box 35, 'Sep–Dec 1941', Dorothy Thompson Papers • 7 SOE Survey of Global Activities, July 1941, HS 7/218 • 8 Gallup, 17

December 1941 (survey period 15–20 November 1941), 'Do you think the U.S. will go into the war in Europe sometime before it is over, or do you think we will stay out of the war?' Would go to war sooner or later with Germany – 85%; *Public Opinion Quarterly*, Vol. 6, (Oxford: Oxford University Press, Spring 1942), p. 149 • 9 OPOR (Roper), 19 November 1941, 'The biggest job facing this country today is to help defeat the Nazi Government', Agree – 72%; Gallup, 17 December 1941 (survey period 15–20 November 1941), 'Which of these two things do you think is the more important – that this country keep out of war, or that Germany be defeated?' Defeat Germany – 68%; *Public Opinion Quarterly*, Vol. 6 (Oxford: Oxford University Press, 1942), p. 151 • 10 Gallup, 17 October 1941, 'In general do you approve or disapprove of President Roosevelt's foreign policy?' Approve – 76%; *Public Opinion Quarterly*, Vol. 6 (Oxford: Oxford University Press, 1942), p. 163 • 11 Cull, *Selling War*, p. 185

PART FIVE

1 Losses to the end of November 1941 calculated from Donald P. Steury, 'The Character of the German Naval Offensive', Timothy J. Runyan & Jan M. Copes (eds), *To Die Gallantly* (Boulder, CO, San Francisco & Oxford: Westview Press, 1994), pp. 75-94; Data retrieved from https://en.wikipedia.org/wiki/Battle_casualties_of_World_War_II#The_Battle_of_Britain_July_1940-May_1941 on 23 March 2019 • 2 Gallup, 17 December 1941 (survey period 15–20 November 1941), 'Do you think the U.S. will go into the war in Europe sometime before it is over, or do you think we will stay out of the war?' Would go to war sooner or later with Germany – 85%; *Public Opinion Quarterly*, Vol. 6, (Oxford: Oxford University Press, Spring 1942), p. 149

Chapter 47

1 Donald Stratton with Ken Gire, '"This Is No Drill": A Powerful Firsthand Account of What Really Happened at Pearl Harbor', *Reader's Digest*, retrieved from https://www.rd.com/true-stories/survival/pearl-harbor-firsthand-account/ on 30 November 2018 • 2 Charles Lindbergh, Diaries, 7 December 1941, Series V, Box 216, Charles A. Lindbergh Papers • 3 '"Just What Britain Planned For Us" Sen. Nye Declares', *Morning Call*, 8 December 1941, p. 7 • 4 Lindbergh, Diaries, 8 December 1941 • 5 Ibid. • 6 C. P. Trussell, 'Congress Ready for All-Out Vote', *New York Times*, 8 December 1941, p. 6 • 7 Marc Wortman, *1941* (London: Atlantic), 2017, p. 309 • 8 Dorothy Thompson quoted in Peter Kurth, *American Cassandra* (Boston: Little, Brown, 1990), p. 341 • 9 William Stephenson quoted

in H. Montgomery Hyde, *The Quiet Canadian* (London: Hamish Hamilton, 1962), p. 213 • 10 SOE Survey of Global Activities, November 1941, HS 7/222

Chapter 48

1 Mark Chadwin, *The Hawks of World War II* (Chapel Hill, NC: University of North Carolina Press, 1968), p. 265 • 2 'Attack Laid to Hitler by Fight for Freedom', *Courier-Journal* (Louisville, KY), 8 December 1941, p. 5 • 3 'Germans Hint Break with US, Fast Aid to Japs', *Brooklyn Daily Eagle*, 8 December 1941, p. 2 • 4 William Donovan to Franklin D. Roosevelt, Folder 123, Record 123, M1642, RG 226; Donovan to Roosevelt, 9 December 1941, Subject File "C", Box 141, President's Secretary's File • 5 'Axis Aliens Held with Japanese', *New York Times*, 10 December 1941, p. 30 • 6 'The President's Address', *New York Times*, 10 December 1941, pp. 1 and 4 • 7 Ian Kershaw, *Fateful Choices* (London: Penguin, 2013), p. 416 • 8 Douglas C. Waller, *Wild Bill Donovan* (New York: Free Press, 2010), p. 87 • 9 Thomas Fleming, 'The Big Leak', *American Heritage*, Vol. 38, Issue 8 (December 1987) • 10 Stephen Early quoted in Douglas M. Charles, *J. Edgar Hoover and the Anti-Interventionists* (Columbus: Ohio State University Press, 2007), p. 121

Chapter 49

1 Karl Dönitz, *Memoirs* (London: Cassell, 2000), p. 195 • 2 Jodl quoted in Thomas Fleming, 'The Big Leak', *American Heritage*, Vol. 38, Issue 8, December 1987 • 3 Geoffrey P. Megargee, *Inside Hitler's High Command* (Lawrence, KS: University Press of Kansas, 2000), p. 137 • 4 Ian Kershaw, *Fateful Choices* (London: Penguin, 2013), p. 419 • 5 Adolf Hitler, Reichstag Speech, 11 December 1941, translated by Mark Weber, retrieved from http://www.ihr.org/jhr/v08/v08p389_Hitler.html on 18 March 2019 • 6 Ibid. • 7 Adolf Hitler quoted in Kershaw, *Fateful Choices*, p. 411 • 8 Ernst von Weizsäcker quoted in Gerhard L. Weinberg, 'Hitler's image of the United States', *American Historical Review*, Vol. 69, No. 4, pp. 1006–21

Chapter 50

1 Washington War Conference, Memorandum, 14 January 1942, CAB 99/17 • 2 Charlotte Coe Lemann quoted in Marc Wortman, *1941* (London: Atlantic, 2017), p. 332 • 3 Harry S. Truman quoted in Albin Krebs, 'William Stephenson, British Spy Known as Intrepid, Is Dead at 93', *New York Times*, 3 February 1989, p. 17

Epilogue

1 Douglas C. Waller, *Wild Bill Donovan* (New York: Free Press, 2010), p. 320 • 2 Adolf Berle quoted in H. Montgomery Hyde, *Secret Intelligence Agent* (London: Constable, 1982), p. 179; Berle quoted by Thomas F. Troy in Bill MacDonald, *The True Intrepid* (Vancouver: Raincoast, 2001), p. 1 • 3 Ernest Cuneo quoted in Timothy J. Naftali, 'Intrepid's Last Deception', *Intelligence and National Security*, Vol. 8, Issue 3, 1993, pp. 72–99 • 4 Nigel West, 'Fiction, Faction and Intelligence', *Intelligence and National Security*, Vol. 19, Issue 2, 2004, pp. 275–89 • 5 Hugh Trevor-Roper, 'Review of A Man Called Intrepid: The Secret War by William Stevenson', *The Secret World* (New York: I. B. Tauris, 2014), pp. 136–42 • 6 Maurice Buckmaster quoted in David Stafford, 'Intrepid: Myth and Reality', *Journal of Contemporary History*, Vol. 22, Issue 2, April 1987, pp. 303–17 • 7 Thomas F. Troy in MacDonald, *The True Intrepid*, p. 6

Afterword

1 Thomas Rid, Tweet, 11 November 2017, retrieved from https://twitter.com/RidT/status/929341523887616000 on 6 February 2018 • 2 'Directorate of Security Coordination in America', Part III: Special Operations (SOE), HS 7/72 • 3 Walter Bell interviewed in Bill MacDonald, *The True Intrepid* (Vancouver: Raincoast, 2001), p. 230 • 4 Churchill quoted in Martin Gilbert, *Churchill and America* (London: Free Press, 2005), p. 254 • 5 Thomas F. Troy in MacDonald, *The True Intrepid*, p. 5

INDEX

Credit: Jeff Overs

Henry Hemming is the author of five works of nonfiction including most recently *Agent M* and *The Ingenious Mr. Pyke*, which landed on the *New York Times* monthly espionage bestseller list. He has written for the *Sunday Times, Daily Telegraph, Daily Mail,* the *Times, The Economist, FT Magazine,* and the *Washington Post*, and has given interviews on Radio 4's Today Programme and NBC's Today Show and spoken at schools, festivals, and companies including RDF Media, the RSA, Science Museum, Frontline Club, and the School of Life. Henry lives in London with his wife, daughter, and son.

PublicAffairs is a publishing house founded in 1997. It is a tribute to the standards, values, and flair of three persons who have served as mentors to countless reporters, writers, editors, and book people of all kinds, including me.

I. F. STONE, proprietor of *I. F. Stone's Weekly*, combined a commitment to the First Amendment with entrepreneurial zeal and reporting skill and became one of the great independent journalists in American history. At the age of eighty, Izzy published *The Trial of Socrates*, which was a national bestseller. He wrote the book after he taught himself ancient Greek.

BENJAMIN C. BRADLEE was for nearly thirty years the charismatic editorial leader of *The Washington Post*. It was Ben who gave the *Post* the range and courage to pursue such historic issues as Watergate. He supported his reporters with a tenacity that made them fearless and it is no accident that so many became authors of influential, best-selling books.

ROBERT L. BERNSTEIN, the chief executive of Random House for more than a quarter century, guided one of the nation's premier publishing houses. Bob was personally responsible for many books of political dissent and argument that challenged tyranny around the globe. He is also the founder and longtime chair of Human Rights Watch, one of the most respected human rights organizations in the world.

·   ·   ·

For fifty years, the banner of Public Affairs Press was carried by its owner Morris B. Schnapper, who published Gandhi, Nasser, Toynbee, Truman, and about 1,500 other authors. In 1983, Schnapper was described by *The Washington Post* as "a redoubtable gadfly." His legacy will endure in the books to come.

Peter Osnos, *Founder*